The Economic Ascent of the Hotel Business

Paul Slattery

(G) Goodfellow Publishing

(G) Published by Goodfellow Publishers Limited,
Woodeaton, Oxford, OX3 9TJ
http://www.goodfellowpublishers.com

British Library Cataloguing in Publication Data: a catalogue record
for this title is available from the British Library.

Library of Congress Catalog Card Number: on file.

ISBN: 978-1-906884-03-1

 Design and typesetting by P.K. McBride

Printed by Lightning Source, www.lightningsource.com

Contents

Preface

There are three gaps that this book seeks to narrow. First, the ideal combination for corporate executives in hotel chains is to have both a conceptual understanding of a business discipline and a conceptual knowledge of the hotel business. However, hotel chains frequently populate their corporate structures with executives drawn from the disciplines of accounting, marketing, finance and the other general business disciplines, but without a conceptual understanding of the hotel business. Once they have taken-up their position in a hotel chain their emerging understanding of the hotel business is only experiential and this can limit the effectiveness of their creativity. This book is designed to narrow that gap by providing a systematic analysis of high level strategic issues that confront the hotel business.

Second, most of the advisors to the hotel business: investment bankers, equity analysts, lenders, equity investors, management consultants, real estate agents, lawyers, accountants, developers, architects, construction companies, the media and a host of others have been sent to work on hotel projects, they have not chosen to work on them. As a result, there is a very high turnover of advisors involved in the hotel business. Only a few are sufficiently attracted to remain committed to it for a significant part of their careers, but even these stalwarts only have a piecemeal rather than a conceptual understanding of the hotel business, which constrains their interpretation of the challenges and can limit the effectiveness of their advice. This book is designed to narrow that gap and to help advisors gain a more comprehensive understanding of the dynamics of the hotel business.

Third, undergraduate and postgraduate degrees in hospitality management throughout the world pay too little attention to the understanding of the economic development of the hotel business, to the dynamics of economies, the hotel demand that they generate and the hotel supply needs that follow. Given that hotel chains dominate hotel development it is of concern that most graduates in hospitality management enter the business with inadequate understanding of hotel chains, their drivers, strategies and structures. This book is designed to narrow that gap and help academics and graduates to comprehend and get excited about one of the most dynamic and growing businesses in the world.

Acknowledgements

The hospitality business has been the thread that has bound my three different careers as an academic, as an equity analyst and as an investment banker. Throughout, there have been countless colleagues, clients, corporate executives, competitors and students, most of whom are unaware that they sparked ideas, demanded solutions, inspired me and punctured the crazier ideas that I have had about the hospitality business. The 16 years to 1987 at the University of Huddersfield was a period of broad creativity with colleagues and friends such as Rita Carmouche, Keith Johnson, David Litteljohn, Ray Pine, Angela Roper and George Wilson, all of whom have left distinguished marks on the development of hospitality management in the academic world. We were very young academics charged with developing a degree in Hotel and Catering Administration and in pursuing research in hospitality management. It was at this time that my commitment to the analysis of hotel chains and to the creation of the hotel supply database was established.

At Kleinwort Benson Securities from 1987 to 1998 Simon Johnson and Greg Feehely were two graduates in hospitality management who crafted very successful careers in the investment community and worked with me when I first developed the idea that economic structure was a critical influence on the size, shape and performance of the hotel business.

Since 1998 my immediate colleagues in corporate finance at Kleinwort Benson and my close colleagues at Otus: Simon Read, Andrew Boshoff and Ian Gamse stretch my thinking because their talents are both wide and deep. It is with these colleagues and friends that I have been able to extend the wider strategic analysis of hotel chains and the hotel business.

As I was completing this book I received the news that Greg Dillon had died. Greg was one of the great statesmen of the hotel business who served as Vice Chairman Emeritus of Hilton Hotels Corporation after his retirement from the main board. His involvement with Hilton stretched from the acquisition of Statler Hotels in 1954, which was at the time the largest ever hotel chain transaction. He was responsible for the development of Hilton from the 1960s and was one of the executives who understood and drove the economic ascent of the hotel business in the US and elsewhere. Greg was also a great friend, a grand host and an inspiration.

Thanks also to Tim and Sally at Goodfellow Publishing, who have always been thoughtful and helpful.

My preoccupation with the hotel business is exceeded by my preoccupation with my family who have provided so many highs, a sprinkling of lows and a few scares. Libby has shared my whole adult life, wonderfully. Stephen and Natalia and the Ms – Martin, Millie and Markus – know that the time I spend thinking about, reading about, talking about and writing about the hotel business is secondary to my love for them.

Paul Slattery

About Otus

Otus focuses on three sectors: Hospitality, Travel and Transport. Otus directors and partners are sector experts and experienced bankers with long experience in the strategic analysis of the hospitality, travel and transport businesses and an unrivalled record of advising on key transactions of all sizes, national and international in hospitality, travel and transport.

Otus Corporate Finance offers advice on a full range of corporate finance activities including: mergers and acquisitions, disposals, joint ventures, MBOs/MBIs and financing transactions.

Otus & Co provides independent, high level and innovative strategic advice drawing on a range of proprietary data and analytical tools.

For the hotel business we own and operate the Otus Hotel Brand Database, the most sophisticated hotel brand supply database covering all of Europe, the Middle East, Africa and Asia. We provide systematic analysis of hotel brand supply with consistent classification of hotel market levels, hotel configurations and hotel locations each economy.

We track developments in economic structure for each economy and economic policies to assess their implications for the hotel business. We also track the volume of domestic business demand, domestic leisure demand, foreign business demand and foreign leisure demand into hotels.

We use these resources to advise on portfolio and performance strategies of hotel brands to enable main boards to make more secure decisions about the medium to long-term directions of companies.

Our clients include international and national hotel companies, online travel agencies and capital providers in Europe, North America and elsewhere.

Otus & Co Advisory Ltd
1 Cornhill, London EC3V 3ND
+44 20 7375 2604
www.otusco.com

Introduction

This book is about the hotel business and the economic contexts in which it has evolved. The central thesis is that the size, structure and growth of the hotel business in a country are functions of the prevailing economic structure. Thus, fundamental to comprehending the economic ascent of the hotel business is an understanding of the structural development of the economies in which hotels operate and which provide the fertility for hotel demand and supply to grow. The book draws on contemporary data and events to chart the historic development of economies and of the hotel business to illustrate patterns in this fundamental relationship. The book also focuses on the economic conditions that produced hotel chains of different sizes, structures and growth patterns and it seeks to provide a more comprehensive basis on which future developments in hotel demand, supply and performance can be contemplated.

The economic ascent of the hotel business has not been uniform because the development of economic structures has not been uniform. Europe and North America are the centre of the hotel universe, so that, with a combined population of around 700 million and with around 10 million hotel rooms, they have a supply ratio of 14 hotel rooms per 1,000 citizens. The rest of the world accounts for a population of around 6 billion with 6 million hotel rooms, a supply ratio of one hotel room per 1,000 citizens. The fundamental question is: what is it about the economies of Europe and North America that generate a much higher volume of hotel supply, and by implication hotel demand, than the rest of the world? Those economies from Africa, parts of Asia, parts of South America and parts of Eastern Europe that are grounded in agriculture and basic manufacturing generate the lowest volume of demand for hotels, have the lowest supply of hotel rooms and throughout history the economic ascent of their hotel businesses has been minor. At the other end of the continuum of economic structure, the most advanced economies such as the US and Britain, have progressed to be driven more by service businesses. They generate the highest volumes of hotel demand and need the highest volumes of hotel room supply per citizen to accommodate them. It is in these countries that the economic ascent of the hotel business has been greatest. Thus, identifying the historical development of the economic structure of these countries and the parallel development of their hotel businesses is necessary to make sense of the different size, shape and prospects of their hotel businesses.

In the most advanced economies the hotel business has existed and grown throughout their economic history and has been dominated by two major trends. First, the provision of hotel facilities and services has developed from small inns, which were an extension of the home of the innkeeper, with primitive communal sleeping and eating facilities for handfuls of travellers at any time to modern mammoths such as Wynn Las Vegas, opened in 2005 with a development cost of $2.7 billion in 2,716 rooms and suites, an 111,000 square-foot casino, 22 restaurants and bars, an 18-hole golf course, approximately 223,000 square feet of meeting space, an on-site Ferrari and Maserati dealership and approximately 76,000 square feet of retail space.

Second, from the middle of the 19th century in Britain, hotel chains emerged. They developed gingerly during the next 100 years, but the emergence of chains and therefore the growth in concentration of the hotel business was a feature of the second half of the 20th century, most notably in the US and Britain as Figures 1 and 2 illustrate.

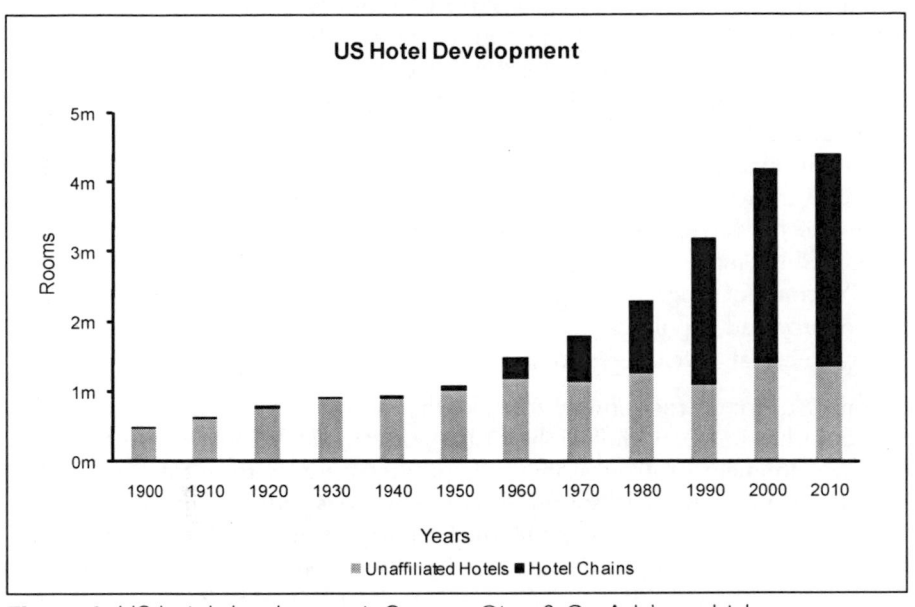

Figure 1: US hotel development. Source: Otus & Co Advisory Ltd

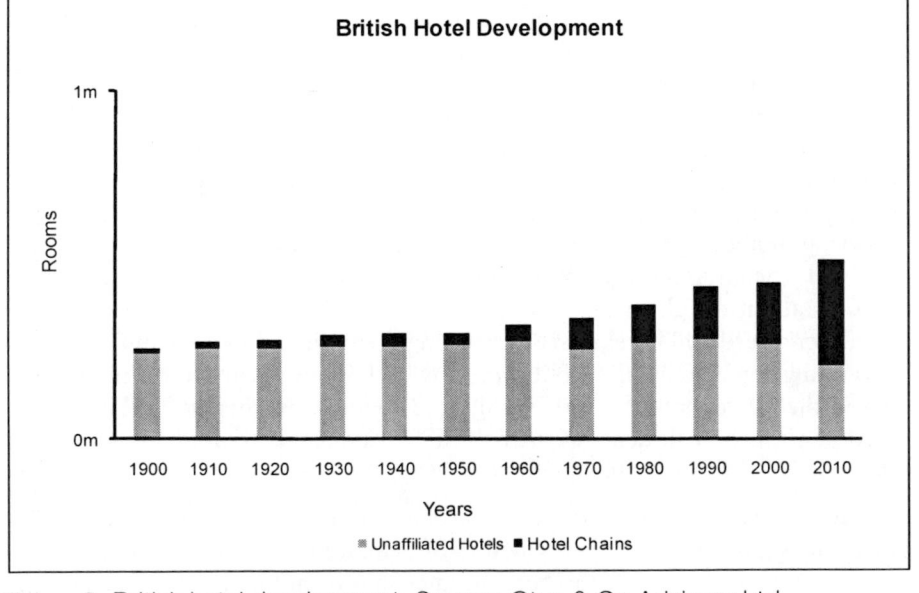

Figure 2: British hotel development. Source: Otus & Co Advisory Ltd

The experience of the US and Britain is that hotel chains come to prominence when the development in economic structure is driven most by the growth of service businesses. Of the two countries, the US has by far the larger hotel room stock, because it is the larger economy with a larger and faster growing population and the larger physical size, but also, crucially, because throughout the 20th century the structural development of the US economy progressed at a faster rate than Britain's. At the start of the 20th century both economies were grounded in manufacturing and their hotel businesses were closer than they have been since. In 1900, the US, already the world's largest economy, had 500,000 hotel rooms and a supply ratio of 6.6 hotel rooms per 1,000 citizens, while Britain had 270,000 rooms and a supply ratio of 7.1, higher than the US. Britain started the 20th century with a higher level of concentration in the hotel business than the US due to the vertical integration of railway companies and of brewers, which accounted for most of the hotel chains. However, throughout the 20th century, the US economy progressed more speedily to be driven by service businesses and the country had a political philosophy of small government, which facilitated faster structural development of the economy.

In contrast, Britain took longer to make the transition to service businesses and did so with a political philosophy of big government, which slowed the structural development of its economy. The progressive growth in total hotel room supply and in hotel chain supply in both countries reflected the divergence in their economic structures. By 2008, the US hotel business had grown to 4.7 million hotel rooms, a supply ratio of 15.5 hotel rooms per 1000 citizens and hotel chains accounted for 69% of total room stock. In contrast, British hotel room stock had grown to 510,000 rooms, a supply ratio of 8.4 hotel rooms per 1000 citizens and a concentration of only 57%.

Hotel chains have also grown internationally. At the end of 2008, global hotel chains such as Hilton Hotels Corporation, Intercontinental Hotels Group, Marriott International and Wyndham Worldwide each accounted for around half a million rooms. However, hotel chains are still at the early stages of their global growth and demand and supply are accelerating as the structural balance of more economies progresses. Although it has taken all of economic history to develop the first hotel chains with half a million rooms, the rate and pattern of growth in hotel chains means that if these chains maintain their recent growth, they will reach a million rooms each by 2020. Yet, the growth of hotel chains is not only about the global majors. At the end of 2008, in the 52 countries of Europe, there were 700 hotel brands operating portfolios of more than four hotels, accounting for a total of 14,000 hotels with 1.7 million rooms. Otus projects that in the 10 years to 2018 they will need to add a further one million rooms to stay in touch with demand growth that is the result of developments in the structures of the European economies.

The hotel business and its sisters in travel and tourism are now of too great an economic significance for the dynamics of demand and supply to be only casually understood. However, the hotel business has been lured into a reliance on a narrow range of short-term and general macroeconomic metrics such as changes in total GDP, changes in interest rates and movements in currency exchange rates. Sadly, the analysis gets no deeper than the superficial assumption that rises in GDP, reductions in interest rates and reduction in currency exchange rates are positive for the hotel business and movements in the opposite directions are negative. At the micro level the depth of analysis is not much more than a dependence on short-term hotel operational measures such as historic revenue per available room (RevPAR) and tracking of future pipelines of hotel construction. These macro and micro output indicators are necessary tools, but without a more comprehensive understanding of inputs into economies, the drivers of hotel demand and supply, and the economic context in which the outputs occur, they are insufficient to make real sense of developments. Thus, it is no accident that too frequently, hotels have delivered sub-optimal returns on invested capital, because their development strategies and marketing strategies have not been grounded in effective analysis. Along with greater economic significance comes greater responsibility to investors and other stakeholders in the hotel business. An understanding of the structural development of economies enables us to identify more effective ways to measure the hotel demand and hotel supply needs of economies and enables us to plan investments more effectively. This book is about these big economic and investment issues. It presents a consistent understanding of the dynamics of economic structures as well as the patterns and volumes of hotel demand and supply that they generate and the development of hotel chains that follows.

There are three purposes to this book. First, to demonstrate that the Otus approach to the strategic development of the hotel business is an advance from the conventional approach. Second, to argue that the structural balance of economies are in the process of shifting to segments that yield higher demands into hotels. Third that if the structural balance of economies move as anticipated, then the global hotel business will enter a golden age.

The book tracks six stages in the economic ascent of the hotel business.

Chapter 1, Economic structure: The building blocks of economic structure are introduced and used to explain how economies develop.

Chapters 2 and 3, Historic primary economies and the emergence of the hotel business until 1850: The economic structures of the historic agricultural economies and the Industrial Revolution are reviewed. The economic development of the hotel business during these periods is tracked and the ways in which the patterns of hotel demand and supply were influenced by the prevailing economic structures are illustrated.

Chapters 3, 4 and 5, Historic secondary economies and the emergence of hotel chains: 1850 to 1945: The segmentation of hotels is shown to have paralleled the economic and social structures as they evolved in industrial economies. The severe impact on the hotel demand and supply of world wars, ideological shifts and the Great Depression are tracked and the emergence of hotel chains is explained.

Chapters 6 and 7, The emergence of the service business economy and the growth of hotel chains: 1945 to 1960: The transition of the US to a service business economy is examined, as is the fast growth in hotel demand and supply that it engendered. The meteoric growth of US hotel chains and innovations in the structure of hotel chains that set the patterns for the rest of the century are explored. This is contrasted with the struggles of the European economies to recover from World War II and the sluggish progress of their hotel businesses.

Chapters 8 and 9, The establishment of the service business economy and the acceleration of hotel chains: 1960 to 1980: The growth in the significance of service businesses in the US is traced and compared with the growth in the volume and diversity of hotel demand and the growth in the significance of hotel chains. The slower development in the structural balance of the European economies is charted and its impact on the growth in the size and structure of their hotel business is examined.

Chapters 10, 11, 12 and 13, The expansion of the service business economy and the dominance of hotel chains beyond 1980: The most dramatic growth of the hotel business occurs within service business economies because they produce the widest diversity, volume and frequency of hotel demand and this has been matched by the greatest significance and diversity of hotel brands.

The book draws on data from the Otus Hotel Brands database and its precursor that I started at the University of Huddersfield in the early 1980s and expanded at Kleinwort Benson Ltd until the end of the millennium, to illuminate the dynamics of the economic ascent of the hotel business.

1 Economic Structure

Introduction

There are many ways to differentiate economic structures, but in this analysis the most potent approach is to profile the activities in which the population of a country is employed, the numbers employed in each economic activity and how they change over time. In addition, the focus on patterns of consumption, patterns of travel, the main currents in the social and political structures of a country and the economic policies it pursues illuminate the patterns of development in the structural balance of economies.

Economies can be classified into five segments: agricultural, industrial, citizen services, market services and experience businesses. A view of the different pattern of consumption that derives from economies with different structural balance is expressed by Pine and Gilmore's review of birthday cakes:

> As a vestige of the agricultural economy, mothers made birthday cakes from scratch, mixing farm commodities (flour, sugar, butter and eggs) that together cost mere dimes. As the goods-based industrial economy advanced, moms paid a dollar or two to Betty Crocker for premixed ingredients. Later, when the service economy took hold, busy parents ordered cakes from the bakery or grocery store, which, at $10 or $15, cost ten times as much as the packaged ingredients. Now ... parents neither make the birthday cake nor even throw the party. Instead, they spend $100 or more to outsource the entire event to Chuck E. Cheese, The Discovery Zone, The Mining Company or some other business that stages a memorable event for kids – and often throws in the cake for free. Welcome to the emerging experience economy.
>
> (Pine and Gilmore, 1998)

A more developed version that links economic structure to demand and supply is as shown in Table 1.1.

The more developed the economic structure, the more personal spending there is on hospitality events, the more complex the processes involved and the more frequently people engage in the events. Economic ascent is accompanied by the provision of more facilities, services and products, which are used to create the context in which people experience hospitality events.

Table 1.1: Economic structure and the birthday party.

Economic structure	The Birthday Party	The Cake
Experience	Mum takes the child and 20 friends to McDonalds, which organises the whole vent with food, drinks and entertainment. Cost € 200	McDonalds provides the cake
Market Service	Party at home with 20 of the child's friends and a clown. Cost € 50	Mum buys the cake. Cost €15.
Citizen Service	The child invites a few friends home for tea and birthday cakes. Cost €10	Mum buys cake mix and bakes the cake. Cost €5
Industrial	Family sings 'Happy Birthday" at evening meal and eats the cake. No party cost.	Mum buys flour, eggs, sugar and makes the cake. Cost €3.
Agricultural	No party. No cost	No cake. No cost

The classification of economic activities

Economic activities have been classified and periodically revised by the United Nations Statistics Division, International Standard Industrial Classifications, into three groups (United Nations Statistics Division, 2006).

♦ Primary industries include: cultivation of crops, livestock production, fishing, forestry and hunting.

♦ Secondary industries include: construction, manufacturing, mining, quarrying and utilities.

♦ Tertiary services include: banking, bars, betting shops, bingo clubs, casinos, cinemas, communications, distribution, education services, financial services, health services, hairdressers, hotels, insurance, personal services, professional services, public administration, restaurants, retailing, security services, sports clubs, storage, transport, travel, theatres, visitor attractions and welfare services. Within each of these activities there are sub-divisions that extend tertiary activities throughout the lives of citizens of advanced economies and establish the tertiary segment as the most diverse and complex of the three economic segments.

Employment in each economic segment is different. It requires different knowledge and skills and it involves different relationships with the land, with machines, with colleagues and with the buyers of their output. As the balance of an economy ascends through the economic stages, so its structure becomes more complex and diverse. At any one time within any economy there are skills and jobs that are in demand to deliver economic output, others that are in decline and vanish and others for which demand has yet to materialise. As a result, the availability of products and services is not constant and their provision and consumption is not uniform.

Except during the earliest pre-economic period of history, each country had some involvement in primary, secondary and tertiary economic activities and its economic structure was determined by the amount and types of activity in each segment. Historically, tertiary was the least significant activity since most tertiary services existed only as a necessary support to the production, distribution and sale of agricultural and manufactured goods. Personal markets for services were minor in the historic agricultural and industrial economies. As a result, tertiary services were small and grew, generally in line with primary and secondary activities. It was not until after World War II that the US economy reached the stage at which tertiary activities took on a life of their own. Not only did the corporate market for service businesses expand, but the most significant change was the growth in personal demand for services. No longer was their existence dependent on their historic role as support services to primary and secondary activities. This was uncharted territory for economists since new economic activities emerged and others grew to dimensions never previously thought possible.

Tertiary activities are different in kind from primary and secondary activities. At the core of the difference is that tertiary activities are concerned with the provision and distribution of services whereas primary and secondary activities produce durable and non-durable goods. Tertiary activities are more complex than secondary activities, which in turn are more complex than primary activities. Within primary activities the dominant work interaction is between the worker and the land. Within secondary activities the dominant interaction is between the worker and the machine. In tertiary services, the crucial relationship is between people. The operational interaction with colleagues is necessary for the provision and delivery of services as is the interaction between the providers and the consumers of services. Reflecting this, services involve more mental work than the manual work that is characteristic of primary and secondary activities and consequently more white-collar work than blue-collar work.

Economists traditionally assumed that the range of tertiary activities is more homogeneous than it is in reality. The diversity and complexity of tertiary services has meant that to understand the role and dynamics of services and to plan and manage them effectively it has been necessary to classify services. The problem has been that most classifications have not been practical. Two examples illustrate the point. One attempt by Banton (1968) was to differentiate the range of tertiary activities between commerce and direct services. Commerce was seen by Banton to include: transport and communication; distributive trades; insurance; banking and finance; and storage, while direct services were seen to include: professional and scientific services; sport and recreation; personal services; and public administration. There is no obvious analytical base for this distinction between commerce and direct services and no more homogeneity within commerce and direct services than there is within tertiary activities as a whole.

Another attempt to classify services was provided by Foote and Hatt who proposed three sub-divisions of services (Foote and Hatt, 1953). In the tertiary sector they included: restaurants and hotels; barber and beauty shops; laundry and dry cleaning establishments; home repair and maintenance; handcrafts once performed in the home and other domestic and quasi-domestic services. For Foote and Hatt, the quaternary sector encompassed transportation, commerce, communication, finance and administration; and the quinary sector involved health-care, education and recreation. According to Foote and Hatt, tertiary activities are, "devoted simply to the maintenance of individuals in the style to which they have become accustomed". Quaternary activities "facilitate and effectuate the division of labour" and quinary activities are about, "the cultivation of behaviour to which they are not accustomed". This is a rather tortuous distinction in which the classifications are not mutually exclusive. Many other analyses of the growth and development of economies do not even address the issue. For Jay (2000), and Bernstein (2004) and Kay (2003), services are presented as little more than activities in addition to secondary activities.

The classification of tertiary services must accommodate two influences: one is the inherent features and functions of the services and the other is the influence of the political system on its economy. The political influence is crucial. Under Communism, the government controlled all services, whereas in a free-market economy many services are businesses with only light control exerted by the government. The more that the supply of and demand for services within an economy are controlled by the government, then the weaker the structure, performance and growth of the economy as a whole and services in particular. In the first instance, I present the tertiary activities in two stages: citizen services and service businesses. Then, for the more advanced economies service businesses are split into citizen services, market services and experience businesses.

Citizen services are controlled by governments. They include public education, public health, social services and the full range of public administration. It was not until the mid-19th century that governments in the historical industrial economies such as the Western European countries and North America considered that the provision of a broad range of these services was one of their core duties. From the late 19th century the role and significance of government grew, particularly in Western Europe, to the extent that citizen services became the largest segment of several economies. In the more advanced modern economies, access to many citizen services such as public education, public health care and social services are available to all as a right of citizenship and many are free at the point of delivery. As a result, some citizen services such as public health and public education have grown to be among the largest employers in a country. As the structural balance of an economy becomes tertiary, citizen services expand. Education expands as childhood and adolescent education become mandatory and a higher proportion of the population has access to further education, higher education, continuing education and pre-school education. Health care improves to sustain longer life expectancy and diversifies to include preventative as well as curative medicine. Community health grows and paramedic disciplines such as nutrition, physiotherapy and holistic medicine advance and the prison service seeks to reform criminals in addition to its basic custodial role.

The extent to which citizen services dominate the tertiary segment is both a political and an economic matter. Indeed, the main theme in political economy throughout the 20th century in Europe and North America was about the most effective way to provide citizen services. Europe emphasised the moral responsibility of governments not only to provide citizen services, but also to ensure that all citizens had equitable access to them. In contrast, the American approach emphasised the role of citizen choice in accessing many services with the implication that when choice is involved a market is created. Thus, the American approach was to involve business in the provision of many citizen services. The distinction between Europe and the US in the role of the government in the provision of citizen services was at the core of the distinction between the left wing and the right wing in politics. The more left-wing a government the more its commitment is to managing citizen services and to big government. The bigger the citizen services segment the more income the government needs to generate from other parts of the economy to fund the provision of citizen services. The result is that when service businesses are minor, a higher tax burden falls on the primary and secondary segments and the poorer the quality and scope of core citizen services such as health and education. The more right-wing an elected government the less it is committed to the management of citizen services, the more that some citizen services are privatised and become service businesses and the more it is committed to smaller government.

Market services

The first category of service businesses consists of market services including: banking, communications, distribution financial services, personal services, professional services, real estate management, retailing and wholesaling. Unlike citizen services, market services are not inherently managed by the state. They are businesses whose size, range and performance are driven by prevailing conditions in the two broad markets that they serve: the corporate market and the personal market. As the structural balance of an economy progresses, the growth in market services is fast because personal markets become mass markets.

As industrial economies grow and prosper there is increasing growth in the range of consumer goods produced and retailing emerges as a distinct skill to maximise the sale of goods. There is the recognition that manufactured goods do not sell themselves to the public and that advertising, marketing, merchandising and in-store facilities are necessary to sell more goods. Shops become larger and retail chains grow nationally. There are differences in the patterns of purchase and use of durable goods and non-durable goods. Consumer non-durables such as food and drink involve frequent repeat purchase because they have a high degree of perishability and once consumed cannot be re-used. Once consumer durables such as brown goods, white goods, cars and houses have been acquired there can be continued gratification from their use and re-use. Repurchase of consumer durables depends on the goods wearing out, falling out of fashion or becoming obsolete. Moreover, the consumption of many consumer durables, particularly brown and white goods, is private consumption, which occurs within the home.

As secondary economies grow and prosper so does the demand for financial services from both corporate and personal customers. The proportion of the population with bank accounts increases and financial services diversify. The provision of mortgages to enable citizens to own their homes rises and provides the source of ownership of a generally appreciating asset. The access to personal credit is eased so that the volume of unsecured loans increases as does the supply and use of credit cards, which accelerates personal spending on both goods and services. There is also an expansion in savings through pension schemes, insurance policies, stock market investments and other forms of saving. The communications industry was transformed in the historic industrial economies by the inventions of the postal service, telephone, radio, motion pictures and television. In the late 20th century there was a further explosion in communications for both the corporate and the personal markets with the invention of mobile telephony, personal computers and the Internet.

Personal demand for domestic services such as housekeeping, home repairs, home maintenance, gardening and car maintenance increase with prosperity and contribute to the shift in the structural balance of an economy to service businesses. As an economy develops its tertiary sector so the range of asset classes increases.

As well as land and industrial real estate, which are the preserve of the primary and secondary segments, domestic housing increases with population growth and with the growth in prosperity. Citizen service expansion produces an increase in the number of schools and hospitals. Commercial real estate increases with the market service economy as a result of the greater need for offices, warehouses, retail outlets and other venues.

Professional services operate as free-standing businesses and they also exist as a service function within corporations. Such jobs include white-collar and professional jobs in accounting and finance; marketing and selling; human resource management and other professional services. The larger the size of a business the larger the corporate structure and the wider the range of professional service careers within companies, irrespective of the industry or service in which they operate.

Experience businesses

The second category, experience businesses, include: airports, bars, bingo clubs, casinos, cinemas, cruise ships, events management, hairdressers, health clubs, hotels, nightclubs, passenger airlines, passenger coaches, passenger trains, private hospitals, private schools, private prisons, restaurants, sports businesses, theatres and visitor attractions. Experience businesses provide contexts in which their customers, students, patients, clients, passengers, prisoners, audience, players and spectators are participants in events that are designed for them to experience sensations such as enjoyment, anticipation, knowledge, health or remorse. The widest diversity of real estate occurs as the experience segment of the economy grows because experience businesses are based in venues. As the experience segment grows to become a significant part of the economy so experience properties emerge to become significant asset classes. The prime market for experience businesses is the personal market. Corporate demand for experience businesses is limited to business travel and the use of hotels, restaurants and other experience venues for subsistence and business entertaining. The frequency of personal demand for a wide range of experience businesses accelerates when ownership or at least access to the gamut of household and personal consumer goods and to market services has been achieved. The only economies in which personal markets for experience businesses have become economically significant are those in which government intervention has been slight.

There are four features of experience businesses that differentiate them from market service businesses:

♦ Consumption in experience businesses occurs in specific venues outside of the home. Central to the management of experience businesses is the creation of the conditions for consumption in the venue and the management of the consumption process. This is different from market service businesses. In retailing, for example, consumption occurs away from the point of sale and outside of the control of the retailer. Retailers do not manage the consumption of the products that they sell.

♦ Each experience business is defined by the configuration of facilities, services and products it offers for on-site consumption. This is the basis on which a hotel is different from an airport or a bingo club is different from a theatre and so on.

♦ Buying from experience businesses involves short-term renting, but not buying the ownership of the facilities and services.

♦ Because the buyer of services from experience businesses does not own the facilities or services, further gratification from consumption can only be gained by buying again.

The transition from primary to secondary industries

Having worked out the classification of economic activities, the next step is to seek explanations of the changes that occur in economic structure over time, the pace and patterns of those changes, the economic conditions and social structures that they support and that supports them and ultimately to reach an explanation of how economies develop. The significance of the shifts in the structural balance of economies should not be underestimated. Political systems have been developed to promote them and to prevent them, wars have been fought over them, economic traumas have been endured when an economic segment has matured and economic booms have emerged when new segments emerge and grow. The first shift in the structural balance of economies was the progression of the historic agricultural economies to become industrial economies. The progression began around the mid-18th century when a catalogue of technical, social and economic changes prepared the way for the most advanced economies to enter the historic industrial period proper around the mid-19th century. This transition period was the Industrial Revolution and it emerged after two centuries of slowly improving agricultural productivity, critical technical inventions such as steam power, the increase in jobs in manufacturing and mining, an acceleration of trade, and the increase in the range of industrial and consumer goods produced. Bernstein has identified four factors that provide the necessary conditions for the structural balance of an economy to shift from primary to secondary activities: property rights, scientific rationalism, capital markets and improvements in transport and communications (Bernstein, 2004: 7).

Property rights ensure that economic efforts will not be arbitrarily confiscated by the state or by criminals. According to Bernstein, "The medieval serf had little incentive to produce a crop in excess of his manorial obligations or increase the productivity of the land he worked...The feudal system not only failed to protect ownership and recognise equality under law; it also throttled basic consumer activity" (2004: 29) The introduction of property rights for the population was achieved slowly. The US was one of the last western countries to introduce property rights across its population and it took the Civil War to achieve it. The southern states, which formed the Confederacy, clung on to slavery to shore up their declining competitiveness in agricultural production in the face of the faster growing and more competitive industrial economy of the northern states.

Scientific rationalism refers to the systematic procedures for examining, measuring and interpreting the world. It underpins invention and production methods. In Bernstein's analysis secular and scientific ideas were traditionally not welcomed by the Catholic Church and its hostility was most notably seen in its reaction to Copernicus's conclusion that the earth moved around the sun. Until later in the historic agricultural period the churches were a major influence on what was taught in schools and universities and only when that control was loosened did the flow of inventions and innovations, protected by property rights, materialise and enable the structure of economies to change. Secondary activities moved to centre stage in the 100-year period from the mid-18th century driven by technological innovations such as steam power, iron and steel production, textile technology, gas light and the telegraph. Scientific rationality and property rights afforded investors the motivation and security to develop their ideas and to profit from their sale and use.

In the transition from primary to secondary industries, the capital markets were involved in providing funds for the development and production of new inventions. Economic development during the historic agricultural period was hampered, according to Bernstein, by Christianity's blurred distinction between lending and usury, which originally was seen as lending with interest, and Islam's opposition to interest. It was not until the advent of the historic industrial period that inventors had access to sufficient capital to put technological ideas into practice, transforming industry. The harnessing of steam power and the other landmark technologies of the Industrial Revolution did not come free. Before the end of the historic agricultural period fundamental capital market processes had been introduced. Money, double-entry bookkeeping, banking, insurance and stock markets were established and formed an important non-governmental component of tertiary activities. The more that manufacturing and trade grew, the more industrialists and traders needed access to capital markets. Improvements in transport and communication were necessary to accelerate trade and to sell the increased output resulting from the technological developments. During the transition period, steamships and railways emerged and materially reduced the time taken for journeys and materially increased the volume of freight and numbers of passengers transported.

By the mid-18th century in countries such as Britain and Holland, Bernstein's four factors prevailed sufficiently for the transition of the structural balance of the economy from primary to secondary activities to proceed naturally. The feudal period had long since ended. New inventions and new technologies were improving agricultural output and productivity. Agricultural unemployment was increasing. New technologies, most notably factories, were emerging with the need for workers and the capacity to produce basic goods in greater mass. The capital markets opened to fund these industrial developments and thus, the Industrial Revolution brought a 100-year period of great change to economies for which agriculture and its supporting structures had been central for almost 10 millennia. The economies that emerged as full-blown secondary economies in the mid-19th century were characterised by an explosion in the volumes, diversity and development of manufactured products, of the volume of coal and other materials extracted from the earth, and the provision of nationwide public utilities such as water, gas and electricity to homes, workplaces and public buildings. The period was also characterised by the substantial growth in productivity in all secondary activities until the stage was reached in the US in the 1920s at which market demand for the range of products could be delivered by significantly fewer employees. When the growth in productivity exceeded the growth in demand for goods, structural unemployment in the secondary economy became a central problem that was only resolved by creating new tertiary sector jobs. However, so powerful was the development of the historic secondary economy that it was regarded until the last quarter of the 20th century as the engine room that created wealth. This thinking was at the bottom of the concerns by many in the US, Britain and elsewhere between the 1960s and 1990s when agriculture and manufacturing were declining in economic significance and there was insufficient understanding of the sources of wealth that would emerge from service businesses to replace them.

From secondary industries to tertiary services

As the diversity and complexity in tertiary services are much greater than in primary and secondary activities so the transition of an economy through citizen services to market service and experience businesses is not easy. There are two fundamental requirements that provide the context for the transition to be achieved: the quality of performance of its economy and the political system of a country. The USA, Britain and the USSR, each of which had different political systems and levels of economic performance, produced different outcomes in the development of their economic structures.

The transition to tertiary in the US

The USA, achieved the most successful transition in the structural balance of any economy to tertiary activities. During the first half of the 20th century the US diverged both economically and politically from other economies in ways that made it easier for it to make the transition to be a full-blown service business economy. The structural unemployment in primary and secondary industries in the 1920s were key causes of the Great Depression because there were too few tertiary services that were growing and creating new jobs. A priority for the first Roosevelt administration was to reduce unemployment, which had reached an all time high of 25% by 1932 *(source*: US Government Census 1932). The solution, the New Deal, was designed to re-establish economic equilibrium at lower levels of unemployment and it achieved this by the federal creation of new jobs, many of which were service orientated and this provided the early signs that a structural shift in the balance of the economy towards services was under way.

The unique feature of the US management of the Great Depression was that, within the free market culture of the US, the New Deal was designed as a short-term initiative to allow the free market economy to find a more acceptable long-term solution and it succeeded. Citizen services were centre stage in the US economy for only 10 years from 1932 to the entry of the US to World War II. The US considered citizen services to be little more than a safety net and in the debate about the role of government it came down firmly on the side of small government. The US pursued the idea that central government should only control core citizen services such as health, education, welfare and security, but that even within these there was room for free market initiatives. The practical dimension of this belief was that the free market would do a better job of managing services than the government and the philosophical dimension was that citizens should have choice about which services to buy in the same way that they have with any other purchases. Throughout World War II, the US economy continued to grow and after the war moved even further ahead. As a result of superior economic performance and easy access to consumer goods, the demand for services grew materially and service businesses expanded to a degree not achieved by any other significant economy. By 1950, the majority of the US workforce was employed in tertiary activities since when the economic history of the US has been about the continuing growth of the tertiary segment and in particular the size and scope of mass market service and experience businesses.

The transition to tertiary in Britain

The lead that Britain achieved over other economies in the transition from primary to secondary was under strain by the end of the 19th century and the decline continued into the 20th century. All of the administrations over the first 80 years of the 20th century increased citizen services to the extent that it had become political orthodoxy. When the US was initiating the New Deal as a short-term solution to the Great Depression, British politicians were being entranced by the ideas of John Maynard Keynes, and produced long-term solutions to the Great Depression that set the British economy off on 50 years of increasingly bigger government and that grew the citizen services segment till the 1980s when it was unable to be supported by the rest of the economy (Keynes, 2007).

The collapse of manufacturing in the 1960s and 1970s, accompanied by an escalation in unemployment marked the relegation of secondary activities from their position as the driver of economic growth in Britain. The Harold Wilson and James Callaghan Labour administrations in the 1960s and 1970s tried to solve the problems with more big government initiatives by extending government control over increasingly large parts of the secondary economy. Already, industries such as coal, railways, electricity, gas, telephony and waterways had been nationalised and so also had companies such as British Airways. Wilson and Callaghan added the steel industry, Rolls Royce, shipbuilders such as Upper Clyde Shipbuilders, vehicle manufacturers such as British Leyland and aerospace companies such as Vickers, ostensibly to save the large number of jobs that would have been lost if the firms had collapsed. At the same time, core citizen services were expanding fast. New and larger schools were built throughout the 1950s and 1960s to accommodate the bulge in the birth rate in the 10 years after World War II, then to provide for the pupils when they reached 18 years of age, higher education exploded with the creation of a raft of new universities and polytechnics during the 1960s and 1970s. At the same time, the National Health Service was expanded not only by the building of more and larger hospitals, but also by the extension of the service into community health through the growth in health visitors, district nurses, district midwifes and social workers. The Government also became the largest landlord by building around 2.5 million council houses throughout the 1950s and 1960s (source: United Kingdom, Office of National Statistics)

The initiatives failed to bring about the recovery of the economy. The nationalised industries did not perform well and too much tax was being taken from weakening primary and secondary business at a time when service businesses were still relatively small and most were very fragmented. The Callaghan government was replaced by the Margaret Thatcher Conservative administrations that stretched from 1979 to 1992 and was followed by the John Major Conservative administration till 1997. During this 18-year Conservative period the government control of industry was unwound, substantially. The victory in 1982 over the yearlong miners' strike was crucial in breaking the downward spiral of heavy reliance on the government to provide full employment and all other economic benefits. There was a series of successful privatisations of utilities such as gas, electricity and water as well as British Telecom, the national telephone company, British Airways and BAA, which owned and operated the main airports. Government ownership of shipbuilding, vehicle manufacture and other smaller businesses was sold.

Bureaucratic hurdles were reduced for start-up businesses, most of which were service businesses and the infrastructure was put in place to extend home ownership among the population. Importantly, as part of the process of making government smaller, key citizen services such as health, education and prison services developed market driven elements, that is, they became experience businesses. Private education expanded throughout the full range: nursery schools, preparatory schools, secondary schools and universities. Private curative health expanded, as did the insurance schemes to fund it. In addition to lifesaving drugs, lifestyle drugs, such as the birth control pill, became more prominent and cosmetic surgery became more readily available as an experience service. Private security companies were contracted to manage parts of the prison service. All of these initiatives succeeded in reducing unemployment, most new jobs were created in service businesses and the structural balance of the economy progressed to service business.

The transition to tertiary in the USSR

The USSR and communist states as a whole were examples of a political system whose economics was entrenched in agricultural and industrial activities, it was no accident that the emblem of the Soviet Union was the hammer and sickle, and it considered service businesses to be peripheral to their ideology. The establishment of the first communist government following the Russian Revolution in 1917 meant that for the first time in economic history, the state took control of all economic activities and removed free market influences on demand and supply. The pre-revolutionary economy had been focused on primary and secondary activities, which were performing badly and the economy as a whole was in a dire state. When the USSR was created, the primary and secondary economic focus continued. Tertiary activities were a minor element of the economy and the government limited the scope of service businesses to those that were required by primary and secondary producers under communist domination. Thus, throughout the communist era, service businesses stagnated, travel was curtailed and poverty was widespread. The economy did not progress beyond the subsistence level and came nowhere close to reaching the stage at which it was strong enough to make the transition in its structural balance to service businesses. Indeed, no other communist country has ever been able to progress beyond the secondary stage of economic development and many have struggled to make the transition from primary to secondary. The paradox of Communism is that sea changes introduced by the political system aimed at reducing poverty and social injustice prevented the development of the economy in ways that would have enabled it to deliver the prosperity needed to reduce poverty and social injustice.

Factors in the transition to the tertiary

The examples of the US, Britain and the USSR illustrate the extent to which the political ideology of a country determines the rate at which an economy can progress from secondary to tertiary and through citizen services to market services and experience businesses. The US showed that it was able to make the transition sooner, faster and more completely than any other economy, while Britain had to endure almost a century of big government before it was able to develop mass market service businesses. Communism was a non-starter. The effective transition to tertiary is not a naturally occurring event, it needs to be managed and part of the management is the creation of the necessary economic and social conditions to enable the transition. Bernstein identified four factors that provide the necessary conditions for the structural balance of an historic primary economy to shift to secondary activities. In addition to the political and economic determinants of the transition to tertiary, the necessary conditions for an economy to make the transition are adapted from Bernstein's originals to fit the service context.

First, Bernstein's property rights are elevated to human and civil rights. The greater diversity and complexity of service economies requires political, legal and social frameworks that are more open than in primary and secondary economies. Enfranchisement of the adult population; free speech; the establishment of legal institutions that are not subsidiary to government; mandatory access to a wide scope of education, healthcare and welfare services; the decline in hereditary priviledge; the protection of gender, age and disability rights are all examples of rights that exist more extensively in service economies than in primary and secondary economies. They mark out the differences in the social structure of a service business economy compared with a secondary or primary economy.

The more explicit and the wider the range of human and civil rights, the less control that a government can exert over the lives of its citizens, the greater the egalitarianism, the greater the social mobility and the more effective the transition to mass market service businesses. The second Bernstein factor, scientific rationality, is reflected in the transition to services by the growth of the social sciences. As societies become increasingly open due to the extension of human and civil rights and economies become more service orientated, so they become more diverse and more complex and this requires the utilisation of social scientific understanding, interpretations and explanations of events. A feature of service business economies is the significance of pure and applied social sciences in education, particularly the growth vocational degrees in business, which involve an element of the social sciences. Hospitality management is an example with more than 120 universities in the US and 40 universities in Britain offering undergraduate degrees in the field. No other economy, irrespective of its size, comes remotely close to these levels of provision.

In Bernstein's four factors, the capital markets to which he referred were corporate capital markets. For economies to develop into mass-market service businesses the requirement is the additional development of personal capital markets with easier and more widespread access to credit through loans and credit cards. The ownership of appreciating assets such as homes, insurance policies and other savings products enables the capital markets to adjust risk to lend for service activities such as holidays and entertainment as well as for capital goods that they can recover in the event of default. The extension of access to personal capital markets provides a boost to aspirations for the consumption of goods and services and is instrumental in growing the mass service business economy.

The fundamental requirement of the transport and communications factor in the Industrial Revolution was for the transport of freight and it relied on the efficiency benefits of steam trains and steam ships, whereas in the transition to service businesses the central focus is on the transport of people. The major increase in volume and frequency of personal travel resulted from the introduction of paid annual holiday leave and the material increase in the volume and frequency of business travel resulted from the growth of mass market service businesses. The boost to spending was not only in travel, but also in hotels, restaurants and other goods and services at destinations. This practice grew for short holidays as well as for long holidays. Indeed, it was not only holidays and business travel that boosted spending. Experience businesses entail participation in out-of-home leisure activities and thus, they also involve some form of travel. All of these factors contribute to the increasingly cosmopolitan perspective in service business economies and the reduction of the narrow parochialism that is more prevalent in primary and secondary economies.

Economic performance and economic structure

Economies with low GDP per capita in primary and secondary activities also have low GDP per capita in tertiary activities because there is not enough government revenue to fund more than basic citizen services and there is not enough corporate and personal income to generate demand for more than the most basic service business. The prime economic condition for an economy to make the transition in structural balance from secondary to tertiary is a sufficiently high GDP per capita in primary and secondary activities to generate enough government income to fund more extensive citizen services and to generate demand from the population and from corporates for mass market service and experience businesses. For the year 2000, the Russian GDP per capita reached $3,140. In the same year the US economy achieved $37,640, 12 times more and Britain achieved $32,400, 10 times more. Also in 2000, Russian GDP per capita in agriculture reached $202 at a time when the US achieved two and a half times more and Britain one and a half times more. In the same year, Russian secondary industries achieved GDP per capita of $1,190, while the US and Britain each achieved more than four and a half times as much, but the sharpest differences were the tertiary segment. Russia delivered tertiary GDP per capita of $1,750, while the US bettered it by 16 times and Britain by 13 times (*source*: World Bank Country Statistical Information Database, 2005).

2 Historic Agricultural Economies and the Hotel Business to 1750

Introduction

The practice and study of economics emerged during the historic agricultural period, which lasted until the mid-18th century. This was also the period when even the most advanced economies were simple and their structural balance was embedded in agriculture and fishing. Hotels and their early equivalents emerged, but remained small venues of little economic significance, with little national capacity serving small markets of traders and pilgrims as well as sundry and intermittent other travellers.

Historic agricultural economies

From the first appearance of man to around 8,000 years bc, life was concentrated on survival by hunting and gathering food. Economics as we know it played no part in differentiating lifestyles or standards of living. Progress was slow; surpluses did not emerge in the early millennia neither did trading, which at first was based on barter when hunting and gathering activities were progressively supplemented by cultivation and herding. The historic agricultural economy, which emerged gradually in the Fertile Crescent, the area between the Tigris and the Euphrates in modern Iraq, spread to the other parts of the known world. Agricultural activities became economic activities and dominated the economic focus of man in almost all countries for the remainder of the period. Progressively, but still slowly, surpluses were produced that enabled the sale of products and the start of trading. The progress of technology and innovation in agricultural practices were slow and uneven. They involved tools such as the plough, practices such as crop rotation and towards the end of the period, the introduction of property rights so that by the end of the agricultural period in the most advanced economies such as Britain output and productivity had improved substantially and fewer agricultural workers were needed. New technologies, new products and new markets were needed to utilise the increasing levels of unemployment among agricultural workers. This was a serious problem since rural agriculture workers accounted for the bulk of the workforce even in the most advanced historic agricultural economies. As Bernstein reminds us, "By 1500, the largest city in Europe was Naples with a population of 150,000. Only 865,000 Europeans, or about 1% of the continent's population lived in cities of more than 50,000. Another 6% lived in towns of more than 10,000. More than 90% of Europeans, then, were engaged in agriculture in the medieval period" (Bernstein, 2004: 21).

From the feudal medieval era, trade in agricultural products and spin-offs such as cloth, basic household goods and shipbuilding expanded from local to regional, national and in a few cases international markets, but they were all minor economic activities at the time. As trade grew, small-scale manufacturing and construction emerged. Cottage industries and new occupations evolved, which were not agricultural and involved different skills in jobs such as metal work, carpentry, textile production and tailoring. They also involved different work relationships between man and machine as well as man and materials rather than man and the land. They occurred in workshops rather than in the fields and they served different markets, being more affordable to those who had sufficient disposable income. During the historic agricultural period these secondary economic activities were in the minority, but were growing and in the most advanced agricultural economies accelerated the emergence of tertiary activities such as banking and transportation, which were the smallest parts of economies. The balance of the most developed agricultural economies was shifting away from agriculture as secondary and tertiary activities grew. In the last 200 years of the agricultural period in England, the most advanced agricultural economy of the time, new innovations appeared which contributed to the introduction of new products and the growth of more surpluses, which in turn required more tertiary infrastructure for support. These developments were reflected in the doubling of agricultural output between 1600 and 1800 (Jay, 2000: 180). The agricultural period produced only ponderous economic development, a pattern that was reflected in the social structure that was based on heredity and class, which constrained progress and opportunity and relegated the mass of the population to subsistence living. Human rights and services such as education and health care were minimal at best and organised leisure was all but absent. For the vast mass of humankind, life in the historic agricultural economy was oppressive and short.

Inns during the historic agricultural period

The historic agricultural economies were invariably subsistence economies and their inns were simple businesses with the prime aim of satisfying only the subsistence needs of customers and their horses as well as serving as the home of the innkeeper. Demand volume in the historic agricultural economies was small because populations were small and only a minute proportion travelled far enough to need to stay in an inn. The very low level of demand was a function of the structure of the historic agricultural economies that relied almost entirely on demand from agricultural traders and later in the period from traders in basic manufactures as well as occasional other travellers such as pilgrims. The main economic activity, agriculture, involved very little travel. Predominantly, arable farmers took their products to local markets and had little need for inns, while serfs, the mass of the population, endured a subsistence existence and were not a market for inns. Pastoral farmers, particularly those located far from larger conurbations of the time, needed to travel farther to market than arable farmers and were a larger market for inns.

Early inns

One early example in Britain involved pastoral farmers in a practice that lasted for almost 800 years to the 19th century. Each year from May to October waves of cattle and sheep farmers from the Scottish Highlands would drove their livestock southward as far as the English markets at the approximate rate of 10–15 miles per day. There developed over time a string of drovers' inns that stretched over the routes (Haldane, 1995: 40). Each was located around one day's drove apart and on the way south the drovers would stay overnight with their livestock and their dogs and would return with their dogs and the money from the sale of their livestock to the inns as they walked home. The early versions of the drovers' inns were rough places providing no more than bothy facilities and many drovers preferred to sleep outside with their cattle. Eventually, the safety of the hospitality improved and drovers took to the inns, but the demand for drovers' inns was not great. Their locations, mostly in rural areas, attracted little demand over the centuries. Their defining market was active for only half of the year. During the winter months there was practically no demand for accommodation and as a result, the drovers' inns relied on local demand for drinks, but still were barely effective economically. Drover's inns such as the Clachaig Inn, Glencoe, the Kings House, Rannoch and the Bridge of Orchy Inn at Bridge of Orchy were each separated by a day's drove and they survive today still with heavily seasonal demand, but from leisure travellers rather than from agricultural traders.

Drovers were an example of both farmers and traders who were key customers for inns; they were the business travellers of the historic agricultural economies. There are examples from the Middle East where traders stayed in khans, from North Africa where they stayed in caravanserai, from France where they stayed in auberges, in Spain where they stayed in posadas and Japan where they stay in ryokans. Hotels in the historic agricultural economies were culturally specific in terms of the facilities, services and products that they provided reflecting the common practice of the country or region in which they were located. Although they were developed in different centuries, in different cultures and provided various patterns of hospitality, they bore a family resemblance. In keeping with the slow change in the social structure of the historic agricultural economy, changes were also slow in inns and in the style and substance of the hospitality that they provided. Inns differed from other businesses in any location since they were established to serve customers on-site and to serve customers who were not local.

The only alternative to inns that rented sleeping accommodation and sold meals and drinks were monasteries, which catered mainly for pilgrims as a backup to their prime religious function. Pilgrims also used inns and in the 14th century Chaucer's pilgrims in The Canterbury Tales met at the Tabard Inn, Southwark, London "theis gentil hostelrye" (Chaucer, [1400] 1934: 3). Because inns were small and because of the subsistence hospitality they provided, the relationship between the customers and the innkeeper and his family helpers was utilitarian. Demand was generated because of to the location of the inn and its capacity to accommodate travellers and their horses.

Inn supply and demand 1577

The 1577 census for England and Wales identified 1631 inns that rented short-term sleeping accommodation and sold basic meals to travellers as well as selling drinks to travellers and the local public (source: Census for England and Wales, 1577) At this time Shakespeare was a teenager, Elizabeth I had been on the throne for 19 years and Sir Francis Drake was setting off on his voyage around the world. Thomas Burke recorded in The English Inn, that the inn of this period, "had stone or earthen floors strewn with rushes. In the main room a number of mattresses were laid around the walls, and here the guests slept" (Burke, 1930). The historic agricultural period was characterised by a narrow range of reasons for customers to stay at inns and their stays were rarely more than one night at a time. The homogeneity of the subsistence level facilities, services and products reflected the low level of demand and customer selection of inns was determined by the mode of transport and the availability of accommodation at the end of a day's travel since there were few locations where there was a commercial alternative to a single inn. Collectively, these features of the interrelationship between inn supply and inn demand meant that a customer's decision to stay at an inn was dictated by circumstances rather than based on a choice from a range of alternatives.

Table 2.1: English and Welsh Inns 1577.

Inns	1,631
Rooms	1,631
Room nights available (m)	0.6
Room occupancy %	40%
Room nights sold (m)	0.2
Average customers per room	4
Customers per year (m)	1
Customers per inn	584
Inn supply ratio	0.3

Source: Otus & Co Advisory Ltd.

The communal sleeping facilities meant that for analytical purposes each inn had only one bedroom and given the population of England and Wales at the time, the supply ratio of only 0.3 inn rooms per 1,000 citizens illustrates their marginal economic significance. On the assumptions that each inn accommodated, typically, one coach load of five including the driver, each received a coach during the four mid-week nights rather than at the weekend and that the demand in winter was at its lowest, then it is unlikely that total annual occupancy would have exceeded 40%. On this basis, the total number of customers staying at all inns in England and Wales in 1577 was probably less than one million.

The miniscule average number of resident customers per inn in 1577 of around 580, or an average of less than two customers per night is another measures of their marginal economic significance in the late 16th century. To boost income, inns also sold a daily meal to resident customers, provided stables for the horses of travellers and sold drinks to resident customers and locals. Even with the inn doubling as the home of the innkeeper and his family, they were still only marginal businesses with very low levels of invested capital. Before the 17th century, meal provision in inns was both basic and communal. Meals were provided at one table to all travellers together (Burke, 1930). There was little or no choice of dishes and travellers helped themselves from a communal pot, from which practice the term "potluck" is derived. At the same time in French inns the term "table d'hôte" referred to a communal table at which travellers sat to eat a communal meal. Invariably, inns catered for customers at only one meal per day, the timing of which varied according to coach arrival and departure times.

The emergence of coaching inns

In the later part of the historic agricultural period when trading grew, tertiary activities expanded from a very low base, smoother road surfaces were created between the larger cities, more frequent horse-drawn coach services were introduced and the volume of travel increased. Inn demand from traders grew and a minor leisure demand emerged, largely from wealthy individuals travelling between country houses. The demand for inns during this period was subsidiary to the demand for travel. Inns were a necessary element of travel for traders and others to reach their destinations. The function of travel was not to stay at an inn. The coaching inn era also saw an increase in the quality of provision compared with the drovers' inns. They began to evolve bedrooms rather than communal sleeping facilities and the one communal meal with potluck was replaced gradually by the provision of limited menus. In response, inn facilities became less basic, but there was not a structured or differentiated market at this time. In England, the coaching inns were situated further apart than the drovers' inns, because horse-drawn coaches travelled further in a day than farmers on foot. The coaching inns were more elaborate because they catered for more wealthy travellers and their locations within and between the larger towns and cities catered for a higher volume of demand. During the period, inns remained independently owned and continued to function as the home of the innkeeper. Thus, the capital requirements, although greater than in previous centuries, remained small. At the end of the historic agricultural period, innkeeping was still a small, wholly fragmented business used by only a tiny minority of the population as a support service on their journeys, but some of the coaching inns including the

George, Stamford, the Red Lion, Colchester and the Angel, Guildford that were established during this period, continue to operate today as hotels.

Inn supply and demand 1750

By the end of the historic agricultural period, around 1750, there had been a significant growth in the number of inns in operation in England and Wales compared with the position in 1577. The population had grown 16% to 5.5 million. Otus estimates that in broad terms, the number of inns increased to 2000 as new coaching inns with bedrooms were built increasing total room stock to around 8,000. If the inn supply ratio had remained constant, then, given the growth in population the room stock in 1750 would have increased to only 1900 rooms. Otus estimates that secular growth in room stock over the period amounted to 6,100 rooms. The volume of hotel demand had grown too, but the pattern of demand had not changed much. The demand for coaching inns remained more concentrated on mid-week rather than weekend demand and customers were at their fewest in the winter. The resulting room occupancy declined to 30% as the additional room stock accelerated faster than demand and sharing bedrooms was commonplace. In 1750, the supply ratio of inn rooms per 1,000 citizens had risen to 1.5, up from 0.3 in 1577. Although the supply ratio shows a significant improvement, the inns were still not a material part of the economy.

Table 2.2: English and Welsh Inns 1577–1750.

	1577	1750	GAGR %
Inns	1,631	2,000	0.1%
Rooms	1,631	8,000	0.9%
Room nights available (m)	0.6	2.9	0.9%
Room occupancy %	40%	30%	
Room nights sold (m)	0.2	0.9	0.8%
Average customers per room	4.0	2.6	
Customers per year (m)	1.0	2.3	0.5%
Inn supply ratio	0.3	1.5	
Secular growth in inn room supply		6,100	

Source: Otus & Co Advisory Ltd.

3 The Industrial Revolution and the Hotel Business: 1750–1850

Introduction

By the middle of the 18th century the range of non-agricultural technical innovation in the most advanced historic agricultural economies such as Britain and Holland triggered a new industrial economic era. The Industrial Revolution, which lasted for 100 years until the middle of the 19th century, was the transition phase when the structural balance of the most advanced agricultural economies shifted to become industrial. The emerging industrial economies became more technological, more manufacturing orientated, more urban and economically more complex. The significance of the developments in the structural balance of the economies was codified in landmark texts in classic economics. In 1776 Adam Smith published the first modern economic text book on the systematic division of labour, economic growth and progress (Smith [1776] 1904) Thomas Malthus produced his first economic analysis of population in 1798 and David Ricardo published an economic analysis of employment in the new industrialising era in 1817. (Ricardo 1817) The emergence of new secondary industries that accelerated the rate of growth, size and complexity of the economies as well as the increase in wealth was accompanied by a stepped growth in the demand for and supply of hotels. It was also accompanied by the first explicit stratification of hotel demand and of hotel supply. The economic ascent of the hotel business was under way. Even the use of the term hotel emerged during the Industrial Revolution. It refers to those establishments that in the historic agricultural period were known by a variety of titles such as inns, khans, caravanserai, auberges and posadas. Its use emerged in post-revolutionary France and spread to become a global word that transcends all major languages and cultures.

Developments in economic structure during the Industrial Revolution

The 100 years of the Industrial Revolution saw an accelerated growth in economic activity and the expansion of new, larger and more efficient forms of production, most notably the factory. Migration to cities increased, as did population. The British population increased from 5.5 million to 20 million and life would never be the same again. From 1760 to 1840 in Britain male employment in agriculture fell from 53% to 29% and in industry it increased from 24% to 47% Jay, 2004: 184). The growth of factories, mills and mines needed manpower, which was provided during this period by mass migration from the countryside to towns and cities. The migration to the cities was driven by increases in agricultural productivity and the increase in the importation of foodstuffs. Both caused agricultural unemployment to rise and the migration to cities was driven by the search for employment. As the population of the towns and cities escalated so the construction industry grew over the period to build the homes, factories, commercial properties and public properties that defined the urban areas. The first application of steam to machinery for spinning cotton was made in Manchester in 1789 and contributed to the establishment of the cotton industry in the area, which was close to Liverpool the port at which raw cotton arrived in the country. In 1800, the population of Manchester was 75,000. By 1850 it had reached 225,000 due largely to migration from the countryside to the mills and factories (source: www.visionofbritain.org.uk). In 1830, there were over 560 mills in the area employing more than 110,000 workers, of which 35,000 were children (source: www.ourwardfamily.com) As Jay records, "Britain in the late eighteenth and early nineteenth centuries acquired as a result of technical change (innovation and application) a competitive advantage through higher productivity in tradable manufactures that was even greater than its advantages in farm products. Cotton textiles were the panzers of this onslaught" (Jay, 2004: 194).

Similar developments were occurring in other key cities. In 1800, the population of New York was 60,000 (source: www.census.gov/population). By 1850, it had reached 515,000 through a mixture of migration from the countryside and most significantly migration into the US (source: www.census.gov/population) There were other technological transformations too. In Britain in 1800, the net tonnage of steamships registered was 24,000, the highest in the world and a reflection of Britain's economic power and its empire (Mitchell, 1988). In 1793 there were around 400 banks in Britain and by 1810, there were around 700 (Court, 1964). Exports also flourished during the Industrial Revolution. Free trade grew after the repeal of the Corn Laws in 1846 and maintained momentum in the international markets so that by 1850 British exports reached a record level (Court, 1964). The increase in the volume and range of manufactured goods, the migration to towns and the movement to mass employment in factories produced an urban social structure that was more formal and more complex than in the historic agricultural economy. This fast and mass movement also produced the dreadful problems of child workers, inadequate education, deficient healthcare provision and hovels for homes. Governments of the period were not active in the provision of these services although the larger local authorities were. Apart from the 1834 Poor Law, which was the last resort for the destitute, the state did not manage social services. However, in Britain, by the middle of the century, women and boys under 10 years old were forbidden from working underground in mines and the 10-hour working day was introduced in 1847 (Court, 1964). By the middle of the 19th century the structural balance of the British economy had shifted fully from agriculture to industrial activities, the Industrial Revolution was complete and other advanced economies such as the US were not far behind.

Hotel business demand in the Industrial Revolution

The first and most significant source of hotel demand that grew during the Industrial Revolution was business demand. The hotel demand generated by agriculture in the historic agricultural period continued during the Industrial Revolution, but agriculture demand for hotels was minor. Most of the new and additional hotel business demand was generated by the growing secondary industries and the follow-on growth of tertiary businesses such as banking and transport. Of the secondary activities – manufacturing, construction, public utilities and mining – the most important for hotel demand during the Industrial Revolution was manufacturing. The period produced an increase in the range and volume of manufactured goods, which entailed growth in the frequency of business travel by the rising numbers of owners, directors and merchants predominantly selling their manufactured goods and buying raw materials. Manufacturers in the US at the time produced a greater proportion of their output for the domestic market than for export while in Britain the balance tilted the other way. The Americans also sold their products and imported goods over a wider domestic area than did British manufacturers and thus required more salesmen travelling who stayed in hotels more frequently. Owners and directors of other secondary and tertiary businesses also increased the frequency of their business travel, but it was on a much smaller scale than manufacturers. The growth in construction was in the expanding towns and cities as were location-specific construction companies and thus they generated less regular business demand into hotels than manufacturers.

Public utilities were emerging during the period, but were also location-specific and generated less regular business demand into hotels. Similarly, the growth in coal mining produced the prime power source of the period, but the small size of mining companies and their focus on local markets limited the need for their owners to stay in hotels for business. In the tertiary segment, banking and retailing were highly fragmented and local. Thus, although the volume and frequency of domestic business demand into hotels from banks, retailing, construction, public utilities and mines increased compared with the historic agricultural period it was still less than the demand from manufacturers. Otus estimates that by 1850, business travel was the main hotel market accounting broadly for 5 million room nights, up from half a million in 1750. The volume of foreign business travellers increased over the period, but it was a minor source of hotel demand that came from suppliers of raw materials into Britain, buyers of raw materials and manufactures from the other advanced economies who concentrated on London and the main manufacturing cities.

Hotel leisure demand in the Industrial Revolution

The other source of hotel demand during the Industrial Revolution was from leisure travellers. The increase in wealth over the period was a key factor in the growth of domestic leisure demand into hotels. Even so, domestic leisure travel was not a mass market and the volume of domestic leisure customers in hotels remained low relative to the populations of Britain, the USA and the advanced economies of continental Europe. Throughout the period there was no mass holiday taking. In the early part of the period, the leisure travel market was dominated by wealthy families visiting relatives and friends, which occurred mainly during the spring and summer months and less frequently during the winter months. Then, in 1845, there was a crucial change in leisure travel. Thomas Cook organised his first formal tour from Leicester to Liverpool, which proved so successful that by 1846 he had expanded his tours to Scotland (Brendon, 1991: 36). Coaching inns were used by this market as a necessary element of that travel rather than as a destination and the length of stay was rarely more than one night in any inn. Otus estimates that by 1850, leisure demand in Britain accounted broadly for 2.7 million room nights in hotels, up from 0.3 million in 1750. International travel was boosted in 1841 when Cunard started its regular crossings of the Atlantic in steamships. These were not only of greater capacity than sailing ships of the day, they reduced the time taken for the crossing to two weeks, and also reduced the cost thus boosting international tourism across the Atlantic and to other parts of the British Empire (Johnson, 1987: 11). Foreign leisure travellers who were drawn from the wealthiest in their home countries constituted a small demand category, but they stayed in the host country for long periods and to meet this demand, hotels in capital and other prominent cities had to provide enhanced facilities compared with the coaching inns. Thus, towards the end of the period the stratification of hotel demand emerged.

Hotel supply in the Industrial Revolution

The growth in the volume of hotel demand and the changing pattern of demand required growth in supply, which brought with it the first explicit stratification of hotel supply into coaching inns, hotels and gentlemen's clubs. Most of the new development was in coaching inns, which was a continuation of the hotel provision from the historic agricultural period. They were built mainly in provincial cities, in industrialising towns and on arterial roads between cities and were a response to the stepped increase in demand for travel. In 1815, 22 million coach journeys were taken in Britain (Taylor, 2003: 23). Not unexpectedly, London had some of the largest coaching inns in the country, because it also had the highest volume of demand and included establishments such as La Belle Souvage, the White Bear and the Golden Cross (Taylor, 2003: 23). At the start of the Industrial Revolution, the journey from London to York took a week and involved at least six nights in coaching inns along the route. Journeys of more than 35 miles would have needed an overnight stay in a coaching inn. Provincial inns were small, few provided more than 10 bedrooms and there was more space for the upkeep of horses and coaches than for customers. Predominantly, their concentration in the provinces meant that they accommodated foreign travellers only rarely. Coaching inns provided facilities for customers to sleep, eat and drink, but there was little in the range of facilities, services and products to differentiate among the coaching inns. Customers arrived by coach or on horseback and it was of little significance to the innkeeper whether they were domestic or foreign, business or leisure travellers and it was rare for women to travel other than in a family group. There was little impetus to change inns since customers did not make explicit choices to stay at any one inn rather than another. They stayed wherever the coaches stopped and stayed typically for only one night at a time in any inn. Thus, the key relationship was between the innkeeper and the coach operators that stopped at the inn, not between the innkeeper and the customers. It was the coach operator who delivered the customers and importantly the coaches, horses and drivers that were also sources of income to the inn.

The coming of the railways

The Industrial Revolution was the heyday of the coaching inn, but their growth did not last for the whole of the period. Like many developments in the Industrial Revolution the threat to coaching was technological. Their decline was caused by the introduction of passenger train travel which emerged late in the period. One of the world's first railroads, the Liverpool and Manchester, opened in 1830 and by 1845, 30 million passenger rail journeys were being taken in Britain. Jay puts the development of railways in context when he says that "by 1840 Britain had almost 1,500 miles of railway, the US nearly twice as much and continental Europe including Russia, less than 900" (Jay, 2004: 214). Room occupancy at coaching inns along the train routes fell sharply. It was the first major secular correction in travel supply and it produced the first major change in the demand for and supply of hotels. By the end of the period the one-week coach journey from London to York was replaced by a one-day train journey and one night in a hotel in York. The trains also carried many more passengers than the coaches and this transition required the first major change in the location of hotels, their size and their provision of hospitality. To compensate for the room nights lost in coaching inns, there would need to be a major increase in the length of stay in hotels and/or a significant increase in the total volume of travellers staying in hotels at train destinations. To achieve these there would need to be an increase in the construction of new hotels in the locations where the market now needed them and with new forms of hospitality that the market demanded. These were not achieved within the Industrial Revolution. At the end of the period there were probably no more than 10,000 of the new city hotel rooms in Britain, but they were larger and more extensive establishments than the coaching inns.

Inns in the US

The development of coaching inns during the Industrial Revolution in the US paralleled Britain's in terms of location, size of the inns and facilities provided. The first recorded coaching inn in America was in Jamestown, Virginia and was similar in its provision to the British coaching inns. Others such as Hancock Tavern in Boston and the Blue Angel in Philadelphia opened throughout the colony and after independence, when the West was being opened, modest wooden hotels serving early stage coaches were among the first buildings constructed in the new towns. In 1805, Manhattan recorded 274 boarding houses and six hotels including the City Hotel, the North American and the Washington in lower Manhattan, but as the century unfolded significant changes occurred (Pillsbury, 1990: 18-20).

In the first half of the 19th century in the major US cities, larger and more elaborate hotels were developed even before the introduction of passenger rail networks. In 1829, the 170-room Tremont House in Boston opened. It was designed by the architect Isaiah Rogers who is credited with establishing the configuration of facilities in urban hotels that lasted at least for the rest of the 19th century (Kaplan, 2007). The Tremont was one of the early hotels to have a lobby where checking-in and checking-out occurred, a dining room for up to 200 customers as well as private dining rooms, a reading room and separate drawing rooms for ladies and gentlemen. The hotel provided single and double bedrooms at around $2 per day for transient customers and also provided a range of apartments for longer-term residents. In addition it incorporated the new innovations of indoor plumbing and steam heat (Bachin, 2005). When John Jacob Astor, the founder of the real estate dynasty, decided to build a hotel in New York he commissioned Rogers as his architect due to the success of the Tremont House. In 1836, the 309-room Astor House was opened on Broadway as the premier hotel in New York City. Its architectural style and configuration reflected the Tremont, but with more new developments. The Astor House had 18 shops on its ground floor, was lit by gas from its own plant and had its own printing facility. The hotel cost $400,000 to construct, $1,300 per room. It had over 100 employees in addition to servants who often accompanied customers and its dining room was opened 24 hours per day to accommodate the increasing number of transient customers and New York glitterati (Kaplan, 2007: 19). When the Astor House opened, John Jacob Astor leased the hotel to Simeon and Fredrick Boyden from the family that successfully ran the Tremont House. The rent for the first year was $16,000 and rose to $20,500 in year four (Kaplan, 2007: 21), which represented a return to Astor of 5% per year on his investment. The trend in large and luxurious urban hotels continued with other examples such as the Adelphi and Howard hotels in New York; the American House, the United States Hotel and the Adams Hotel in Boston and the Wendell House in Cleveland, Ohio (Donzel et al., 1989: 19). All of these new urban hotels were prominently situated in the affluent city centres and were architecturally imposing buildings, heralding a major change in hotel provision away from coaching inns and becoming significant in the social, cultural and economic lives of the cities.

Railway hotels

British railway companies were quick to see the opportunity to extend their control over travel by building, owning and managing hotels adjacent to key railway stations. At first, the railway companies acquired coaching inns close to stations around the country, but the much higher volume of passengers carried by trains and the longer length of stay at the destinations meant that the coaching inns did not provide the facilities and services that the new market demanded. In 1839, the first new railway hotel, the Victoria, was opened at Euston Station in London and before the end of the year the Euston Hotel opened next door. In 1848, the Midland Hotel, Morecambe opened and other hotels were added in Stoke-on-Trent, Furness Abbey and Newhaven before 1850 (Wooler, 1987: Appendix IV, Table A). As Taylor asserts, "Hotel development during the 25 years between 1837 and 1862 was geared to the progress of the railways" (Taylor, 2003: 35). The new hotels were among the largest hotels in the country at the time and were the start of a notable era of railway hotels in Britain that was to last for more than a century.

The new city hotels

Taylor also lists some of the independent hotels developed in London during this period which included: Pulteneys, the Clarendon, Longs, Durants, Limmers, Stephens, Grillons and Mirvats as well as Browns in Mayfair, which was opened in 1837 by John and Sarah Brown who had been valet and lady's maid to Lord and Lady Byron (*source*: www.brownshotel.com). The hotel continues to operate today as a deluxe Rocco Forte hotel. These and other independent hotels provided a wider range of facilities, services and products than the coaching inns and thus required more capital. However, investment capital in Britain was not yet covered by limited liability and this was a constraint on the size of independent hotels constructed during the period. Although larger than provincial coaching inns, most of the independent hotels of this period had less than 20 rooms. In contrast, in the main cities in the US there was greater access to capital and investors displayed a greater appetite for hotels.

The new city hotels in Britain and the US attracted wealthier domestic business and leisure travellers and a much higher proportion of foreign travellers than the coaching inns. The customers stayed in the hotels for longer and needed a wider range of facilities and services than in the coaching inns. Typical of the additional facilities were: laundry, the provision of breakfast, lunch and dinner as separate meal occasions as well as facilities to occupy the time of customers between meals and these included writing rooms, reading rooms and lounges. There was a sense in which the new city hotels sought to replicate the quality and facilities of the homes of their customers and this involved superior quality of provision than the coaching inns, nonetheless, they were primitive by today's standards. There were no rooms with private bathroom, lighting was mainly by oil lamp and candle; heating was by open fire and building quality and life safety standards were questionable. Dining rooms were an innovation and it was not uncommon for customers to arrive with their own servants who also needed to be accommodated, thus, most of the major hotels at the time provided servants quarters. The emergence of larger and more luxurious urban hotels with a wider range of facilities and services than the coaching inns marked the transition of hotels from the extension of the home of the innkeeper to larger and more formally organised businesses. It was the hotel version of the transition during the Industrial Revolution from cottage manufacturing to factories.

Gentlemen's clubs

In addition to the new coaching inns and new city hotels built during the Industrial Revolution a unique variation on the hotel, the private gentlemen's club, emerged in London. The clubs were mainly located in St James's and Mayfair and fulfilled the functions of a hotel for their aristocratic and wealthy members. Examples included: Boodles, established in 1762; Brookes, 1764; the Oxford and Cambridge Club, 1821; the Athenaeum, 1823; the Carlton Club, 1832 and the Reform Club, 1836, all of which and more continue to function today. The clubs were private member clubs and like the new urban hotels, they provided a greater range of facilities to eat, drink and interact with like-minded people than coaching inns. The clubs had the advantage of the membership fees that the hotels did not have and thus they were lower risk enterprises. In London, the clubs remain as a variant on the hotel theme that has survived while they stoically sought to resist the adoption of new technology, styles and innovations. Members of the Oxford and Cambridge Club complained so strongly about the introduction of electricity to the club that it became a right for diners to have candelabra on their table, a practice that is retained today.

Hotel supply and demand performance: Britain

Table 3.1 illustrates the indicative position of the hotel business in Britain in 1850 compared with 1750.

The economic ascent of the hotel business progressed during the Industrial Revolution. If the supply ratio of hotel rooms per 1,000 citizens remained constant at the 1750 level of 1.5 throughout the period then, with the actual growth in population, the room stock would have risen to 30,000. However, Otus estimates that in 1850, total hotel room supply grew to 80,000. Thus, there was a secular growth of 50,000 hotel rooms and the fundamental driver of this growth was the structural development of the economy. Hotel room occupancy in 1850 was probably lower than in 1750 because of the reduction in efficiency of coaching inns.

Table 3.1: British Hotels 1750–1850.

	1750	1850	CAGR
Rooms	8,000	80,000	2%
Room nights available (m)	2.9	29.2	2%
Room occupancy %	30%	27%	
Room nights sold (m)	0.9	7.9	2%
Domestic business	0.5	5.1	2%
Domestic leisure	0.3	2.7	2%
Foreign business	0.0	0.0	2%
Foreign leisure	0.0	0.0	2%
Hotel rooms supply ratio	1.5	4.0	
Secular growth in hotel rooms supply		50,000	

Source: Otus & Co Advisory Ltd.

4 Economic Developments and the Hotel Business: 1850–1900

Introduction

The central events of the second half of the 19th century for the British and US economies were the growth of secondary industries and the development of the social structures that emerged from the new economic context, which provided the main boost to business demand and the emergence of mass leisure demand into hotels. The economic significance of agriculture declined. Tertiary activities grew from a very low level, primarily as backup to the growing secondary businesses, and by the end of the 19th century the provision of citizen services was emerging as a core responsibility of central government. These developments produced growth in domestic business demand for hotels. However, the most significant progress in hotel demand and supply during this period resulted from the introduction of paid annual holiday leave for senior white-collar and professional employees. This development saw the expansion of hotels to resorts and the enhancement of the range of hospitality provided in hotels to meet the new holiday demand. The stratifications of the economy and of the social structure were reflected in the stratification of hotel demand and hotel supply. During the period, hoteliers sought to match the assumed social position of customers with the provision of facilities, services and products in hotels. The co-alignment of hotel demand and hotel supply stratification became a central tenet of hotelkeeping during this period and a driver of the economic ascent of the hotel business.

Economic structure and hotel demand

Agricultural development and hotel demand

The decline in significance of British agriculture during the Industrial Revolution continued throughout the second half of the 19th century. In 1800, farming accounted for 40% of British national output and a third of the labour force. By the end of the 19th century both had fallen to less than 10% (Jay. 2004: 211). The decline in British agriculture, encouraged by cheap imports of foodstuffs from the Empire, had only a marginal impact on domestic business demand into hotels because fewer agricultural employees travelled on business than those in any other segment due to the small size of farms as well as the local markets for arable products. Over the period a similar trend occurred in the US.

Industrial development and hotel demand

The Great Exhibition in London in 1851 was a marker in the movement of the British economy to a full-blown industrial economy and was followed by a similar transition in the US after the Civil War. The Great Exhibition displayed over 13,000 exhibits and was visited by more than 6.2 million people, an astonishing number given that the population of Greater London was only around 3 million (source: www.wikipedia.org, The Great Exhibition, 1851). It also signalled the movement in the industrial economy from an emphasis on basic industries such as coal, iron and steel to a greater focus on manufactured goods such as textiles and household goods. The impact of the growth in secondary industries on the economies of Britain and the US can be seen in the change in the pattern of global production. In 1800, China accounted for 33% of industrial output, but by 1900 it had fallen to 6% (Jay, 2004: 237). Similarly, India accounted for 20% in 1800, but by 1900 it had fallen to 2%(p. 238). The advantage of size that these economies had during the agricultural period was lost because the structural balance of their economies had not shifted to secondary activities.

In the period from 1850 to 1875, Britain was the largest producer of coal, iron and steel in the world (Court, 1964: 1183). The woollen industry trebled its intake of raw materials and as a result the 300,000 power looms in operation in 1856 increased to 560,000 by 1885 (Gregg, 1965: 298). These and similar statistics from other industries present the picture of a vibrant economy, but its global leadership was in decline. The impetus of technological developments and the larger size of manufacturing companies in the US as well as more effective capital markets boosted economic growth, while the opening of the West and strong population growth established it as the world's industrial powerhouse. As Jay records, "in the 35 years before World War I the US increased its... output per head (at 2.4 times)... Germany (double)... Britain (1.5 times)" (Jay, 2004: 233). The root of the slower growth that Britain achieved was the domination of its economy by family firms, which were limited in their willingness to invest in new technology to grow. Moreover, the convenience of the Empire as a captive market for up to one third of British exports enabled manufacturers to become lazy in comparison with the US, which did not have an empire. The development of the industrial economy in Britain and the US generated new domestic business demand for hotels. The US produced more industrially generated business demand into hotels and grew faster than Britain because it is a larger country geographically and had a larger and faster growing population as well as having more and larger industrial companies selling their products over a wider area. Owners and salesmen were the main business travellers from industrial companies, but accounted for only a minute proportion of total industrial employees.

Citizen services development and hotel demand

The growth in the secondary industries caused growth in the tertiary segment in two ways. First, it was later in the period before central governments became involved in social services. The migration from rural to urban areas that occurred during the Industrial Revolution continued during the second half of the 19th century, for example, the population of Manchester grew from 225,000 in 1850 and to 450,000 by 1901 (source: www.visionofbritain.org.uk). Over the same period the population of New York City grew from 515,000 to 3.4 million (source: www.census.gov/population). As the population of British cities grew local authorities became more active in public services providing running water, gas and sewerage services to households. Services such as education, health and the care of the elderly remained rudimentary until the 20th century, but in hospitals more effective surgery and professional nursing care emerged during the period. Education provision also changed. At the half century, only 2 million British children were believed to be attending elementary school and half of these for less than a year (Gregg, 1965: 506). Over 80% of children had left school before the age of 12 and it was not until 1880 that school attendance was compulsory for under-13-year-olds. Science and technology were growth areas of study in universities because they were needed for the developing industrial economy, but university students were a miniscule proportion of the population and they were predominantly male. Women rarely had the opportunity to advance beyond compulsory education and thus, were limited to low-skill work and family duties. During the period, mass trade unionism became established among the workforce of secondary businesses. In the face of laissez-faire government policy of the period and inadequate provision by employers, trade unions played a crucial role in providing social services to their members in addition to their role in wage and conditions negotiations. The hotel demand generated by health, education and the other social services was minor during the period because the focus was on activities within hospitals and schools and within the local authority areas so that the professionals hardly travelled on business.

Service businesses development and hotel demand

Transport and banking also grew in response to growth in secondary industries. The introduction of steam power had an escalating effect on rail and sea travel, which were characterised by sharp increases in the volume of freight and passengers carried. Jay illustrates the growth of railways during the 19th Century. "By 1870 Britain had almost 13,400 miles of railway, the US had 52,600 miles and continental Europe including Russia, had around 44,000. By 1914, the numbers were respectively 20,300, 255,000 and 252,000" (Jay, 2004: 214). The growth in supply was reflected in demand. "In the United States the freight carried rose from 39,000 million ton/miles in 1866 to 142,000 million ton/miles in 1900" (Mitchell, 1988). This picture was mirrored in steamships. In 1859, there were 168,000 net tons registered in Britain, up from 24,000 in 1800 and by 1900 it reached 7.2 million net ton. By 1880, there were 263 banks in Britain down from 800 in 1825 as a result of consolidation driven among other things by the growing demand for corporate debt that could not be provided by small single-branch banks (Court, 1964: 186).

As a result of the changes in economic structure, Otus estimates that total domestic business demand into hotels in Britain grew at an average annual rate of 2% from 5 million room nights in 1850 to 11 million in 1900. Over the same period domestic business demand in the US grew at an average annual rate of 2% from 8 million room nights to 25 million. The growth in the volume and range of products in international trade produced an increase in foreign business demand into British hotels in gateway cities and industrial centres, most notably from North America and the continent. By the end of the period less than 1% of hotel demand was from foreign business travellers. Foreign business demand into the US was also marginal accounting for 1% of total demand in 1900.

The development of social structure and its impact on hotel demand

In parallel with the structural developments in the economy during the second half of the 19th century there were significant developments in the social structure of the most advanced economies that had a marked impact on hotel demand. The explicit and hierarchical social structure of the historic industrial economies was expressed in Veblen's Theory of the Leisure Class. Veblen identified the leisure class as standing, "at the head of the social structure in point of reputability and in its manner of life and its standards of worth therefore afford the norm of reputability for the community. The observance of these standards, in some degree of approximation, becomes incumbent on all classes lower in the scale" (Veblen, [1899] 1971: 66). He also introduced the notion of "conspicuous consumption" of expensive goods and services, which was the preserve of the leisure class. The leisure class was an elite drawn from the aristocracy, old money families and the new industrially wealthy that accounted for around 1% of the British and US populations. At the bottom of the social structure were the menials or working class who were limited to subsistence consumption and accounted for up to 80% of the population earning their living from manual work and low-grade white collar work. They were only briefly educated and had neither the cash nor the cultural capital to afford a lifestyle beyond subsistence. In the 19th century, Europe and the US saw the growth of the middle class, located between the leisure class and the working class, as a significant and influential social group comprising the families of owners and managers of smaller businesses as well as professionals such as doctors, lawyers, teachers and civil servants amounting to less than 20% of the population. Their jobs were white-collar rather than blue-collar and involved more mental than manual work. They were better educated than the working class and their lifestyle was characterised by higher income careers, which enabled them to amass more material goods. During the period, consumer goods were produced mainly for in-home, private consumption and consequently, standard of living was based on what people owned. The middle class also consumed more services than the working class and their whole experience of life diverged from the working class.

Growth in leisure demand into hotels

Over the period, the biggest boost in hotel demand and hotel supply was from domestic leisure demand that was tied to the emerging social structure. At first it grew in a trickle-down fashion from the aristocracy to the growing numbers of industrially wealthy and then to the emerging white-collar middle class. The single most important initiative of the period that boosted the volume of leisure demand into hotels was the introduction of paid annual holidays from work. Paid annual vacations started in the US after the Civil War and expanded for the remainder of the period, but were limited to white-collar, middle-class workers. The introduction of paid annual holidays came later in Britain and like the US, white-collar middle-class workers were first to benefit and also like the US, the main response was to take summer holidays in resorts. In Britain, coastal resorts such as Blackpool, Brighton, Scarborough and Clacton emerged as did many others largely because they were within a two-hour train journey of major industrial conurbations. In the US, equivalents included Atlantic City, New Jersey, St. Augustine, Florida and Virginia Beach, Virginia. By the end of the century, the impact of the introduction of annual holiday pay made summer holiday demand in Britain and the US the largest source of hotel demand. As the volume and speed of cross-Atlantic and cross-Channel travel increased so the volume of foreign leisure demand into hotels also grew, but it remained subsidiary to domestic demand. As wealth increased, the middle class emerged as a market in foreign leisure travel evidenced by the global growth of Thomas Cook Ltd, the travel agency. After establishing his travel business in the middle of the century Thomas Cook expanded to become the largest travel agent and tour operator in the world. By 1891, 50 years after the business was started Thomas Cook Ltd organised tours throughout the known world and had 84 offices throughout the world (Brendon, 1991: 219).

Hotel supply overview

During the second half of the 19th century, the three social classes, the leisure class, middle class and working class came to be reflected in the segmentation of the hotel business into grand hotels, mid-market hotels and quasi-hotels. Broadly, grand hotels catered for the leisure class and mid-market hotels targeted the middle class. The vast bulk of the working class lived their lives without spending any time in short-term commercial lodging. However, as the US and British economies grew and paid annual leave began to be extended to some of the skilled working class they emerged as a summer holiday market towards the end of the period and their congruent lodging facilities were quasi-hotels such as guest houses, boarding houses, lodging houses and rooming houses.

A preoccupation of the period was to preserve the congruence between the social stratification and the hotel stratification by matching the class position of customers with the appropriate form of commercial lodging available. The practice of hoteliers managing the congruence between the provision of specific forms of hospitality and the customers admitted to their establishments became a central tenet of British hotel law. Legal precedent going back to 1820 laid two conditions for a hotel customer: that they were willing to pay a price adequate to the type of accommodation provided and that they were in a fit state to be received (Bull and Richardson, 1962: 21). In its basest form this gave hoteliers the power to manage the congruence between the facilities, services and products that a hotel provided and the values and lifestyles of the customers who were admitted. The form of hospitality in grand and mid-market hotels and the prices that were charged were designed to attract leisure class and middle class Anglo-Saxons and they were beyond the means of the working class. This practice was sustained by the reluctance of the middle class and leisure class to share leisure activities with the working class. Current British law has changed little. The 1956 and still current Hotel Proprietor's Act provides the legal definition of a hotel in Britain as, "an establishment held out by the proprietor as offering food, drink and if so required sleeping accommodation, without special contract, to any traveller presenting himself who appears able and willing to pay a reasonable sum for the services and facilities provided and who is in a fit state to be received".

Quasi-hotels were the most modest architecturally, the most modest in terms of the materials used in construction, furniture, fixtures and equipment, the narrowest in the range of services provided, the most modest in the style of service and the most modest in the products sold. They existed at the bottom of the commercial short-term lodging market and came to be considered as entities separate from the grand and mid-market hotels. Hotel customers were regarded as people who did not frequent quasi-hotels, while the working class customers of quasi-hotels invariably did not visit mid-market or grand hotels. It was then a short step to exclude quasi-hotels from the accepted conception of the hotel and for the social profile of hotel customers to exclude the working class. What were differences in degree became perceived as differences in kind reflecting the explicit class structure of the historic industrial economies.

As the volume of hotel demand grew from all sources so the rate of new hotel development increased further and the total capital invested in new hotel development over the period increased substantially, aided by the introduction of limited liability. Three locations dominated the developments.

♦ Urban hotels in Britain and the US were constructed throughout the country in most cities and towns with a population of over 50,000 as the rail networks expanded and fewer coaching inns were able to compete.

♦ The development of resorts in which hotels were among the first buildings constructed.

♦ The opening up of the American West, which saw the creation of new towns in which hotels were also among the first buildings serving the relatively low levels of business demand generated by agriculture, the prime economic activity of the region, from salesmen and distributors delivering construction materials, hardware and farm implements as well as from some immigrants to the West.

The major market for hotels in industrial towns and cities was domestic business demand, which was year-round demand, but it was concentrated on Monday to Friday nights and there was little demand from any source at the weekends. The market for hotels in resorts was heavily skewed to the summer season from Easter to September when, invariably, the hotels closed until the following Easter. Among the larger and more notable resort hotels constructed in Britain over the period were: the Grand Hotel, Scarborough, the Metropole Hotel, Brighton, the Grand Hotel, Eastbourne, the Royal Bath Hotel, Bournemouth and the Imperial Hotel, Blackpool, which were positioned at the top of the market in the resorts. The vacation market in the US concentrated on coastal and rural resorts where hotels were built including: The United States Hotel in Cape May, New Jersey, the Breakers in Palm Beach, Florida and the Greenbriar in White Sulphur Springs, West Virginia. Capital for businesses that, like most urban hotels, had little or no demand for 30% of the week or, as was the case with resort hotels, were closed for up to half the year was more difficult to raise and successful ventures needed to attract very high levels of demand during the active seasons to compensate for the inactive seasons. In spite of this impediment, capital was made available in Britain from railway companies to construct new hotels, from brewers that acquired coaching inns and from the stock market, but capital for most hotels in resorts was very idiosyncratic. Capital was also attracted, mainly in the US from syndicates of investors and single investors who calculated that the seasonality risk was offset by the secular growth in demand and limited liability. By the end of the century, 108 hotels, of which 42 were in portfolios, were listed in the hotel sector of the London Stock Exchange (source: Stock Exchange Year Book 1900). In addition, other hotels were part of listed companies such as 57 hotels owned by railway companies and a range of coaching inns owned by brewers. By 1900, hotel chains in Britain had increased their room stock to around 15,000, up from a standing start in 1850, bringing hotel concentration at the turn of the century to 6%. By the start of the 20th century, the US also had around 15,000 hotel rooms affiliated to short chains, the most prominent of which was the Harvey System, linked to the railroad routes.

Grand hotels

Grand hotels of the period were the most expensive type of hotel to develop. Their imposing architecture was influenced by royal palaces of Europe and the private mansions of the leisure class. Through their architecture and their names as well as the range, combination and quality of the facilities, services and products that they sold, grand hotels set the benchmark for and became a byword for luxury. In the social structure of the day, the leisure class provided the benchmark for quality of life and the grand hotels provided the benchmark for quality of hotels. All other hotels were lesser versions of the grand hotels not only in terms of the substance of the built fabric and of the hospitality provided, but also in terms of the prices they charged and the customers they attracted. They were among the largest hotels created in the largest cities and in resorts during the period. Their large size and their luxury produced palatial lobbies, lavish restaurants and ballrooms that acted as public stages for the leisure class to display conspicuous consumption.

Grand hotels in Europe

An example of the larger grand hotels that were developed in Britain at the time was the Langham hotel, London that opened in 1865 with 234 rooms at a cost of £300,000, almost £1,300 per bedroom. At the time, the Langham was the largest hotel in London and is still in operation as the flagship of Langham International Hotels. When the Langham opened it was not only the largest hotel in London, it was also filled with technical innovations and extensive services. It claimed, as did the Fifth Avenue hotel in New York, to be the first hotel in the world with elevators, "rising rooms". It avoided the problems of water contamination by pumping water from its own artesian well below the hotel. It had 14 public lavatories and 300 toilets, which was well ahead of the proportion typical in contemporary hotels. Each bedroom had hot and cold running water. It had its own steam laundry, four firemen, postal and telegraph offices, the facility to buy railway tickets and theatre tickets as well as a coach service to and from the London railway stations. In addition to its bedrooms and suites, it had a dining room, coffee room and a separate ladies' coffee room, a ballroom, a library and reading room, a smoking room, a billiard room and to mark it out as a hotel for the rich it had quarters for customers' servants (Steel, 1990). When it opened, the daily room rate for a standard room, which also set it apart as a grand hotel for the rich, was 10 shillings – 10 days' wages for a lady's maid at that time (Hibbert, 1987).

Before the end of the 19th century, many capital cities in Western Europe had created landmark grand hotels, which remain today and include: the Amstel Hotel in Amsterdam; the Hotel Grand Britagne in Athens; the Hotel Metropole in Brussels; the Hotel Angleterre in Copenhagen; the Shelbourne Hotel in Dublin: the Savoy Hotel and Claridges Hotel in London; the Hotel de Paris in Monte Carlo; the Grand Hotel in Oslo; the Hotel Ritz, and the Hotel Plaza Athenee in Paris; the Grand Hotel and the Hotel Excelsior in Rome; the Grand Hotel in Stockholm and the Hotel Sacher, the Grand Hotel and the Imperial Hotel in Vienna.

Grand hotels in the US

Grand hotels were also constructed in US gateway cities over the period, but their longevity was not great. The Tremont House in Boston, the first grand hotel in the US, had a life of only 66 years, closing in 1895. Before the Astor House, the first grand hotel in New York, was 40 years old it had become overshadowed by the more advanced technology and facilities of newer hotels further up Manhattan. In the late 1850s, the Fifth Avenue Hotel at Fifth Avenue and West 24th Street opened with a private bath and a fireplace in all of its 800 rooms. It had an early form of elevator, "the vertical railroad", which as Kaplan points out changed the economics and status systems within hotels since, "instead of being less favoured because of the stairs involved, upper-story rooms and suites, distant from street noises and street smells and now conveniently reached by elevator, offered comfort and prestige at premium rates' (Kaplan, 2007: 25).

The Waldorf=Astoria

William Waldorf Astor and John Jacob Astor IV, the grandsons of John Jacob Astor, who owned the Astor House, were competitive and feuding cousins who became significant developers and owners of grand hotels in New York. William H Hume built the New Netherland hotel on Fifth Avenue and Fifty Ninth Street, which on completion in 1892 was the tallest hotel in the world at 17 stories and the first to have telephones in every bedroom. At the same time William Waldorf Astor developed the Waldorf hotel on Fifth Avenue and Thirty Third Street on the site of his parents' mansion. The 450-room Waldorf Hotel opened in 1893 at a cost of $4 million, $9,000 per room. Like the New Netherland, the Waldorf was a grand hotel designed for the leisure class. It included all of the latest technology and its public areas were lavish, yet although each bedroom had trompe l'oeil ceilings, just more than half had en suite bathrooms. It was one of the first hotels with a concierge and its Palm Garden restaurant, according to Kaplan, established itself as the most expensive and exclusive in the city (Kaplan, 2007: 76). The development of the Waldorf caused a severe problem for John Jacob IV's mother whose mansion was immediately next door to and dwarfed by the gable end of the hotel. Consequently, the building of the Waldorf heightened the animosity between William Waldorf Astor and his cousin John Jacob Astor IV. Nonetheless a contract was agreed between the two factions which saw John Jacob demolish his mother's mansion and built a 550-room grand hotel, the Astoria, on the site so that both hotels occupied the entire block on Fifth Avenue between Thirty Third and Thirty Fourth Streets. The Astoria, which opened in 1897, was architecturally similar to the Waldorf, but 400 of its bedrooms had private bathrooms. The combined hotel, the Waldorf=Astoria, in addition to its 1,000 bedrooms and apartments, included restaurants, bars, a ballroom, a theatre, a banqueting room, a suite for wedding receptions, lecture rooms, club rooms, rooms for meetings of secret societies, stock broker offices, a photography gallery, hairdressing salons for men and women, Turkish and Russian baths and a roof garden. Thus, when it opened, the Waldorf=Astoria was certainly the largest, most complex grand hotel in the world and probably the most lavish as well. It was leased and managed by George C. Bolt, the manager of the Waldorf, but the Astor family feud was not far from the surface. As Kaplan (2007: 79) relates, "corridors connecting the two buildings could be sealed off if the fragile truce, uncomfortable for both parties, failed to hold."

Other US grand hotels

The Astors were not the only wealthy people who built and owned grand hotels in the US. Alexander Turney Stewart, the merchant, built and owned the Metropolitan on Broadway and the Grand Union in Saratoga Springs, the upstate New York resort. William Chapman Ralston, the banker, opened the 755-room Palace Hotel in San Francisco in 1875, which at a cost of $5 million was the largest hotel investment at the time. Henry Cordis Brown, the real estate magnet, opened the Palace Hotel in Denver, Colorado in 1892. Potter Palmer, the dry goods retailer, rebuilt the Palmer House in Chicago after the fire of 1871. The New Palmer House was the tallest building in Chicago and occupied a block of

State Street. Grand hotels emerged not only in major city centres, but also in resorts where wealthy customers sought summer and winter vacations away from the industrial cities. Henry M. Flagler, a partner in Standard Oil, developed three grand resort hotels, the Ponce de Leon, Royal Poinciana and the Breakers, all in St Augustine, Florida.

A novel feature of grand hotels that grew over the period was that their residential demand was not only derived from transient customers, but also from permanent and semi-permanent residents who might stay for several months. Grand hotels included a range of apartments that attracted wealthy customers able to use the full range of hotel facilities and services rather than owning a mansion and managing servants. As more grand hotels emerged during the period, more apartments were occupied by wealthy residents. The style, lavishness, excitement and convenience of the hotel attracted key members of the leisure class as permanent and semi-permanent residents. Notables who followed this route included John D. Rockefeller and Andrew Carnegie who lived in apartments in the Windsor hotel on Fifth Avenue. Grand hotels attracted business demand predominantly from the owners and directors of larger companies. Leisure demand came from the wealthiest and the nobility, who stayed mainly in the gateway cities where, invariably, the grand hotels were located. Grand hotels were not just about bedrooms. It was crucial to the success of the venture that their extensive non-room facilities attracted the local leisure class to eat in the restaurants, drink in the bars, dance and dine in the ballrooms and parade through the lobbies.

The social chasm

In their scale, their complexity and their lavishness the grand hotels of the second half of the 19th century were monuments to the success of the industrial economy and the wealth that it created for the elite of the most advanced economies. Grand hotels were funded by the leisure class for the leisure class and reinforced the social chasm between the leisure class and others. The Astors highlighted the point. The Astor family were the largest landlords of slum tenements in New York at one stage owning the buildings that housed three-quarters of the city population (Kaplan, 2007: 33). } When the Waldorf opened William Waldorf Astor collected around $6 million per year in rent from his real estate in New York City and his cousin similarly earned from renting real estate(p. 118). In their tenements of the Lower East Side poor immigrants were crammed into confined space that had minimal heating, lighting, plumbing or ventilation. As Sante reports:

> the basic unit of calculation for the tenement is the 25-by-100-foot lot. If we assume four apartments per floor, six floors per building (the maximum that reform laws finally permitted to be constructed without an elevator), this gives us lodging for twenty-four families, perhaps a hundred people. Around the turn of the century such an edifice could be built for $25,000.
>
> (Sante, 1991)

The price to build one tenement to house 100 people was not enough to build three bedrooms at the Waldorf. Yet, the cost to build the Waldorf with all of its size, complexity and lavishness amounted to only eight months' rental income for William Waldorf Astor. Large, lavish grand hotels were a way that the Astors and others could spend significant proportions of their income.

Hotel employees

While the customers of grand hotels were drawn from the leisure class and the nobility, the employees were drawn from the working class. Hotel jobs were solidly grounded in the role of servants in private mansions and palaces and the relationship between grand hotel customers and hotel staff was conceived as being and was managed as a master–servant relationship. Nowhere was this more prevalent than in a deluxe restaurant in a grand hotel. Eating in such a restaurant was seen as a cultural experience for the leisure class customer and like art, it needed the customer to have the cultural capital for it to be enjoyed. In parallel, it needed the waiters to play the role of a menial servant. The most atmospheric description of life in a deluxe restaurant early in the 20th century was George Orwell's account of his experiences as a plongeur in Paris.

> It is an instructive sight to see a waiter going into a hotel dining-room. As he passes the door a sudden change comes over him. The set of his shoulders alters; all the dirt and hurry and irritation have dropped off in an instant. He glides over the carpet with a solemn priest-like air.

> (Orwell, 1970: 61)

The absence of formal training for hotel employees and the heavy seasonality of demand required that regular job changes was the prime basis for widening the experience of hotel managers and workers. This was further reinforced in the almost entirely fragmented structure of grand hotels in which hotel workers had jobs rather than careers. The managers of grand hotels were considered to be the linchpin in the provision of hospitality to customers and they needed to have extensive experience of providing the type of hospitality demanded by the leisure class and nobility. Cesar Ritz, the foremost grand hotelier of the period, held jobs in 13 different hotels and restaurants before he became a hotel manager. His first job as hotel manager was at the Hotel de Nice in San Remo, Italy, from which he went on to manage another eight hotels before he bought his first hotel in Cannes at the age of 37, until then his average length of stay in his 22 jobs was one year (Ritz, 1981). The peripatetic career structure of hotel workers was reinforced by the common practice of the day that they lived-in at the hotel and did not have local roots or strong ties to the district. In fact, it was difficult for them to build local roots due both to the need for job mobility and for the reliance on tips to create a living wage.

Individuality of early grand hotels

The creation of larger and more complex grand hotels was also a further step in the establishment of hotels as formal businesses rather than the extension of the family home of their owner and paralleled the shift in manufacturing from cottages to factories, but during the second half of the 19th century there was practically no concentration among grand hotels. The Savoy Hotel Group, which included the Savoy Hotel and Claridges Hotel in London and the Grand Hotel in Rome, along with the three Flagler hotels in the US, were the only examples of owned and operated grand hotel portfolios at the time. While the grand hotels of the Astors were owned by the family members, the hotels were leased to independent operators. One of the reasons for the extreme fragmentation was that each grand hotel was created as a unique venue and grand hotel owners needed to have faith in their architects to create the uniqueness. Thus, prominent hotel architects such as Isaiah Rogers, the architect of the Tremont House, the Astor House and a string of other grand hotels in the mid-nineteenth century and Henry Janeway Hardenbergh the architect of the Waldorf=Astoria and the Plaza hotels, New York and the Copley Plaza, Boston around the turn of the 19th/20th centuries were major influences on the style and substance of the hospitality provided in grand hotels. The architects concentrated on the high investment that the owners wanted to make so that the choices of style and substance of the built fabric and of the facilities and services available to hotel customers were conditioned by the need to be expensive, decorative and rare. An implication of this approach is that there was little attention paid to the size of hotel that the market required and even less to the return on investment that the hotel would provide for its owners.

Hotels and investment

The approach to the development and management of grand hotels during the period reflected the logic of manufacturing that provided the economic growth momentum at the time. Capital and effort was invested in developing the hotel as it was for durable goods; once created, the grand hotels wore out as did durable goods. The lavishness of the built fabric, the wide range of facilities and services and the products were expected to compensate for any other means to generate demand and commitment by customers to specific grand hotels. However, the progressive physical redundancy of a grand hotel generated a loss of demand and commitment by its customers. Thus, grand hotels were a fashion and they stayed popular with the leisure class for only as long as they remained fashionable. At the end of the 19th century, grand hotels were firmly established at the apex of the hotel business. They were in tune with and reflected the economic, political and social structures of the period. The approach to the creation and management of grand hotels was the major legacy of the grand hotels of the second half of the 19th century. The belief that there was a causal relationship between the level of investment in a hotel, the generation of demand to the hotel and the level of customer satisfaction with the hotel experience endured for at least a century. Consequently, the return on investment in grand hotels was relegated to be an incidental outcome. Indeed the impact of this belief within the hotel business lasted for longer than many of the grand hotels.

Mid-market hotels

The mid-market hotels were a reflection of the middle-class quality of life and standard of living and the middle class hotel demand was predominantly domestic and mainly provincial. Throughout the year most of the demand in mid-market hotels was from domestic business travellers mostly in urban hotels complimented by holidaymakers during the spring and summer months in resorts. Thus, mid-market hotels were located in most of the cities and larger towns throughout Britain and the US. Because the middle class accounted for a far greater proportion of the population than the leisure class there were many more mid-market hotels than grand hotels in spite of the more frequent use of hotels by the leisure class. Mid-market hotels were less grand than the grand hotels and cost less to build. They had fewer and lower quality facilities, services and products, they had fewer employees per customer, the hospitality provided was less bespoke and consequently the mid-market hotel prices were lower than grand hotel prices. Mid-market hotels were a much less homogeneous category than grand hotels and included hotels with a range of non-room facilities as well as coaching inns that continued to trade.

During the second half of the 19th century, the middle class was the main passenger market for longer train journeys and thus, the railway companies in Britain accelerated their development of station hotels designed to provide more services and attract more demand from the middle class. Notably they created hotels at the mainline stations in London including: the Great Western Royal Hotel at Paddington Station, the Great Northern at King's Cross, the Grosvenor Hotel at Victoria Station, the Charing Cross Hotel at Charing Cross Station, the Cannon Street Hotel at Cannon Street Station, the Midland Grand at St Pancras, the Great Eastern at Liverpool Street and the Great Central at Marylebone Station. All of these hotels except for Cannon Street continue to operate today. Moreover, in many of the significant industrial towns and cities in the provinces, the railway companies developed hotels adjacent to the railway station. Most of these hotels such as: the Queens in Birmingham, the Central Hotel, Glasgow, the Adelphi Hotel, Liverpool, the Royal Victoria Hotel, Sheffield and the Midland Hotel, Derby were focused primarily on business travellers, which meant that hotel rooms were quiet at the weekends.

The development of the railway hotels also reinforced the crucial relationship between travel and demand for hotel accommodation. The involvement of the railway companies in hotels was an example of vertical integration. They had significant control over the demand since invariably their hotel customers were also train customers. The hotels developed by the railway companies were an improvement in the quality, range and style of facilities, services and products available previously in the industrial towns and cities where they became the main hotel. Moreover, in the provincial industrial towns and cities, the railway hotels were among the most significant buildings and their existence pressurised the smaller, less formal, less well located, independently owned coaching inns left over from the Industrial Revolution. This process was reinforced since these coaching inns did not have the availability of capital of the railway companies and consequently, many of the coaching inns in industrial towns and cities were removed from the market or simply had the bedrooms closed so that they operated as pubs. However, not all coaching inns suffered in this way. Many in small rural towns and along secondary roads that were not on the rail network continued to operate as hotels.

The mid-market railway hotels in Britain were the first examples of hotel chains. In the later stages of the 19th century, other examples of mid-market hotel chains emerged, the largest of which was the British based Gordon Hotels whose portfolio reached 15 hotels at its height. The approach to the development of mid-market hotels during the period mirrored that of the grand hotels. Architects designed the hotels in line with the investment available, which in the case of mid-market hotels was less than in grand hotels. The hotels were architecturally diverse, but there was a greater uniformity in the range and style of facilities, services and products sold in mid-market hotels and as a result they were more utilitarian than lavish. Like the grand hotels, the approach to the management of mid-market hotels reflected the logic of manufacturing. Once the hotel was created little effort was invested in generating demand and commitment from its customers, but the railway hotels had the benefit of synergies between hotels and trains, which gave them an edge over other hotels. The social distance between the middle-class customers of mid-market hotels and the hotel workers was less than that between grand hotel customers and its workers. Nonetheless, the role model for mid-market hotel employees was also the private servant. The configuration of facilities in mid-market hotels established during the period – bedrooms, restaurant, bar and ballroom – endured as the dominant configuration of hotel facilities throughout the 20th century.

Hotel supply and demand performance: Britain and the US

During the second half of the 19th century the population of Britain grew from 20 million to 38 million. At a constant 1850 supply ratio of hotel rooms per 1,000 citizens, the market would have needed 150,000 rooms by the end of the period. However, Otus estimates that British hotel room supply grew to 270,000 rooms illustrating the extent of the secular growth achieved during the period and the supply ratio grew to 7.1, up from 4.0. Over the half century, room nights sold grew by an average annual rate of 2% and room occupancy fell to a very inefficient 27% for three reasons: the continuing existence, but progressively declining demand into coaching inns; the significant growth in resort hotels that closed for up to six months of the year and the very low level of weekend resident demand in urban hotels. Otus also estimates that, thanks to the introduction of paid annual holidays, domestic leisure demand grew to be the main market for hotels. Foreign demand increased over the period but still remained marginal.

Table 4.1: British hotels 1850–1900

	1850	1900	CAGR
Total rooms	80,000	270,000	2%
Room nights available m	29	99	2%
Room occupancy %	27%	27%	
Room nights sold m	8	27	2%
Domestic business	5	11	2%
Domestic leisure	3	15	3%
Foreign business	0	0	4%
Foreign leisure	0	1	5%
Concentration %	0%	6%	
Hotel supply ratio	4.0	7.1	
Secular growth in hotel room supply		120,000	

Source: Otus & Co Advisory Ltd.

The US population grew by 53 million to reach 76 million by 1900. At a constant supply ratio the country would have needed only 260,000 hotel rooms, but room stock grew to 500,000 entailing secular growth of 240,000 rooms over the period and the supply ratio reached 6.6, up from 3.4 in 1850. Room occupancy declined by less than Britain's aided by the permanent and semi-permanent residents in many grand hotels and the greater volumes of business and leisure demand. As in Britain, domestic leisure demand became the major market for hotels and although foreign demand grew it remained marginal. Like Britain, the economic ascendancy of the hotel business during the period was achieved by the overall increase in supply and demand. One area in which the business in Britain and the US was on par was in the presence of chains. In 1900, in spite of Britain having many fewer hotel rooms it had around the same number of chain rooms as the US due to the vertical integration of railway companies and brewers.

Table 4.2: US hotels 1850–1900

	1850	1900	CAGR
Total rooms	80,000	500,000	4%
Room nights available m	29	183	4%
Room occupancy %	35%	33%	
Room nights sold m	10	60	4%
Domestic business	7	25	2%
Domestic leisure	3	34	5%
Foreign business	0	1	4%
Foreign leisure	0	1	4%
Concentration %	0%	3%	
Hotel supply ratio	3.4	6.6	
Secular growth in hotel room supply		240,000	

Source: Otus & Co Advisory Ltd.

5   Critical Events and the Hotel Business: 1900–1945

Introduction

The economies of the US and Europe and their hotel businesses were dominated in the first half of the 20th century by four critical events – World War I, ideological shifts in Europe, the Great Depression and World War II. The governance of the four critical events was different for each of the main economies as was the impact of the events on each economy and on its patterns of recovery. In turn, these critical events produced different impacts on hotel demand and hotel supply. At the start of the period the US hotel business was the largest and fastest growing in the world and it suffered the least severe downturns over the period, Britain suffered more severe downturns and the continental European hotel business, which started the century in the least developed state, endured the most severe downturns. In parallel, US hotel demand and supply recovered the soonest, developed the most and grew the fastest after each event and thus the economic ascent of its hotel business was greatest. British hotel supply took longer to recover and its development and growth was marginal, but its hotel demand declined over the period and thus there was no economic ascent of its hotel business. In the cases of France and Germany, the most significant continental economies, their hotel demand and supply suffered sharp decline and as a result their hotel businesses regressed.

The rate of growth in population reinforced these trends. In 1900, the population of the US was 76 million. By 1945 it had nearly doubled to 140 million, boosted by significant immigration and the least loss of life among any of the major combatants in the two world wars. In contrast, the population of European countries was characterised by greater proportionate loss of life in wars and more emigration. Over the period, the British population grew from 38 million to 48 million. The German population grew from 56 million to 70 million, while in France the population fell by one million to 38 million. Thus, the US with an economy that was already the largest and fastest growing in the world had added boosts from fast-growing population and greater structural development, which was reflected in hotel demand and hotel supply over this traumatic period.

World War I

World War I was centered on the European continent, most of the battles were fought in Belgium, France and Germany and they suffered the greatest loss of life as well as the greatest degradation of land, property and transport infrastructure causing the suspension of their economic development. The impact on the British economy was less because it was not invaded and did not suffer the degradation of its land, property and transport infrastructure. When World War I was declared in 1914, conventional domestic business demand into hotels in the battling countries collapsed as military production was given priority over consumer production, holiday taking crumbled and new hotel construction was stopped. Battle damage reduced hotel supply in France, Germany and Belgium, but not in Britain or the US, and throughout Europe conventional hotel demand took longer to recover after the war was over. The impact of World War I on the US economy and its hotel business was less severe than it was on any of the other combatants, not least because the US was involved for only 19 months of the 55-month duration of the war. The US also had a lower proportion of its population engaged in the fighting and it endured lower loss of life than the other major combatants. Moreover, its territory was not invaded and it avoided degradation of its land and infrastructure. By staying out of the war until 1917, the US economy achieved three years of growth as did its hotel business when the European economies and hotel businesses were in shock. The US economic momentum did not cease when the war ended. Apart from a hiccup in 1920, US manufacturing continued to grow apace rising by almost 50% between 1913 and 1925, and the US share of world trade rose from 20% to 33% over the same period (Jay, 2004: 247). In contrast, during this period, output in Europe was flat as the European countries struggled in the postwar period to re-establish their civilian economies and their hotel businesses.

Ideological shifts in Europe

The suffering in the European economies during World War I was not their only problem. Politics in Europe changed. It started with the simmering trend towards socialism, which asserted that the only effective way to eradicate poverty and social injustice was for elected governments to take control of the economies. Socialist ideology and big government went hand in hand. Both had grown in the latter decades of the 19th century and came into the mainstream of European politics with the formation of the British Labour Party. Left-wing political parties emerged in other European economies and were united in the promotion of state planning and control of economic activities. In 1918, the British Labour Party adopted clause IV of its constitution, which committed it to, "common ownership of the means of production... of each industry and service" and this was not revoked until 1995 (source: http://www.labour.org.uk). The employment of the blue-collar working class who dominated the membership and support of left-wing political parties was predominantly in primary and secondary industries. Traditionally, tertiary businesses required more wealth as the basis for consumption and reflected more of the lives of the white-collar middle class and leisure class who were the bedrock of the right-wing political parties. This was the clear blue water between the left wing and right wing in European politics in the 20th century which was not paralleled in the US, where the distinction between the Democrats and the Republicans was much less explicit.

USSR and Communism

The most radical political development in Europe was the Russian Revolution in 1917 and the establishment of the USSR, the first communist state. In terms of economic structure, Communism involved state control of all of the means of production. It differed from democratic socialism in that it was a single party, non-democratic system and as such introduced a difference in kind between the USSR on the one hand and the elected governments of western European economies on the other as far as control of primary and secondary economic activities were concerned. Similarly, service businesses such as retailing, banking, hospitality and travel were controlled by the state in the USSR, but were market controlled in the other industrial economies. Communism also involved the state control of the provision and distribution of citizen services and in comparison with the other European economies the difference was less obvious since most of the citizen services, such as public education, public health and social services in the free market economies were state-controlled by elected governments. The USSR was a poor agricultural economy when it was formed. Communism made a virtue out of the poor availability of consumer goods and promoted materialism as a capitalist evil. Its emphasis on commitment to the communist ideal as an alternative to material aspirations and consumption of discretionary services masked the lack of economic progress. Under Communism the capital markets, also controlled by the state, remained primitive and personal credit was absent. Consequently, no communist economy ever managed to progress to become a service business economy and several were unable even to make the transition to become a secondary economy.

Fascism

The second political movement that took power in Europe at this time, Fascism also had dubious democratic credentials and included Mussolini's Italy where he took power in 1922; Germany, where following a long period of hyperinflation and political instability, Hitler and the Nazi Party were elected in 1933; and Spain where the Revolution in the mid-1930s brought Franco to power. Like Communists, Fascists came to power with radical and populist promises to solve the economic turmoil after World War I. Fascist dictators enacted nationalist and racist policies with little tolerance shown to those who opposed them, but as with Communism they exerted significant influences that were not easily removed. It took a second world war to remove the Fascist regimes of Hitler and Mussolini. Franco's regime lasted in Spain until the 1970s and the Soviet empire, which, after World War II stretched as far west as West Germany, did not collapse until 1990. The economic turmoil on continental Europe after World War I was not a fertile context for growth in hotel demand and supply. The ideological shifts in Russia, Germany, Italy and Spain further impeded growth in hotel demand since the controlling regimes pursued economic policies that did not generate growth in domestic business demand into hotels and their less developed standards of living limited the growth in leisure demand into hotels.

The Wall Street Crash and the Great Depression

Events in agriculture, events in manufacturing and events in the capital markets triggered the Wall Street Crash and initiated the Great Depression. Over the first three decades of the century, American farmers more than achieved the significant increase in output needed to feed the fast-rising population, while simultaneously improving agricultural productivity. At the centre of these two successes was the increased use of agricultural technology and improved farming methods, which required farmers to raise debt to acquire the machines and introduce the new work methods. As the 1920s progressed, two outcomes of these changes were the production of agricultural surpluses and the increase in agricultural unemployment. The continuing excess of supply over demand caused prices of crops and livestock to fall. In turn, the income of farmers declined leaving them unable to service the debt they had raised for the new machinery. The subsequent increase in defaulted loans caused the small rural banks that provided the debt to foreclose on failed farms, reducing bank income. The position became so onerous that the rural banks were unable to provide cash to depositors or to service the wholesale sources of their capital and at its height it forced the closure of rural banks at the rate of two per day (Olson, 2001: 26). The failure rate of rural banks in the late 1920s caused investors to fret about the national implications and Wall Street sought to anticipate these implications by the first sharp downward correction in the market in September 1929.

In parallel, the size of the manufacturing industry as well as its growth in output and productivity outstripped that achieved in agriculture. As Galbraith has recorded:

> between 1925 and 1929 the number of manufacturing establishments increased from 183,900 to 206,700: the value of their output rose from $60 billions to $68 billions. The Federal Reserve index of industrial production which had averaged only 67 in 1921 (1923-5 = 100) had risen to 110 by July 1928, and reached 126 in June 1929. In 1926, 4,301,000 automobiles were produced. Three years later, in 1929, production had increased by over a million.
>
> (Galbraith, 1929: 31)

The fast expanding manufacturing industries needed manpower, which they got from two main sources: immigrants and unemployed agricultural workers. The high growth in manufacturing employment and output fuelled the higher demand that marked the "roaring twenties" and this was fine as long as demand continued to grow, but it came under pressure. The growth in productivity from the widespread introduction of the assembly line and more rational work methods limited the manpower needs of manufacturers and so as output rocketed, manufacturing unemployment increased. The structural problem was that whereas some of the agricultural unemployment created as a result of increasing productivity was soaked-up by expanding manufacturing businesses, the growing and larger manufacturing unemployment after the crash, brought about by rising productivity and plummeting demand, was confronted with the fact that there were few emerging tertiary businesses hungry for new employees. Neither were there economic policies to stimulate tertiary growth and consequently, the real economy spiralled into the Great Depression.

As the capital markets funded the corporate demand for debt and equity so they also funded the personal markets and the speculators' market. Professional and white-collar workers, whose income and savings allowed them access to credit to fund large purchases, spearheaded the demand for higher value goods, such as homes and automobiles. In contrast, the demand from the mass of blue-collar workers was for smaller ticket household items, which were funded out of income and small debt sources such as buy-now-pay-later programmes. In the late 1920s when blue-collar demand for credit to fund larger purchases such as automobiles and household electrical goods was growing, manufacturing unemployment was rising and the traumas in agriculture were accelerating. The growth in cheap money during the 1920s reached its limit in 1929, when brokers' loans collateralised by securities that had been bought on margin reached $6 billion, up from $1.5 billion in the early 1920s (Galbraith, 1929: 48). In 1914, there were 250 securities dealers in the US, but by 1929 this had increased to around 6,500, yet less than 3 million Americans, less than 2.5% of the population, invested in stocks and shares. Of these less than 1 million were estimated to be speculators using credit to buy shares on the margin (p. 102). The oversupply of goods, falling demand, growing unemployment, falling prices, business failures and the failure of rural banks as well as the growth in speculative loans, triggered a response by Wall Street. On Wednesday 4th September 1929 the Dow Jones Index peaked at 381. The following day, Black Thursday, the stock market started to crash. From then the downward spiral in both the economy and the stock market fed off of each other.

The New Deal

Austerity initiatives failed to solve the problem. The Dow Jones Index bottomed on 8th July 1932 at 41, a loss of 89% since Black Thursday and was accompanied by the failure of 2,000 investment houses. In 1929, US GDP reached $104 billion. By 1932, GDP had fallen 43% to $59 billion. Total manufacturing had fallen to 54% of its 1929 peak. Food fell 42%, furniture and household equipment fell 56% and transport suffered with a 39% fall. By 1933, almost half of the 25,000 banks in the US had become insolvent, whereas a rare example of growth during the period was electricity and gas, which rose by 4%. By 1932, US unemployment reached 25% against only 3.2% in 1929. Franklin Roosevelt was elected President in 1933 with a mandate to end the Great Depression and he introduced the New Deal as a systematic programme of recovery, which was a radical departure for the US. The structure of weak federal government and strong state government limited the imposition of national economic policies and limited the growth of big government compared with the European countries. When President Roosevelt introduced the New Deal in his first administration it was a big government initiative to provide citizen services that the free market was unable to provide at the time. The first task was to provide economic relief for farmers who had been most severely hit. The government acquired agricultural surpluses and provided grants to farmers not to produce, but by 1940, 6 million farmers were receiving federal funding.

The Social Security Act of 1933 established a system of insurance for the aged, the unemployed and the disabled based on employer and employee contributions. It mirrored the systems put in place in Britain, France and Germany more than 20 years earlier. During the same period Blue Cross and Blue Shield were established as non-profit health insurance schemes. The Works Progress Administration sought to provide work rather than welfare and its recipients were engaged in activities such as building schools and transport infrastructure. In addition, there were the Federal Theatre Project, the Federal Arts Project, the Federal Writers Project and the National Youth Administration, which together had established 9 million jobs before they were stopped in 1943. These and other New Deal initiatives expanded tertiary activities for which manpower was required to the benefit of the US economy and society. By 1939 and the outbreak of World War II, US unemployment had fallen from the high of 25% in 1932, to 15%.

The Great Depression had a dramatic impact on hotel demand for as the economies collapsed so did demand into hotels. According to a Horwarth & Horwarth report "in the early 1930's approximately 70% of the hotels in the US were in some form of receivership or financial difficulty" (Davidson, 2005). The depth of the economic collapse and its pervasiveness across the economy devastated the volume of business demand into hotels, while the escalation in unemployment devastated leisure demand. The New Deal initiatives not only steadied the economy and encouraged growth, but also facilitated some growth in hotel business demand. As employment grew so also did hotel vacation demand and gradually, business demand returned.

The Great Depression in Europe

Although the Wall Street Crash was induced in the USA, the already weaker European economies were hit by it and the hike in US import duties in 1930 tipped the European economies into the Great Depression. British exports collapsed to a low of £0.37 billion in 1932 and recovered a little to £0.47 billion in 1939. This pattern was mirrored by the levels of unemployment, 2.7 million and 1.8 million respectively. The political traditions of the US cast the New Deal as a necessary, but short-term flirtation with big government. Thus, by the outbreak of World War II many of the New Deal initiatives, having succeeded in alleviating the impact of the Great Depression, were unwound. In contrast, approaches adopted in Europe to combat the Great Depression were heavily influenced by a mixture of socialism and the thinking of the economist John Maynard Keynes (2007). In the elected democracies of Western Europe, notably Britain and France, the big government initiatives produced the long-term extension of citizen services that lasted for the rest of the century. By the outbreak of World War II social services in Britain had expanded to include public education; national health insurance; unemployment insurance; old age, widows' and orphans' pensions; employment exchanges; unemployment relief and public assistance. Together they serviced the needs of up to 25 million citizens, more than half of the population and cost about 10% of national income.

In 1938 by the provision of paid annual leave for most full-time employees under the Holidays with Pay Act boosted leisure demand. However, the horrid experiences of the Great Depression for the hotel business became etched in the psyche of hotel professionals, manifest by the belief that the hotel business is inherently cyclical. That is, when an economic downturn occurs, hotel demand collapses. It was regarded as a law of nature that could not be avoided and has remained a central feature of hotel orthodoxy ever since.

World War II

Economically, World War II was a re-run of World War I. The European economies were further devastated and the approach of the US to stay out of the war until December 1941 provided a boost to its economy and its hotel business, both of which benefited from two more years of post-Depression recovery not available to Europeans and both the economic and hotel divergence between the US and Europe widened even more. Thus, when the US entered World War II its economy and hotel demand were in a much stronger state than any of the European combatants when they entered the war in 1939. The US was involved in World War II for only 45 months against 70 months for the Europeans, the proportion of the US population involved in the war was much lower than the Europeans and fewer American lives were lost. Again, the US was not invaded or its territory degraded except for the one attack on Pearl Harbor, which triggered their entry into the war. These factors were central to the higher level of hotel demand achieved by the US during World War II than any other of the key combatants. Between 1940 and 1942, new hotel supply continued to trickle on to the US market, but during its involvement in the war this dried-up.

Table 5.1: GDP Relative to US.

	1938	1945
Austria	3%	1%
France	23%	7%
Germany	44%	21%
Italy	18%	6%
Japan	21%	10%
Soviet Union	45%	23%
Britain	36%	22%

Source: M Harrison, The Economics of WWII, CUP 1998

Table 5.1 shows the GDP relative to the US for the main countries involved in World War II for 1938, the last full year before the war and 1945, the last year of the war. In all cases there was a marked reduction in GDP relative to the US.

During the war, world farm production fell by one third, but US agricultural output continued to grow due to the pre-war immigrant-induced rise in population, the growth in agricultural productivity, the export of farm products to Europe, the late entry to the war and the fact that its land was not invaded. In Europe, the rationing of food, clothes and other household goods was introduced and the development of sectors such as retailing, financial services, communications, professional services, travel, hospitality and entertainment were put on hold. Much civilian production was curtailed as the focus of manufacturing turned to armaments, but no country produced and sold as much as the US. According to Krug, between mid-1940 and mid-1945. US manufacturers produced: 86,338 tanks, 297,000 planes, 17.4 million rifles, 41.4 billion rounds of ammunition for small arms, 315,000 field artillery, 4.2 million artillery shells, 64,000 landing vessels, 6500 other navy ships and 5400 cargo and transportation ships (Krug, 1945). In the 12 years after the pit of the Great Depression in 1933, US GDP grew by 3.5 times.

World War II produced six years of the most dramatic reduction in hotel demand in European history and when it started in 1939 new hotel construction stopped and bombing and business failures reduced supply. The conventional functions of hotels also changed during the war. Taylor recounts that in Britain, "in the first two weeks of the war 200 hotels were requisitioned (by the government)...and... many civil service departments were evacuated to resorts and spas" (Taylor, 2003: 159). City-based boarding schools were evacuated to hotels in the countryside away from the threat of bombing. The south coast beaches were mined and hotel demand into the coastal resorts evaporated (pp. 258–259). Many hotels in the South East, in London and in the main provincial cities and ports were bombed and others throughout the country ceased trading, never to reopen. According to Taylor, "In November 1945, there were still 2,700 requisitioned hotels" (p. 256) The still weak economy at the start of the war, the high proportion of the adult population involved in the military and in the war effort, the rationing of food, fuel and most other consumer goods, the bombing of key cities and the battles throughout western continental Europe all contributed to the steep and sustained reduction in hotel demand and hotel supply. The only limit on the collapse for Britain was that it was not invaded Otus estimates that in 1945 when many hotels were used by the government and the military, hotel demand was 20% lower than it was in 1900. In contrast, US hotel room nights sold in 1945 was 70% higher than the level achieved in 1900.

Economic structure and hotel demand in the US

The US governance of the four critical events of the period meant that their impact on the US economy was the mildest of any of the main economies and its recovery was the fastest and the greatest. Over the period, the material conditions of life and life experiences of Americans changed most. The growth in automobile ownership was accompanied by new highways and expressways to accommodate the increased speed of vehicles and enable longer, faster and safer journeys. In parallel, gas stations and auto maintenance shops peppered the country and a spare parts industry grew. In contrast, the rate of motor vehicle manufacture, sale and use in Europe was much less significant. Radio and movies became national US institutions in the 1920s and introduced new and powerfully effective forms of advertising that contributed to the growth in demand, particularly with the introduction of talking pictures. In contrast, radio advertising was absent from the newly-created British Broadcasting Company. In the US, telephones expanded nationally as did modern sewage systems, electrification, domestic refrigeration and air conditioning in public buildings. There was a burst of modernism with skyscrapers and the art deco movement, while jazz emerged as a uniquely American musical form. Participation grew in the full range of sports that were established in the 19th century to the extent that in the first half of the 20th century, playing sport became one of the largest and most frequently undertaken forms of recreation. But it was not only growth in playing sport that was a feature of the period. American football, baseball and ice hockey became major spectator sports.

At the turn of the century there was little difference in the size of the manufacturing workforces of the US and Britain, but the US had many fewer companies and thus benefited from economies of scale to a considerably greater degree than Britain. The largest US company, US Steel, employed 250,000 people, while the largest British company, Fine Cotton Spinners and Doublers, one of over 2,000 cotton firms in the country, employed only 30,000. During the early years of the century, a clutch of US companies emerged which were to become global giants including: Ford Motor Company, Firestone Tire and Rubber, General Motors, Harley-Davidson, Monsanto Chemicals, Pepsi Cola, Philip Morris, Quaker Oats and Texaco. The internationalisation of manufacturing also emerged. US car manufacturers such as Ford and General Motors established factories in UK and Germany to produce vehicles for those markets.

The impact of mass production

In 1900, half of the US labour force worked on farms, but over the period this declined rapidly. Otus estimates that in 1900, agriculture accounted for a minor share of business demand into US hotels and it declined throughout the period as employment in the segment declined.

The first element in the acceleration of the US economy was its commitment to mass production. A surge of technical innovations generated new consumer demand and the US economy was the first to mass produce new inventions such as automobiles. In the US in 1900, there were only 2,475 automobiles produced. By 1913, Ford was producing 80,000 Model Ts (Lacey, 1986: 120). In the same year there was a nationwide network of 7,000 dealers affiliated to Ford. Major growth was also achieved by other automobile companies such as General Motors and Chrysler, and though many fledgling companies collapsed or were consolidated, by 1930 the automobile industry was the largest business in the US. The second element in the acceleration of the US economy was the growth in productivity. In the early years of the 20th century systematic analysis of work practices and the establishment of approaches such as Frederick Taylor's scientific management (Taylor, 1947) and in the 1920s Elton Mayo's human relations approach to the management of production (Roethlisberger and Dickson, 1939). The manifestation of these and other management theories was the greater growth in output and productivity achieved by the US than in any other industrialised country, examples of which were often dramatic. In 1913 it took 728 man-minutes to produce a Model T Ford, but a new assembly line introduced at the start of 1914 reduced assembly time to only 93 man-minutes (Lacey, 1986: 120). The third element in the acceleration of the US economy was the growth in diversity of consumer goods. Early in the 20th century, the Sears Roebuck catalogue already included 10,000 items and by 1908, 3.6 million copies were distributed, largely to households in rural communities (Woloson, 2005). The pace of growth in manufacturing productivity hastened the rise in structural unemployment and was a contributing factor to the Depression because of insufficient growth in citizen services and service businesses to create new jobs.

Industrial companies were the largest employer in the US throughout the period and it was positive for the US hotel business since they provide more business demand into hotels than agriculture.

First, from around the turn of the century the burst of concentration in manu-facturing widened the geographic distribution of the enlarged producers to a regional and national level. This required and produced an increase in the size of the corporate structure of manufacturing companies and in particular in the number of travelling salesmen who were a market for hotel rooms. Second, the increase in the range of consumer goods produced, mostly smaller ticket house-hold equipment, required an increase in the number of salesmen and other cor-porate executives, which was also positive for hotel demand. Third, in addition to the increase in the range and volume of consumer goods there was material growth in the production of goods such as machine tools, component parts and construction materials, the sale of which to other businesses also required a more modest increase in business travellers and provided a further boost to hotel demand.

Other secondary activities such as construction and public utilities also grew as the population grew, but much of the scope of construction and public utilities was limited to individual states, thus limiting the rate at which they generated business demand into hotels. A feature of the period in the US was the expansion of citizen services as government extended the provision of public education, public health and welfare services, particularly during the New Deal. Although this added additional sources and volumes of business demand into hotels, it was not transforming, but it did offset some of the loss of business demand from other segments.

Over the period from 1900 to 1945, service businesses such as retailing, wholesaling, banking, communications, movie theatres, travel and financial services had a roller coaster ride, but all ended the period larger than at the start in spite of the setbacks during the traumatic events and although still a minority of the economy they added new business demand into hotels. Business travellers used automobiles and trains for their work-related travel. Until 1930, the airline industry was dominated by military use. Air passenger travel was small, exclusive, expensive and short-haul. In 1929, 173,000 passengers flew in the US *(source:* www.century-of-flight.freeola.com). Otus estimates that in 1900, domestic business demand into US hotels accounted for 25 million room nights, which grew to 29 million by 1910 and then 34 million by 1920. By 1930, the first ravages of the Great Depression reduced domestic business demand to 28 million room nights and it got worse as the Great Depression worsened, but by 1940 it had recovered to 34 million room nights. In 1945, the civilian economy was cranking-up as victory in Europe became more assured as a precursor to the rapid growth of the post-war recovery.

Leisure demand

US domestic leisure demand grew over the half century as the number of workers receiving annual vacation pay increased, but as with business demand, the growth was not linear, suffering as it did from the collapse that resulted from the critical events. Otus estimates that the volume of vacation room nights sold by US hotels at the end of World War II, 37 million was up only 4 million since the start of the century despite a doubling of population. In the main, white-collar workers provided the increase in demand, but little vacation demand was generated by recently arrived immigrants. The predominant vacation demand was concentrated in the spring and summer months and was boosted progressively by the increase in automobile ownership and passenger trains as driving and train journeys to the vacation destinations became the common practices. The heavy concentration of manufacturing industries in urban areas depressed industrial cities as popular vacation destinations. Over the period, foreign demand into US hotels remained at the margins, never exceeding 2% of total room nights sold. The first half of the 20th century was the golden age of Atlantic liners, which delivered both business and leisure travellers from Europe during the high growth stages of the period, but were eliminated during the two world wars and volumes collapsed during the Depression.

Prohibition

In the US in 1919, the Volstead Acts, the Eighteenth Amendment to the Constitution, banned the production and sale of alcoholic drinks. Prohibition changed the pattern of spending on out-of-home leisure activities at the expense of saloons, which never recovered and impacted the performance of hotels and restaurants. More specifically, its impact was on non-rooms demand into hotel restaurants, bars and banqueting which were forbidden to sell alcoholic drinks. In 1933, the worst year for the US economy, the Volstead Acts were repealed, which removed the main constraint on non-rooms demand and reintroduced bars into hotels. However, the ferocity of the Great Depression and World War II meant that it took a generation to recover demand into hotel bars, restaurants and banqueting. In 1900, domestic leisure demand accounted for 34 million room nights. By 1940, before the US entered World War II, domestic leisure demand accounted for 77 million room nights illustrating the extent of growth despite the critical events.

Economic structure and hotel supply in the US

If the supply ratio of hotel rooms per 1,000 citizens had remained constant at the 1900 level during this period the US would have needed 870,000 hotel rooms in 1940, before it entered World War II. However, Otus estimates that even over this very traumatic period the governance of the critical events and the structural developments in the economy increased the volume of business and leisure demand into hotels, which in turn boosted hotel supply to around 940,000 rooms, a secular growth of 70,000 rooms. Hotel room supply grew during each decade of the period, but by different amounts. Between 1900 and 1920 around 150,000 hotel rooms were added, with only the World War I years from 1917 slowing the growth. A further 130,000 rooms were added during the 1920s, notably with the introduction of motels. The 1930s saw a decline in new supply with only 10,000 rooms added. Early in the decade new rooms that were planned before the Great Depression came on stream and suffered losses for years. Later in the decade, as the economy and hotel demand began to recover, a trickle of new rooms began to emerge, mostly in small motels. This trickle increased into the 1940s until the US entered World War II and by 1945 another 10,000 rooms had been added. Of the 430,000 rooms added between 1900 and 1930, 95% were created by independent hoteliers. It was the last period of raw entrepreneurial hotel development in the US. They chased the trend of automobile travel for which they produced motels. They chased the trend of summer vacations for which they created hotels in resort areas, they chased the trend of growing domestic business travellers for which they constructed urban hotels and they chased the trend in permanent and semi-permanent residents for which they developed apartment hotels. Over the period as a whole, US hotel room supply grew at a net rate of 1.4% per year, fluctuating from a high of 2.7% during the first decade of the century to a low of 0.2% during the 1930s. The supply ratio at the start of the period was 6.6 and stayed above 7.0 until 1940, but fell back to 6.8 in 1945.

There were four notable developments in hotel supply during the first 45 years of the century. All were linked to the developments in the US economic structure and economic policies:

♦ the growth of grand hotels,

♦ the growth of apartment hotels,

♦ the emergence of motels, and

♦ the growth of hotel chains.

Grand hotels

First, the development of grand hotels was a feature of the period and this was particularly the case in New York City where the Astors were more active early in the 20th century than they had been in the 19th century. The Astor House was closed in 1913 after operating for 77 years. The 300-room New Netherland opened in 1892 and was sold by the Astors in 1924 after enduring the reduction in demand imposed by Prohibition and was demolished in 1926 having operated for only 32 years. In 1904, William Waldorf Astor opened the 22-story Hotel Astor in Times Square at a cost of $7 million. It was a dramatic addition to the Manhattan hotel stock. Kaplan described it as follows:

> there were more than 500 bedrooms served by twelve passenger elevators, a banqueting hall seating 500, a 35,000 square foot kitchen described as the largest in the world, dozens of public rooms, each with its own distinct character, and guest suites that drew on a lexicon of styles – art nouveau, Empire, Dutch Renaissance and made inevitable references to Versailles. Some of the Astor's technological innovations were air-conditioning; fire and smoke detectors in every room; electrically controlled fire doors; a "food escalator" connecting the kitchen and banqueting rooms, an ice plant that produced 120 tons each day; an array of dynamos powering elevators and the hotel's 14 thousand lights; and a "crematory", or incinerator, the first of its kind in a hotel, to dispose of trash and garbage.
>
> (Kaplan, 2007: 142)

The Astor was such a success that two years after its opening a further $4 million was invested to double the size of the hotel to include, among other additions the Astor Theatre and the largest roof garden in the world. The Astor remained a feature of mid-town Manhattan until it was demolished in 1967 having lasted twice as long as the New Netherland. Two months after the Astor opened in 1904, John Jacob Astor IV opened the St Regis hotel at the corner of Fifth Avenue and Fifty Fifth Street. At $6 million and with around 200 rooms, the hotel was focused on high luxury and high prices relative to the grand hotel market in Manhattan. Two years later John Jacob Astor IV opened the Knickerbocker hotel at the corner of Broadway and Forty Second Street at a cost of $3.5 million. It never succeeded and relied on local non-rooms demand, which was eliminated by Prohibition forcing the closure of the hotel after only 20 years of operation.

The Waldorf=Astoria may have started the 20th century as the hotel in New York, but its attractiveness waned in the face of the accelerated development of new grand hotels further up Manhattan with more modern technology and new interior design. The Astors sold the hotel in 1916 to Coleman du Pont who installed Lucius Bloomer as general manager. Bloomer and Du Pont formed Bloomer du Pont Hotels to own and manage grand hotels in the 1920s and 1930s. However, the new owners did not halt the decline. They did not invest to keep pace with the developing standards of luxury, design and fashion. The decline in demand was exacerbated by the elimination of alcohol sales during Prohibition and two connected factors finally culminated in its closure: Manhattan real estate values escalated and advances in building technology were enabling the construction of skyscrapers. In the end, the first 1,000-room grand hotel was just too small for the land it occupied in Manhattan. In 1928 it was sold to the Bethlehem Engineering Company for $14 million and a year later it was sold to the Empire State Corporation for $17.5 million. The new owners sold the contents of the hotel, including an astonishing 125 pianos and demolished the building in 1929. The Waldorf=Astoria was replaced after only 32 years of existence by the Empire State Building, which remained the tallest building in the world until 1954.

New York was not without a Waldorf=Astoria for long. Boomer Du Pont acquired the Waldorf=Astoria name for $1 and their plans to construct a new Waldorf=Astoria were advanced when the old hotel was being demolished. The $40 million finance for the new, larger, art nouveau and lavish Waldorf=Astoria was secured before the stock market crash closed the debt and equity markets to hotel developers. The hotel opened in October 1931 as the Depression was deepening. It occupied a block from Park Avenue to Lexington Avenue between Forty Ninth and Fiftieth Streets that was leased from the New York Central Railroad. The new Waldorf=Astoria had around 2,000 rooms, most of which were in the 42-storey main hotel. The 30 story Waldorf=Astoria Towers that faced Park Avenue included apartments for long-stay residents. In addition, the hotel had a clutch of restaurants, private dining rooms, clubs, shops and a complex of ballrooms, the largest of which could accommodate 2,000. The new Waldorf=Astoria was a colossus, even by New York standards. However, opening when the economy was spiralling down in the Depression was disastrous and the hotel spent its first 13 years in the red, not making a profit until 1944.

Another grand hotel in New York City that was re-created was the Plaza Hotel, at the corner of Fifth Avenue and Central Park South. The first Plaza opened in October 1890. The land was acquired for $850,000 and the 400-room hotel cost $3 million to build and fit out. The Plaza was not a failure, but the acceleration in the size, technology and facilities of hotels such as the New Netherland and the Waldorf=Astoria meant that it was not making most effective use of its famous plot. In 1903, the Plaza was acquired for $3 million by a syndicate of investors with a plan to demolish the existing hotel and rebuild a much larger and grander hotel on the same site. Demolition began in 1905, only 15 years after the hotel was opened and the new Plaza, constructed and fitted out at a cost of $12.5 million, opened in 1907. The new hotel had more than double the number of rooms of the first Plaza, it had much more extensive non-room facilities and was one of the world's most architecturally recognisable grand hotels on one of the world's most prominent hotel sites.

Over the 100 years from the mid-19th century, grand hotels, which had the highest investment, were in the most prestigious locations and were regarded as the benchmark for the hotel business were also among the worst performing and the poorest of hotel investments of the period. The first Waldorf=Astoria and the New Netherland lasted for only 32 years each, the Astor reached 67 years before it was demolished, the Knickerbocker only 20 years and the first Plaza a mere 15 years. The Waldorf=Astoria, and the Plaza in New York, the Palace in San Francisco and the Palmer House in Chicago were re-created as larger, more modern and more lavish hotels only to perform precariously during the first half of the 20th century. They were impacted by the four critical events and were unable to adapt to the evolving economic and social conditions.

Apartment hotels

The second notable development in US hotel supply during the period was the rise of apartment hotels. There is no exact definition of an apartment hotel. Predominantly, they were a version of grand hotels or aspirant grand hotels and were distinguished from regular hotels since they contained a proportion of multi-room suites that were rented by long-term residents for whom the apartment hotel became their address in the city. New York City ordinances permitted hotels providing apartments without a private kitchen to be classified as commercial rather than residential buildings enabling apartment hotels to be larger than apartment buildings on the same size of site. One measure of the growth of grand hotels and apartment hotels and the decline in private mansions in the early decades of the 20th century was the sharp reduction in the number of domestic servants. Between 1910 and 1920 the numbers declined by 25% from 1.3 million and in New York City the number fell by one third from 113,400, many of whom transferred their skills to grand hotels and apartment hotels (Smith, 1927: 214). The Volstead Acts produced the closure of hotel bars and the reduction in demand for hotel restaurants and banqueting. Thus, apartment hotels progressively reduced their non-room facilities and progressively fewer non-residents were attracted. By the 1930s, Rutenbaum estimated that there were around 150 apartment hotels in New York City (Ruttenbaum, 1996). The longer that Prohibition lasted and the Great Depression worsened, the transition from hotel to apartment hotel was a means to survive in the harsh environment of fast diminishing transient hotel demand and collapsing non-room demand by shifting the demand focus to long-term residents attracted by the high prestige sites, the cache of the luxury and the range of services rather than the cost of owning a mansion and employing servants. The rise of apartment hotels during the 1920s and 1930s was another example of the widening North Atlantic divide in the hotel business since few apartment hotels emerged in Europe at the time and the proportion of permanent and semi-permanent residents in grand hotels was minor.

The emergence of motels

The third and most significant development in US hotel supply during the first half of the 20th century was the introduction of motels. Traditionally, US hotels provided full life support facilities for resident customers and also sought to attract local demand to their non-room facilities. This pattern continued until the1920s when two factors came together to produce an alternative approach that was based on the reality of the prevailing market rather than on an idealised conception of the hotel. First, in the early decades of the century non-room revenue could account for half of total hotel revenue in medium-sized hotels. Thus, the Volstead Acts were the first fiscally imposed initiative to jeopardise such a significant proportion of hotel demand. Most hotels suffered, but the larger the non-room facilities and the greater the reliance of a hotel on local demand, then the more severe the impact of Prohibition. Coinciding with the introduction of Prohibition was the strong growth in automobile ownership. The increasing use of the automobile by growing numbers of travelling salesmen boosted the volume of business customers who arrived at hotels by automobile and the growing practice of families using their automobile for vacation travel boosted the numbers of leisure customers who arrived at hotels by automobile. The rational response by the US hotel business to the impact of the Volstead Acts and the sharp rise in road travellers was to create the motel.

Motels were a latter-day version of the European coaching inns targeted on a single travel market, the motorist. Motels also sought to avoid the need to attract non-rooms demand that was in jeopardy at the time by providing only limited non-rooms facilities. The first recognised motel opened in 1925 in San Luis Obispo, California followed by a spate of small, new build motels developed by independents along arterial roads and in suburban locations to be a convenient, inexpensive and utilitarian hotel facility for motorists who rarely stayed for more than one night at a time. Their location was the first reason why motels cost less to build than urban and resort hotels. The second reason was that their bedrooms were smaller and had more utilitarian furniture, fixtures and equipment. Motels also included a functional rather than a decorous lobby. The third reason why they cost less to build was that, importantly, motels had few non-room facilities other than a temperance restaurant that was low cost and sold quick-service breakfast and dinner to resident customers. Motels did not rely on attracting local demand to their restaurants. Thus, the motel was the first limited feature hotel of the 20th century in which more than 75% of turnover was derived from renting bedrooms. Their rooms intensity meant that their profit margin for the same room occupancy as urban full-feature hotels was higher despite lower room rates and they delivered a higher return on investment. Motels captured both business and leisure demand and as a result, the seasonality of their demand was less severe than urban and resort hotels. Motels were a unique and successful US hotel format that did not materialise in Europe because there was no equivalent to the Volstead Acts, there was a much lower level of car ownership and Europe had a legacy of coaching inns. Consequently, the conditions that prevailed at the time in the US to produce motels were not in place in Europe and further widened the North Atlantic divide in the hotel business. When the US was creating an innovative and market grounded hotel category for which there was growing demand and which was designed to produce higher returns on investment, Europe continued with an idealised conception of the hotel that was devoid of innovation and produced poorer returns on investment.

Hotel chains

The fourth notable development in US hotel supply was the expansion of hotel chains. Over the period, hotel chains added around 40,000 rooms to reach a total of 55,000, an annual increase of 3%, double the rate of total supply growth, which lifted concentration in the US hotel market to 6%. The first significant hotel chain developed over the period was Statler Hotels. Ellsworth Statler built his first hotel in Buffalo, New York in 1908. The Statler in Cleveland, Ohio opened in 1912 with 800 rooms to which another 300 rooms were added later. Detroit opened in 1915 with 800 rooms all with private bathrooms. In 1916, he leased the Hotel Pennsylvania, New York City in which all of the 2,200 rooms had a private bathroom. Statler constructed more hotels in New York City, St. Louis, Buffalo and Boston before he died in 1928. His widow continued to develop the chain until it was sold in the early 1950s. Statler's legacy is important. He took advantage of the progress in the economic structure in the US early in the 20th century to develop very large urban hotels, mainly in the mid-market and he pioneered the inclusion of private bathrooms in all bedrooms at a time when, in Europe, it was only grand hotels that were considering the idea. Later, in 1927, he added a radio to each room in the Statler Boston, which was another innovation for mid-market hotels. Statler was influenced by the scientific management movement and by assembly line production early in the 20th century and he sought to translate these approaches to the hotel business by building large hotels with a more rational lay-out than the grand hotels and replicated the format in key industrial cities. The first benefit Statler achieved was internal economies of scale from the size of the hotels. The second benefit was from the more limited and more functional non-room facilities, which he geared to the specific demands of mid-market business travellers, his target market, at prices that attracted them. The more limited non-room facilities and the large size of the hotels in urban centres enabled the achievement of high operating margins and higher returns on investment than grand hotels. But that was not all, another innovation that the Statler chain introduced, which distanced it from the management of grand hotels, was investment in generating demand. Advertising was considered anathema to grand hoteliers, but it was a critical element of success for Statler Hotels. His early advertising slogan - "a room and a bath for a dollar and a half" succinctly captured the essence of his offer and created his brand as the undisputed mid-market leader.

Conrad Hilton acquired his first hotel, the Mobley in Cisco, Texas in 1920. It was, at best, a mid-market hotel targeted to business demand. This was followed by a decade of acquisition in Texas. He leased the 68-room Melba hotel in Fort Worth, which was followed by the lease of the Waldorf in Dallas, few of whose 200 rooms had private bathrooms. Others were added such as the Terminal hotel Dallas in 1925, the first to carry the Hilton name; the Beaton hotel in Corsicana; then hotels in Wrotham, Abilene, Waco, Marlin, Plain View, San Angelo and Lubbock. In all of these hotels, Hilton benefited from the growth in business demand as a result of the fast development of the Texas oil industry, the overall buoyancy of the economy, while the limited non-room facilities in the hotels provided Hilton with insulation from the impact of the Volstead Acts. All of the hotels were leased and Hilton made money by improving their performance and attracting higher volumes of demand without adding to hotel supply. The hotels were a mixed bag, none of which traded any higher than the mid-market (Hilton, 1957: 119). It was not until 1930 that Hilton built his first hotel, in El Paso, but by 1931, the Great Depression and Hilton's reliance on travelling salesmen brought the company to bankruptcy, most of the leased hotels were lost and no more hotels were added until 1938. The post-Depression expansion took the business beyond the Texas border for the first time, into larger cities and into hotels with a higher market level. The first new era acquisition was the Sir Francis Drake in San Francisco. This was followed in the early 1940s by a number of acquisitions of larger and more up-market hotels in major US cities and his first venture outside the US. These acquisitions included: the Town House in Los Angeles; the Roosevelt and the Plaza in New York City; the Palmer House in Chicago and the Stephens Hotel in Chicago, the largest hotel in the world at the time with 2,673 rooms. The first venture outside the US was the acquisition of the lease on the Palacio Hotel in Chihuahua, Mexico. This was a remarkable period of development and did not stop with the outbreak of World War II. Hilton was able to access capital on the momentum of the growth of his portfolio and the improvement in performance that he delivered from the hotels. Among the bargains he acquired was the Plaza in New York City, which he acquired for $7 million in 1943, when it had cost $12.5 million to build 36 years earlier. Hilton spent a further $6 million on refurbishment since the hotel had not received effective investment since it opened. The Plaza and the Palmer House as well as the other hotels that Hilton acquired became chain affiliated for the first time. Their performance benefited from the demand generation activities of the chain and also from the more systematic control of operating costs. By the end of World War II, the Hilton portfolio had increased to 14 hotels.

Some of the other chains that became established during this period included Bowman Biltmore, which during the first two decades of the century, developed a chain of nine large full feature and resort hotels. The largest chain that operated during the period was United Hotels, a portfolio of mid-market, urban hotels that operated in cities across the country. At its height, United had almost 30 hotels. Then there was Western Hotels, later to be renamed Westin, which by 1929 had created a portfolio of 17 hotels in the north western states. In 1937, Ernest Henderson and Robert Moore, the founders of Sheraton Hotels acquired their first hotel, the Stonehaven in Springfield, Massachusetts. In 1939 they acquired a further two hotels in Massachusetts, one of which was the Sheraton Hotel after which the brand was named and in 1941 they acquired the Copley Plaza in Boston. In 1922, the Treadway Company established a short chain of college inns adjacent to universities. In addition, Sonnesta and Associated Resort

Hotels emerged in the 1940s. The growth of hotel chains over the period was the first material change in the structure of the US hotel business. The driver of this development was the emergence of hotel chain entrepreneurs such as Statler and Hilton who were opportunistic in their developments and acquisitions, but also realised more than other hotel entrepreneurs of the period that inherently hotel chains had the capacity to provide cost synergies and demand generation synergies that were beyond independent hotels and thus to deliver superior returns on investment.

US hotel demand and supply performance

Otus estimates that in 1900, annual hotel room occupancy was 33%. As supply increased over the period and hotel demand fluctuated due to the impact of critical events and short bursts of growth, total annual hotel room occupancy rarely exceeded this level. In 1940 annual hotel room occupancy was no better than in 1900, but hotel demand grew over the period from 60 million room nights sold in 1900 to 114 million in 1940. Even absorbing the impacts of the critical events of the period, hotel room nights sold in 1945 had grown by half from 1900. The US was the only country in which the hotel business achieved economic ascent over the period, expressed in the growth in rooms supply, rooms demand and the superior rate of growth of hotel chains.

Table 5.2: US hotels 1900-1945.

	1900	1910	1920	1930	1940	1945	1900-1945 CAGR
Total hotels	10,000	12,000	15,000	25,000	26,000	27,000	
Total rooms	500,000	650,000	800,000	930,000	940,000	950,000	1.4%
Room nights available (m)	183	237	293	339	344	347	1.4%
Room occupancy %	33%	34%	34%	28%	33%	30%	
Room nights sold (m)	**60**	**81**	**100**	**95**	**114**	**104**	**1.2%**
Domestic business	25	29	34	24	34	62	2.0%
Domestic leisure	34	50	64	70	77	42	0.5%
Foreign business	1	1	1	1	1	1	-0.3%
Foreign leisure	1	1	1	1	1	1	-0.3%
Concentration %	3%	3%	4%	4%	5%	6%	
Hotel room supply ratio	6.6	7.0	7.5	7.5	7.1	6.8	
Secular growth in hotel room supply		40,000	60,000	0	-50,000	-40,000	

Source: Otus & Co Advisory Ltd.

Economic structure and hotel demand in Britain

The four critical events between 1900 and 1945 produced a more severe impact on the British economy and its hotel business than was endured by the US. Britain was involved in the two world wars for the full duration and although it was not invaded, its main cities and southern ports suffered bomb damage during World War II. It also suffered during the Great Depression and there was a general leftward swing in political orthodoxy reflected in the longer-term big government initiatives enacted to manage the economy. Consequently, between 1900 and 1945 the British economy grew less than the US economy, its recovery between the critical events was slower and shorter lived than the US recovery, its economic structure developed at a slower pace and British hotel demand and supply both declined.

In 1900, the proportion of the workforce employed in British agriculture was already relatively low at 10%, but it declined further after World War I in spite of government subsidies. The decline was due to the continuing switch from arable to pastoral farming as it continued to be cheaper to import foodstuffs particularly from the Empire. As a result, by 1939, less than 5% of the British workforce was employed in agriculture and Otus estimates that hotel demand generated by agriculture also fell to a minor level. The decline in international competitiveness suffered by British textile, iron, steel and coal industries during the late 19th century continued in the 20th century, but they remained significant employers. By 1939, almost 10% of the British workforce was employed in the textile industry, less than 4% worked in coal mining and at least another 30% worked in other manufacturing industries (Addison and Jones, 2005). After World War I, manufacturing recovery was slow and pre-war levels were not reached until the mid-1920s. (Jay, 2003:p247) As a result, the volume of hotel business demand generated by manufacturers in the mid-1920s was not much greater than it was in 1914 and did not compare with the higher volumes and faster growth achieved in the US. The burst of industrial concentration that happened in the US did not happen in Britain to anything like the same degree, thus, British firms were smaller and had a narrower geographic range requiring fewer business travellers than the US and limiting the growth potential of industrially generated demand into British hotels. There was a narrower range of consumer goods produced in Britain, which further limited the volume of business demand into British hotels. The Great Depression was most severely felt in the Midlands and the northern parts of Britain where heavy industries were concentrated and the decline in business demand into hotels was most severe between Scotland and the Midlands.

British citizen services expanded throughout the period as government policies progressively focused on expanding the rights of citizenship. As a result, the balance of employment tilted towards citizen services. The 1908 Pensions Act introduced state old age pensions. The 1911 National Insurance Act introduced benefits for sickness, invalidity and funeral expenses, but it covered only 2.5

million workers. Not until the 1930s did the British Government assume full responsibility to provide incomes to all the unemployed. In 1900, the typical working week was 53 hours, but gradually the eight-hour day became the norm. Thus, for the first time, work, sleep and leisure time came into balance. Education expanded with the raising of the school leaving age to 15 by the end of the period and there was slow growth in the numbers attending universities which remained dominated by the traditional arts and sciences. The citizen service initiatives generated limited hotel demand. Only a tiny proportion of civil servants needed to travel as part of their job and most professional employees in citizen services worked in hospitals, classrooms and offices and did not travel on business. In secondary industries most business travellers were employed in sales and marketing, but in British citizen services there were practically none of those activities.

During the period, the growth in market services such as retailers, banks, communications, wholesalers and professional service businesses was slower than in the US because there was little progress in demand beyond providing as a necessary back-up to the primary, secondary and citizen services activities. British, service businesses were small and their market was local and regional rather than national and this limited the volume of hotel demand they generated. Thus, demand into hotels from services businesses trailed the volume of demand from secondary industries to a greater degree than in the US, which is another implication of a less developed economic structure. Otus estimates that in 1900, total domestic business demand in British hotels amounted to 11 million room nights, by 1910 it increased to 12 million, by 1920 it had fallen back to 11 million due to the impact of World War I and by 1930 the impact of the recession forced it down to 10 million. By 1940, the volume had increased to 20 million and rose artificially to 21 million at the end of the war due to the military and government use instead of conventional domestic business demand. Foreign business demand remained minor throughout the period. International companies were still a marginal part of the British economy so that foreign business travellers, who predominantly were owners and senior executives arrived either to sell or buy and for this they concentrated on the gateway cities and industrial centres.

Holiday demand

Domestic holiday demand into hotels in coastal and rural resorts grew over the spring and summer months until World War I as more white-collar workers received paid annual holiday leave. Domestic holiday customers who stayed in hotels did so typically for less than two weeks and they bought hotel packages such as bed and breakfast, half board or full board. The war ended this demand for the duration, but it picked up in the 1920s only to be devastated again when the Great Depression arrived. Domestic leisure demand in Britain was given a boost in 1938 following the introduction of statutory paid holidays for most full-time employees, but most workers and their families could not afford to stay in hotels. Thus, in coastal and country resorts the numbers of bed and breakfasts, boarding houses, guest houses, self-catering, holiday camps, caravan parks and campsites grew to meet this new demand. The most famous example of holiday camps was Butlin's, which opened its first camp at Skegness in Lincolnshire in 1936 at a cost of £100,000. When the camp opened it could accommodate 2,000 and was expanded in 1939 to accommodate 5,000. By 1939 there were 200 holiday camps opened in Britain. Of course, World War II put a halt to conventional leisure demand into hotels. Between the critical events, weekend leisure demand into hotels increased with the growth in car ownership, but this demand was minor. Foreign leisure demand into British hotels over this period was small. Most overseas holiday visitors to Britain who stayed in British hotels came from the US by ocean liner with a minority from continental Europe, a very small minority of whom flew and their main destination was London.

Otus estimates that total hotel demand in Britain in 1900 amounted to 27 million room nights and that this grew to 30 million by 1910 and that this level was sustained in 1920. By 1930, the volume declined to 28 million nights and during World War II, in 1940, the volume declined to 22 million room nights dominated by military and government use that remained until the end of the War. Thus, in demand terms the first half of the 20th century produced a decline in British hotel demand.

Economic structure and hotel supply in Britain

To maintain a constant 1900 supply ratio of hotel rooms per 1,000 citizens during the period and the actual growth in population, Britain would have needed 340,000 hotel rooms in 1945. Otus estimates that there were only 300,000 rooms at the end of the war. That is, during the first 45 years of the 20th century, hotel supply grew by 40,000 rooms. In the first decade of the 20th century around 20,000 new hotel rooms were added, mainly in coastal resorts and in the main cities. In the second decade, World War I halted supply growth and there were closures of hotels which failed, but in the other years supply grew adding 5,000 rooms to the total. The 1920s produced growth, in resort areas more than in cities and this decade saw 15,000 rooms added to reach a total of 310,000 rooms in 1930. The 1930s was a complex decade for hotel supply. Although London and the Home Counties saw some urban hotel development it was more than offset by the removal from the market of failed unaffiliated hotels in the Midlands and northern parts of the country, then the extension of annual holiday pay during the recovery from the Great Depression produced an increase of room stock in resort areas, but bombing in the first year of World War II depleted room stock in the larger cities and ports. The net effect over the decade was to reduce room stock by 5,000 to a total of 305,000. By the end of World War II hotel room stock in Britain had fallen to 300,000 due mainly to business failures and many of the hotels that remained in business were generally dilapidated having had maintenance and capital expenditure curtailed for at least 15 years since before the Great Depression.

The growth of hotel chains

As was the case in the US over the period, business demand into hotels was mainly rooms demand with the possible addition of dinner and/or breakfast. Hotel-based conferences and meetings were rare and hotels did not have dedicated conference and meetings facilities. Instead some had a ballroom, while larger and more up-market hotels in the larger cities had private dining rooms to attract local functions. As also happened in the US, hotel chains grew at a faster pace than the total market. Over the period, hotel chains added 22,000 rooms, mainly by acquisition of unaffiliated hotels, to reach a total of 37,000, an annual increase of 2%. At the same time unaffiliated room stock, which still dominated the market grew by only 8000. Concentration in the British hotel market grew from 6% in 1900 to 12% in 1945 and this growth was matched by the increase in the number of hotel companies listed on the London Stock Exchange. By 1900, around 165 hotels operated by the railway companies and free-standing hotel companies were listed on the London Stock Exchange and there were coaching inns that were part of brewing companies that were also listed. Among the free standing listed hotel companies there were 13 that operated hotel portfolios, the largest of which was Gordon Hotels with 13 properties. Four of the Gordon hotels were in London, seven were in coastal resorts in the south of England, one was in Cannes and one in Monte Carlo. The next largest portfolio was Fredrick Hotels, whose chairman, Fredrick Gordon, was also chairman of Gordon Hotels. Fredrick Hotels had seven properties of which two were in London and the remainder in English resorts. The other 11 companies owned and operated short portfolios. The most atypical of the hotel companies at that time was Egyptian Hotels Limited, which owned three hotels in Egypt of which two were in Cairo and one in Ismalia. One of its directors was Thomas Albert Cook, the grandson of Thomas Cook the pioneering travel agent, but the significance of the company was that it entered into a management agreement with the Compagnie International des Grands Hotels to manage the Egyptian Hotels for a period of 12 years from 1897. The directors of Egyptian Hotels could terminate the contract every three years. The fee payable to Compagnie International des Grands Hotels was a percentage of net profits and it was also required to guarantee the service of two debentures on the hotels. In addition to these listed companies, the railway companies operated 57 hotels with around 6,500 rooms. In the hands of the brewers many of the coaching inns traded as p,ubs and only in a minority did they make an effort to attract rooms demand. Besides these chain developments, most of the remaining hotel room supply in Britain in 1900 was in small, idiosyncratic, unaffiliated hotels. Just as the emerging chains and listed companies reflected an increase in the efficiency of the hotel capital markets, the unaffiliated hotels reflected their inefficiency.

The most prominent of the hotel chains were the railway companies, Strand Hotels and the brewers, each of which exhibited the triumph of vertically integrated companies at the time. The other major chain development was Trust House Hotels, which was not vertically integrated and grew by consolidating existing coaching inns and other mainly mid-market hotels. The railway companies built on the networks established during the 19th century and in the mid-1920s there was a consolidation of all British railway companies to create four larger businesses. In the early decades of the 20th century they developed 14 prominent new provincial hotels, several of which remain in operation. In 1902, the North British Hotel in Edinburgh opened as one of the most dominant pieces of hotel architecture in the world and it still trades today as the Balmoral, a Rocco Forte hotel. The following year, the Caledonian, Edinburgh opened and is now branded as a Hilton. The Midland Hotel, Manchester was opened with a telephone in every room, but only 100 of the rooms had an en suite bathroom. It is now a Q Hotel. In 1906, Turnbury Hotel in Ayrshire was opened as a hotel resort with a championship links golf course and operates today as a Westin. In 1924, Gleneagles Hotel in Perthshire was opened by the Caledonian Railway Company. Gleneagles was a hotel resort with three golf courses, but of its 216 rooms only 25% had en suite bathrooms. It is now owned by Diageo, the global drinks company, which manages it as a single deluxe hotel.

Amidst its success with the vertical integration of its restaurants and food manufacturing businesses, J. Lyons & Co diversified into the hotel business early in 20th century. It opened its first hotel, the Strand Palace, opposite the Savoy, in London in 1909. It operated in the mid-market and had 470 rooms, none of which had a private bathroom. In the early 1930s the hotel was extended to 1,200 rooms. It still operates as a down at heel unbranded hotel. In 1915, Lyons opened the Regent Palace hotel at Piccadilly Circus, London. Like the Strand Palace it operated in the mid-market and had 1,028 rooms all without private bathroom. These two hotels were the largest built in Britain over the period, but they also reflected the more primitive state of the British hotel business at the time compared with the US where Statler was building equivalent hotels in which all rooms had private bathrooms and radios. In 1933, Lyons opened the Cumberland hotel at Marble Arch, London, another very large hotel with almost 1,000 rooms, but still many of the rooms were without private bathrooms. The Cumberland now trades as a Guoman hotel. The British brewers were preoccupied during the period with surviving the decline in beer consumption and reducing risk in their pub estates. Their small hotels were a factor in attracting the middle class, but they remained focused throughout the period on producing and selling beer and did little to develop their hotel portfolios as recognisable brands.

Trust House Hotels started as a crusade against excess drinking. In 1901, Earl Grey proposed to reduce the drunkenness in coaching inns by making it more profitable for them to sell meals and rooms rather than drinks. He was able to persuade a selection of coaching inn owners to support his proposal that every county should form its own public trust to acquire inns when their leases expired. The new managers were offered incentives on the sale of meals and rooms, but not on the sale of alcoholic drinks. The first Trust House hotel, the Wagon and Horses at Ridge Hill in St Albans, Hertfordshire opened in its new format in 1904 and progressively more were added. In the early years Trust House Hotels lost money, but as the railways destroyed demand for sleeping accommodation at coaching inns in the 19th century so the motor car revived their market early in the 20th century. The early trading difficulties and the Word War I collapse of demand did not deter the company's expansion and by 1919 it controlled 71 hotels and grew to 219 hotels by the outbreak of World War II, all of which were acquired so that Trust House did not add to hotel supply during the period, but needed to invest capital to update the facilities in the hotels.

By 1939, the profile of hotel companies listed on the London Stock Exchange had changed *(source*: Stock Exchange Year Book, 1939). The total of 108 hotels in the quoted hotel companies sector in 1900 had risen to 347 by 1939 and the pattern of concentration had changed. The portfolios that survived did not grow much. Gordon Hotels shrank from 13 hotels to nine. Along the way it developed and managed landmark London hotels such as the Mayfair and the Dorchester. Frederick Hotels retained a portfolio of seven hotels. Early in the century the Savoy Group retrenched into London where it acquired the Berkeley, having sold the Grand Hotel, Rome and the Miraveaux restaurant in Paris. Bournemouth Imperial and Grand Hotels maintained its same portfolio. The major developments came from the new portfolios that became quoted over the period. Trust House dominated with 219 hotels, The Public House Trust had 13 former coaching Inns, Imperial London Hotels had nine hotels in London, but none of the other portfolios had more than five hotels, while 47 hotels had been delisted.

Classification schemes

One area of the hotel business, which emanated from Europe early in the 20th century was hotel grading and classification. The broad segmentation of hotel supply during the second half of the 19th century into grand hotels, mid-market hotels and quasi hotels was implicit and it was not until the early years of the 20th century that the explicit classification of hotels emerged. The first hotel classification scheme was introduced into France by the Michelin Tyre Company and was followed in Britain by the Automobile Association and the Royal Automobile Club in the first decade of the 20th century and established the relationship between hotel demand and the motor car at a very early stage in its history. The new hotel classification schemes were devised to be an information service on selected hotels to enable drivers to make more informed choices of appropriate hotels at which to stay. When the guides to hotels were introduced there were less than 50,000 drivers in Britain, but they included a high proportion of potential hotel customers and the number of car owners increased to around 2 million by the outbreak of World War II. The hotel guides not only sculpted the basis on which the public were able to differentiate hotels, but also were the most important marketing tool for the hotels included in the guides. The schemes classified hotels hierarchically with the most elaborate hotels designated as five-star down to one-star hotels representing the minimum facilities, services and products for a venue to be a hotel. There was a close correlation between grand hotels and five-star and four-star hotels and the former mid-market hotels were repackaged as three-star, two-star and one-star hotels depending on the specific range and quality of their provision. Quasi-hotels were excluded from the classification schemes because the compilers of the guides considered that they did not reflect the standard of living or lifestyle of car drivers and thus could not be recommended as places for them to stay. The influence of the hotel classification schemes was much greater than their size. At their height in Britain they included less than a quarter of all hotels and the graded hotels had to pay for their classification. Nonetheless, customers and hotel professionals adopted the star classifications informally as the defining feature of hotels.

The task of the early classification schemes was to enable customers to make more sense of the existing hotel supply and they were an improvement on the implicit hotel market levels in the 19th century. The extension of the range of market positioning to five market levels was a reflection of the growth in complexity and diversity of the social and economic structures of the more advanced industrial economies and the growth in the complexity and diversity of hotel demand. The main differentiating factors among hotels were their market levels and their locations. The five-star hotels formed the smallest category. There were more in London than in all other cities put together. They were the highest priced, the most luxurious and there was a high degree of similarity in the range and quality of the facilities, services and products they provided. In contrast, one-star hotels, which provided the minimum standards for hotels were mainly coaching inns that had suffered decline from the introduction of rail travel and modest hotels predominantly in rural locations. Many of the three-star hotels were located in provincial towns, smaller cities and coastal resorts. They included many of the new urban hotels constructed during the 19th century and former coaching inns such as the Angel Hotel in Guildford that had been upgraded. Many four-star hotels were located in London and the larger provincial cities and many two-star hotels were in coastal resorts.

The hierarchy of hotels paralleled the class hierarchy. Each hotel star classification carried a set of assumptions about customers and their hotel demands. The congruence that hotel classification established between hotel provision and hotel consumption was never again as close as it was at the start of the 20th century. The problem for hotel classification was that as the social and economic structures of Britain developed, hotel classification did not. Over the period, as more hotels were developed to the hotel classification template, greater homogeneity was achieved within hotels at each star category. An implication of this approach was that over the first half of the 20th century there was little innovation in hotel provision and little change in the definition of each star category. The prime example of the grindingly slow rate of change in hotel classification in Britain is that it took 100 years before classifiers required en suite bathrooms to be mandatory in all classified hotels.

British hotel demand and supply performance

Otus estimates that over the first 45 years of the 20th century, room supply in Britain grew by only 30,000. At the start of the 20th century the supply ratio of hotel rooms per 1,000 citizens was 7.1. Otus further estimates that the British ratio declined thereafter until it reached 6.3 in 1945. In 1900, room occupancy in Britain was only 27% due to the fast rise of heavily seasonal resort hotels and continuing supply growth of urban hotels with no weekend resident demand. The marginal increase in supply over the period and the reliance on military and government demand rather than conventional demand meant that by the end of World War II room occupancy had fallen to a dangerously low 20%. This was the first period in which the British hotel business experienced economic descent, illustrating the strong downward pressure from the four critical events of the period, poor economic performance and slow progress in the structural balance of the economy towards citizen services.

Table 5.3: British hotels 1900-1945

	1900	1910	1920	1930	1940	1945	1900-1945 CAGR
Total rooms	260,000	280,000	285,000	300,000	305,000	300,000	0.3%
Room nights available (m)	95	102	104	110	112	110	0.3%
Room occupancy %	27%	28%	28%	25%	20%	20%	
Room nights sold (m)	**26**	**29**	**29**	**27**	**22**	**22**	**-0.4%**
Domestic business	11	12	11	10	20	21	1.4%
Domestic leisure	15	16	17	17	0	0	-8.9%
Foreign business	0	0	0	1	2	1	3.2%
Foreign leisure	1	1	1	1	0	0	-100.0%
Concentration %	6%	7%	8%	11%	12%	12%	
Hotel room supply ratio	7.1	6.9	6.7	6.7	6.3	6.3	
Secular growth in hotel room supply		-10,000	-10,000	0	-20,000	0	

Source: Otus & Co Advisory Ltd

Continental European hotel demand and supply

As well as starting the 20th century in a less structurally developed state than Britain, continental European economies generated fewer domestic business travellers and less domestic holiday demand into hotels and also had a smaller and even more fragmented hotel business. During the first half of the 20th century, the continental economies and their hotel businesses were overwhelmed by the four critical events, which had a more severe impact on them than was endured by Britain or the US. World War I halted conventional business and leisure demand into continental hotels and supply was depleted by battles and business failures. In Western Europe the recovery of the economies was not straightforward. The French economy began to recover naturally. However, its rate and structural development was slow. Agriculture was of greater significance to the French economy than it was to the US or Britain. In 1900, French agriculture employed half of the workforce. Over the period, it was slow to introduce new technology and new work methods. Consequently productivity growth was also slow producing little structural unemployment and as the population declined over the period there was too little spare manpower for significant expansion of secondary industries and the introduction of citizen services. Thus, the constrained structural development of the French economy was reflected in the slow growth in hotel demand and supply. There was a similar pattern in other economies such as Italy and Spain, which were also heavily reliant on agriculture. The Great Depression in France was less severe than in some other countries since it had been receiving reparations from Germany and relied less on imports and foreign loans. The economic bottom was reached in 1932 when unemployment touched 15%, industrial production dropped 25%, the volume of foreign tourists collapsed and the volume and price of exports declined (source: League of Nations Yearbook of Labour Statistics) This position more or less remained until 1935, when the economy started its slow recovery.

The emergence of Fascism severely limited the structural development of the economies of Italy, Germany and Spain and constrained the growth of their hotel businesses. The Fascist regimes focused their economies on agriculture and manufacturing. As a result of central planning in Germany and Italy in the 1930s, their manufacturing industries were boosted by accelerating armaments production and they further boosted employment by investing in the building of infrastructure, most notably roads. However, service businesses, which were minor at the start of the period, never progressed beyond being a necessary back-up to approved manufacturing and agriculture. The Fascist schemes for economic recovery did not involve service businesses such as hotels and except for citizen services there were few new sources of domestic business demand into hotels. The weak economic conditions also inhibited the growth in domestic leisure demand into hotels. There was little hotel provision in Russia at the time of the Revolution because the economy was agricultural and poor. Hotels were not a priority for the Communists and much hotel demand was directed by the government and the Communist Party. The state control of the economy, the heavy reliance on agriculture and the prime focus in manufacturing on basic and military products, the absence of personal credit and the subsistence standard of living for most of the population created the conditions for very low levels of domestic demand into hotels, but the constraints did not end there. Domestic travel was curtailed and directed by the Communist Party. Foreign travel into the USSR was microscopic because it was strenuously controlled by the government and thus so was foreign demand into Soviet hotels. Once the Communist state was created there was no further structural development of the USSR economy and its hotel business stagnated.

The Great Depression had a severe impact on Germany due to the high level of reparations paid for World War I, which were suspended in 1932, and the reliance on loans from the US, which became onerous in an environment of escalating interest rates. Hyperinflation ensued, then bank failures produced the loss of savings and unemployment rocketed to 30% by 1932. Hitler and the Nazis came to power in 1933 and among other policies focused on reducing unemployment by transferring an increased proportion of manufacturing to military production and instituting the state-directed building of autobahns and other infrastructure. They banned the use of labour-reducing technology and they introduced incentives for married women to stay at home rather than be employed so that male employment could be increased. None of these initiatives were positive for hotel demand. Domestic business demand did not recover in line with the economy since the move to military production reduced the need for travelling salesmen. Domestic leisure demand growth was also low because of the weakened economy and the Nazi propaganda emphasising work as a core value from which leisure was a distraction.

The economic impact of World War II was significantly more severe than World War I and its geography was more widespread. The degradation of land, property and infrastructure was substantially greater and more people were slaughtered. Among the main continental combatants such as Germany, France and Italy, conventional business demand and leisure demand into hotels evaporated. There was a benefit to hotel demand from government use and from the military, but these were only marginal. Hotel supply also declined as they were among the properties that were bombed and degraded, but many hotels also failed due to the prolonged demand collapse. Those hotels that survived the period were generally in a dilapidated state having endured prolonged poor performance and low levels of capital expenditure for most of the period.

Such economic conditions strangled the development of hotel chains on the continent. In Germany, Kempinski Hotels survived, but without much growth and Steigenberger Hotels acquired its second hotel, the Frankfurter Hof, in 1940. In France, there was no greater movement with Société du Louvre and Barriere surviving, but without adding materially to their portfolios. The very high levels of fragmentation in the French and German hotel businesses over the period meant that the supply was mostly in small family owned and managed hotels in highly seasonal markets. In turn, hotels were not listed on continental stock markets and the hotel capital markets were small, local and inefficient. As a result of the hostile conditions during the first 45 years of the 20th century, the continental hotel business at the end of World War II was in peril. The most severe impact of the four critical events was on Germany and its hotel business regressed more than any other among the major European economies. The experiences of continental Europe during the first half of the 20th century is clear evidence of the extent to which wars and dictator-led ideological shifts are major retarding influences on the hotel business. When economic depression is added there could be no other outcome than economic descent of the hotel business. By the end of World War II the gap in the size and structure of the hotel business of continental Europe and Britain had widened and the gap with the US was wider still.

6 The US Economic Structure and Hotel Business: 1945–1960

Introduction

During the 15-year period to 1960, the structural balance of the US economy shifted towards service businesses rocketing the growth in hotel supply and demand and boosting the presence of hotel chains. In parallel, other economies and hotel businesses struggled to shake off the problems of World War II and the legacy of the other critical events of the previous half century. In the US, the four factors necessary to progress the structural balance of an economy towards service businesses progressed.

♦ First, civil and human rights were extended. In 1954, the Supreme Court ruled racial segregation in public schools to be unconstitutional. Women at this time saw a quantum leap in their standard of living and the reduction of drudgery in household chores through the mass ownership of household appliances. In 1950, only 29% of the labour force was female, but as the structural balance of the economy moved towards service businesses so the total number of women employees grew as did the proportion of women entering further and higher education.

♦ Second, the social sciences expanded in university teaching and research and their application to social and business life increased.

♦ Third, the personal capital markets expanded. The increase in the level of personal credit was facilitated by the high levels of employment. Secured loans were extended with the growth in home ownership, unsecured loans increased to buy consumer durables and towards the end of the period, credit cards were introduced.

♦ Fourth, personal travel grew with the significant increase in automobile ownership and the expansion of airline travel.

Importantly, the development in the structural balance of the US economy during the post-war period was facilitated because the citizen services segment was regarded as a safety net for the more vulnerable in the economy and not as a long-term economic equilibrium. Consequently, during the post-war period, service businesses in the US grew in both size and range at a much faster rate than in any other economy and established the American lifestyle as different from and more diverse than in any other country. In parallel, growth in domestic business demand and domestic vacation demand into hotels boomed, which in turn produced accelerated growth in hotel supply and in hotel concentration. For these reasons, the post-war period was a landmark for the economic ascent of the hotel business in the US.

US economic structure and hotel demand

The post-war economy took off, not only in its rate of growth, but also in its diversity as it made the transition from military back to civilian mode. It sustained low levels of unemployment, which remained less than 4% between 1948 and 1953 (*source*: US Bureau of Economic Analysis). The population grew by 22% to 186 million over the 15-year period, led by migration and the baby boom while consumer spending grew by more than in any other country. The structural development of the economy evolved, the proportion of white-collar and professional employees grew at the expense of blue-collar workers and this generated growth in both business and vacation demand into hotels. The 104 million total hotel room nights sold in 1945 escalated to 247 million by 1960, an average annual growth of 6%. Of course, this exceptionally strong growth is flattered by the low level of demand in 1945 and the dynamic of the post-war period is expressed more realistically by the average annual growth in hotel demand of 4% over the 1950s with the addition of 82 million room nights. Domestic business demand into hotels grew from 54 million room nights in 1950 to 74 million in 1960 as citizen services and service businesses increased their share of employment as other sectors declined. Hotel chains captured the lions' share of business demand by locating their hotels in the cities where that market needed to be. Over the period, agricultural employment declined and industrial employment was the slowest growing segment, whereas citizen services and service businesses, the higher yielding segments for domestic business demand into hotels, grew faster.

Table 6.1: Employment by segment in US: 1950 –1960 (millions)

	Agriculture	Industry	Citizen Services	Service Businesses	Total
1950	5.0	17.0	9.0	18.0	49.0
1960	4.9	19.2	11.4	23.7	59.2

Source: US Departmentof Labour 1960, Otus, 1950

Table 6.2: Employment by segment in US: 1950–1960 (percentage)

	Agriculture	Industry	Citizen Services	Service Businesses	Total
1950	10%	35%	18%	37%	100%
1960	8%	32%	19%	40%	100%

Source: US Departmentof Labour 1960, Otus, 1950

Agricultural demand into hotels

Employment in agriculture continued its long-term decline during the 1950s and fell by 50,000 to 4.9 million. Otus estimates that in 1950, 2.8% of agricultural employees were business travellers, producing a total of 140,000. The dominant reason for them to travel was to originate demand for agricultural products on which they spent an average of 12 nights in US hotels generating transient rooms demand of 1.7 million room nights for a 3% share of total business demand. During the 1950s, agricultural productivity rose to meet demand from the growing population and exports, but the decline in agricultural employment had little impact on the demand it generated for US hotels as business travel increased as it competed to sell its products. In 1960 the proportion of agricultural employees who were business travellers, mainly originating demand remained unchanged at 2.8%, which reduced the total marginally, but the number of nights spent in US hotels increased to 13 generating transient rooms demand of 1.8 million nights, up marginally over the decade. However, its share of total domestic business demand fell to 2% as the other segments grew at a faster rate.

Industrial demand into hotels

In 1950, industrial employment in the US totalled 17 million of whom Otus estimates that 3.9% were business travellers, producing a total of 660,000. The main reasons for business travel was originating demand and delivering products on which they spent an average of 29 nights in US hotels and generated mostly transient rooms demand of 19 million room nights for a 35% share of total domestic business demand. Over the 1950s, 2.2 million was added to the industrial workforce and the consumer goods base of manufacturing diversified to produce and sell more and a greater range of goods.

This was matched by the white middle-class enthusiasm for household goods such as washing machines, refrigerators, dishwashers, vacuum cleaners and central heating, which reduced the time and effort needed to keep house. It was paralleled by the attraction and availability of radio, television, record players and telephones, which extended the patterns of in-home entertainment and delivery of information. At the end of World War II there were around 17,000 televisions in the US. By 1950, 10 million US homes had a television, but by 1960, 87 million homes had a television (Bunch and Hellemans, 2004). The progress did not end there. Major items of family expenditure also grew. In 1950, 55% of families owned their home; by 1960 the proportion had increased to 62%

(source: US Census Bureau). In 1950, 59% of households owned an automobile and by 1960, the proportion had increased sharply to 73% *(source*: Gale Encyclopaedia of American Industries, 2005). The range and volume of household goods expanded as did the proportion of the population owning a wide range of household goods so that the material standard of living and the in-home style of life were enhanced, substantially, but that was not all. Over the period, repeat purchases were fuelled by the built-in obsolescence of many consumer goods as well as the expansion of TV, radio and other advertising. The high level of employment in the economy as a whole and the loosening of the personal capital markets were key factors in the escalation of demand for household goods.

The intensifying competition among US manufacturers for share of the growing markets and the on-going growth in concentration among manufacturers produced larger companies with larger corporate structures and wider geographic reach. The increase in productivity was achieved by the improvements in work practices and the introduction of manpower efficient technology, which produced a reduction in the proportion of shopfloor workers, but an increase in the proportion of white collar and professional employees. These developments entailed an increase in the number of travelling salesmen and long-distance truck drivers whose frequency of business trips rose compared with the pre-war period. Travelling salesmen and long-distance truck drivers were the road warriors of the day, selling and delivering to other businesses and to consumers. They were regular users of hotels and they were the most numerous business travellers from industrial companies, but they were not the only ones. Other executives in manufacturing, typically working in the headquarters office were also business travellers engaged in managing their companies and involved in visiting plants, suppliers and external advisors, but their frequency of travel was less than salesmen and truck drivers. Otus estimates that the industrial developments over the 1950s increased the proportion of segment employees who were business travellers originating demand, attending industry-wide conventions and involved in company management to 4.4%, a total of 850,000, up by an average annual growth of 2.6%. They spent an average of 28 nights in US hotels generating both transient rooms demand and packaged conference demand of 28 million room nights for a 32% share of total domestic business demand as citizen services and service businesses grew at a faster rate.

Citizen services demand into hotels

Congress wanted to avoid the creation of bigger government, which was associated with communism and left-wing governments in Europe whose economies were inferior to the US in terms of performance and structure. It sought initiatives that would progress the economy into a full-blown service business economy. The first step was to increase the involvement of private sector companies in the provision of citizen services. It achieved this most in health, security and highways development and least in education. The market for health insurance grew almost sevenfold in the 1940s for which the growth of commercial insurance relative to the non-profit Blue Cross and Blue Shield was largely responsible. In 1951, 42 million people were enrolled in group or individual hospital insurance plans offered by commercial insurance companies, while only 41 million people were enrolled in Blue Cross and Blue Shield plans (Health Insurance Institute, 1965: 14). The 1954 Internal Revenue Code, which exempted from employee taxable income any employer contributions to employee health plans, advanced the commercial plans. There was a major military build-up in the 1950s due to the Korean War and the onset of the Cold War with the rapid expansion of weapons and equipment supplied by private contractors. By the mid-decade there were more than 40,000 defence contractors working on government contracts. Over the decade, military purchases grew 2.5 times and the military-industrial complex accounted for more than half of all government expenditure *(source*: www.us.history.wisc.edu). The 1956 Highway Act allocated $27 billion to build around 40,000 miles of federal roads throughout the country. Although initially paid for out of federal taxes, progressively the construction was contracted to private companies, drivers paid tolls for the use of the roads and private companies often managed the maintenance of the roads.

Two citizen services in which government involvement remained dominant were welfare and education. The public welfare programme grew over the period providing assistance to about 3 million people by 1960. However, even with welfare benefits, a role was found for the private sector as increasing numbers of employers provided pension benefits. By 1951, approximately 8 million veterans had received educational benefits at a cost to the government of $14 billion *(source*: www.gibill.va.gov). The GI Bill had an important impact on further and higher education since it required the expansion of formal vocational training from a low level in universities and accelerated the expansion of business schools. It also produced a raft of mature, newly-qualified graduates, mostly men, seeking more challenging careers, many of which were provided in citizen services and service businesses. In 1950, only 24% of degrees were awarded to women *(source*: US Census Bureau) Thereafter the proportion grew, but it did not reach 50% until the early 1990s.The growth momentum in universities during the post-war period was accelerated by the increasing proportion of high school graduates, and in particular women, entering universities and colleges.

The growth in population and the extension in citizen services, offset by the initiatives to increase the involvement of private sector companies increased employment in citizen services by 2.4 million over the 1950s. It also had a positive impact on domestic business demand into hotels. Most of the employees worked in hospitals, schools and welfare offices and their jobs did not require business travel with hotel stays. Executive and administrative employees were involved in business travel for in-house meetings at citizen service facilities around the country, but there were no business travellers involved in originating demand, which was the main source of business travellers in the agricultural and industrial segments. Professional employees such as medics and academics attending conferences and regional or national internal meetings was an emerging market during the period. Otus estimates that 11.3% of citizen services employees were business travellers giving the segment the highest proportion, with a total above a million, but the average nights they spent in US hotels were lower than in agriculture or industry. In 1950, the segment business travellers spent an average of 10 nights in US hotels generating mainly transient rooms demand of 10 million room nights for a 19% share of total domestic business demand. By 1960, the citizen services workforce had grown to 11.4 million and 11.5% were business travellers increasing the total to 1.3 million mainly involved in segment management and conferences spending an average of 11 nights in US hotels generating both transient and packaged demand of 14 million room nights for an unchanged share of domestic business demand.

Service businesses demand into hotels

The initiatives to involve the private sector in the provision of citizen services was a key factor in the structural progression of the US economy during this period, not only because it focused the federal government away from involvement in industrial activities such as construction and defence manufacturing, but also because it provided the impetus for growth in service businesses such as financial services. This was not the only factor in the growth of service businesses. The high levels of employment, the rising levels of home ownership and the increasing access to personal credit all combined to boost service businesses and to produce a conundrum of economic life in the US in the 1950s. The more that Americans owned household products, the more they wanted to buy services. The major growth in household goods increased demand for service businesses such as retailing, financial services, advertising and communications, which grew in response to the growth in consumer goods. In 1950, service businesses employed 18 million Americans. Otus estimates that 5.2% of them were business travellers involved mainly in originating demand, executing contracts and servicing clients, a total of 940,000 travellers; they spent an average of 25 nights in US hotels generating mainly transient rooms demand of 23 million room nights for a 43% share of total domestic business demand.

Throughout the decade, mass advertising on nationwide television and radio created and fuelled consumer aspirations in the homes of most of the population, which was augmented at movie theatres as well as in the press and on billboards. Retailing developed in size due to the growth in the acquisition of consumer goods and the form of retail outlets also developed. The growth of supermarkets led the way for the establishment of large retail outlets where internal economy of scale benefits and bulk buying contributed to the maintenance of lower prices than in corner shops. This was taken to another level with the emergence of shopping malls. In 1945, there were eight shopping malls in the US and by 1960 the number had risen to 3,840 (source: http://www.icsc.org). There was similar escalation in the telephone service. In 1945, there were 28 million telephones in operation, but this grew threefold by 1960 (source: US Census Bureau). The openness of the consumer capital markets enabled the economic growth momentum to be maintained. Access to small, short-term personal credit increased for the purchase of consumer durables. The Diners Club charge card was introduced in 1951 initially to 200 customers who could use the card in 27 restaurants in New York. The American Express card arrived in 1958, the same year BankAmericard, now Visa, was introduced and was the first to enable the repayments to be made in instalments.

The growth in the volume and the reduction in price of automobiles and air travel accelerated the volume of travel, the distances travelled, the speed of travel and the frequency of travel by Americans during the 1950s. The growth in sport playing and spectating as well as attendance at movie theatres were the main organised out-of-home leisure activities in neighbourhoods, although the attendance at movie theatres suffered from the growth in television. From three billion tickets sold at movie theatres in 1950 the number declined throughout the decade (source: US Census Bureau). The extension of paid annual holiday leave as well as the overall growth in prosperity boosted the growth in vacations. International tourism also grew during the period. PanAm and TWA became the major international airlines from the US, which unlike the airlines from other countries were not state controlled. US hotel chains such as Intercontinental and Hilton began to follow the US airlines to destinations outside the US where US holidaymakers and business people most frequently travelled.

Typically during the post-war period, service businesses were smaller than industrial companies, but they had many more branches than manufacturers. During the period, retail businesses were expanding on a state and regional basis and as the portfolios of retailers expanded so most executives in their corporate structures were involved in business travel. Development teams, recruiters and trainers, merchandisers, marketing executives, accountants and more were all involved in business travel. The pattern was similar for wholesalers, but with fewer business travellers because they operated business to business rather than business to customer. Telephone and television had become established nationwide and like retailers had a high proportion of business travellers among their professional and executive employees. Advertising agencies, market research agencies and other professional service companies also grew materially and had a high proportion of professional employees who were business travellers involved in originating demand, executing contracts and servicing clients. Banking and financial service companies expanded nationally requiring a higher proportion of their employees to travel on business between the headquarters, the regional offices and the branches on matters related to the management of the company. In addition to this business travel, corporate banking and financial services executives also travelled to originate and execute business and to service clients. However, the decline in attendance at movie theatres and in their supply reduced the volume of hotel-using business travellers from that sector.

With the exception of the movie business, all of the post-war business travel from the service segment was either new or substantially increased from the pre-war period and the post-war period marked the start of long-term secular growth in both the size and in the concentration of service businesses and in the growth in demand for hotels that they produced. In 1960, service businesses employed 23.7 million. Otus estimates that the proportion of these who were business travellers, involved in originating demand, executing contracts and servicing clients as well as managing companies and attending conferences, increased to 6% producing a total of 1.4 million business travellers, the most in any segment; they spent an average of 24 nights in US hotels generating both transient rooms demand and packaged conference demand of 34 million room nights for a 45%

share of total domestic business demand and expanding its position as the largest segment for the hotel business.

The dynamics of the post-war development in the US economic structure not only produced an increase in domestic business demand for hotel rooms, but also brought an increase in demand for other hotel facilities, most notably for conferences. The dominant type of business conference was larger industry-wide conferences, conventions, trade shows and exhibitions attended by employees from multiple firms and from the buyers of their products. Such events were held usually in the major cities such as New York, Chicago and San Francisco, which captured this demand through the use of convention and visitor bureaux. As the number of conferences, conventions and exhibitions, mainly from the industrial segment, grew during the post-war period so did the number of convention and visitor bureaux in cities seeking to attract the growing number of events.

Domestic leisure demand

During the post-war period, domestic leisure demand retained its position as the largest market for US hotels, which benefited from the growth in summer vacations. Hotels in summer resorts continued to attract this demand for the season from Easter to September and hotels in winter sports resorts emerged to capture winter demand, while vacation demand to the sunshine states such as Florida also grew during the winter. Moreover, the sharp rise in automobile ownership was reflected in the increase in the use of automobiles as vacation transport sometimes involving the use of hotels and motels for overnight stops on the way to and from the vacation destination. Whereas, Otus estimates that in 1950, domestic business demand accounted for 33% of total hotel room nights sold, it also estimates that domestic leisure room nights at 102 million accounted for 62%. Unaffiliated hotels benefited most from these markets because of their high exposure to resort and arterial road locations, but throughout the period, chains grew their share of this market. By 1960, domestic leisure demand had grown to 146 million nights, but its overall share of demand relaxed. A further distinction between domestic business and leisure demand was the average number of customers per room. Domestic leisure demand relied on couples and families and so the customer density of rooms was higher than for business travellers who, predominantly, had single customer density of rooms. The higher customer density by domestic leisure customers was one of the reasons why the specifications of the Holiday Inn brand, when it was created in 1952, included two double beds in each room and kids under 12 stayed free in their parents' room. The growth in domestic leisure demand was influenced by the pattern of structural development in the economy. The highest volume of domestic leisure rooms demand was generated by families whose main income came from citizen services and service businesses because these segments accounted for the highest number of white-collar and professional employees.

The baby boomers

A defining feature of the post-war period was the arrival of the baby boomers, the generation of 32 million Americans born between 1945 and 1955 when they accounted for 21% of the population. From the outset, the life of the boomers was significantly different from previous generation in the sense that they not only wanted to have things they also wanted to do things. The boomer lifestyle during the post-war period reflected the growth in the US economy and its move towards service businesses. From birth, baby boomers experienced a more enhanced material standard of living than any previous generation and they also experienced more extensive citizen services than any previous generation. They were the first generation to experience a marked reduction in housework and to grow up with a range of in-home entertainment through radio, television and record players. Significantly, television provided a more cosmopolitan view of life than was available to previous generations or was available in their immediate neighbourhood. It built lifestyle aspirations from an early age.

The boomers also sought and consumed a wider range of foods, clothes and toys than previous generations. They had more frequent access to out-of-home leisure such as movie theatres, quick-service restaurants, sports playing and watching, automobiles and annual holidays than had previous generations. Baby boomers were the first generation for which the term 'teenager' characterised not only a period in life, but also a discrete lifestyle in terms of the products they demanded and the activities in which they were involved. The extent to which baby boomers and their families became a market emerged in 1955 when the first Disneyland opened in Anaheim, California and extended the on-screen cartoons and characters to actual experiences. As the decade progressed, the range of products and services targeted directly to boomers escalated so that in 1960 alone $22 billion was spent on them (*source*: US Census Bureau). By the end of the post-war period the oldest boomers were only 15 years old and their only experience of hotels was on family holidays.

Foreign visitors

Otus estimates that foreign visitor hotel demand in the US during the post-war period increased from eight million room nights in 1950 to 27 million in 1960 and their share of hotel demand grew from 5% to 11%. Leisure demand from holidaymakers from the neighbouring countries of Canada, and to a lesser extent Mexico, who arrived mainly by rail and road, was the main source. The post-war period saw progressive decline in cross-Atlantic and other long-haul passenger shipping into the US as air travel grew in frequency and in the volume of passengers carried boosted by the reduction in flight prices. Much of the foreign business demand into the US during the post-war period stayed in the gateway cities, but foreign leisure travellers widened their geographic scope.

Hotel supply and the acceleration of chains

The stepped change in post-war US hotel demand triggered a transformation in hotel supply. At a constant supply ratio of 7.1 in 1940 and with the recorded increase in population, the US would have needed 1.08 million hotel rooms in 1950. Otus estimates that in 1945, the US had 950,000 hotel rooms and by 1950 it comfortably exceeded one million having added 160,000 rooms, producing a secular growth of 15,000 rooms. At a constant 1950 supply ratio and with the recorded increase in population, the US would have needed 1.3 million hotel rooms in 1960. Supply accelerated during the 1950s when 400,000 rooms were added to reach a total of 1.5 million, producing a secular growth of 200,000 rooms. The rapid growth in the volume of hotel supply in the post-war period in the US triggered the number of rooms in hotel chains, which rocketed from 90,000 in 1950 to 310,000 as a result of both new build and the migration of unaffiliated hotels to chains. The development of hotel chains in the US during the post-war period was faster than the overall growth of the hotel business. Whereas hotel chains achieved secular growth, unaffiliated hotels suffered secular decline. Chains were the most effective way to meet the fast growth in demand that characterised the period because of two fundamental features: corporate structure and brand.

Hotel chains and corporate structure

The three primary functions of the corporate structure of hotel chains are: to generate premium demand, to achieve premium operating margins and to attract competitive capital. The corporate structure includes all of the jobs in the company that are within the general business tradition and not within the hotel tradition. It includes those executive functions that are not directly involved in the fundamental customer-facing activities in hotels such as renting bedrooms and selling meals and drinks. It includes functions such as accounting and finance; sales and marketing; human resource management; development and any other executive functions. Typically, they are the functions based at head offices and regional offices, but some junior positions in these functions can be based in hotels that are large enough to require dedicated sales and marketing managers, human resources managers or financial controllers. The more rooms that there are in a portfolio then the more diverse the corporate structure and the more corporate executives required. However, synergies can be created in the corporate structure since it grows at a slower rate than the hotel portfolio so that the resulting higher productivity enhances the performance of the hotel chain.

The first function of the corporate structure is to generate premium volume of demand at premium room rates compared with equivalent unaffiliated hotels. Until the emergence of hotel chains the main means of generating demand for hotels was reactive and included their locations and the level of capital invested in the hotels. The significant growth in hotel chains during the post–war period saw the emergence of demand generating infrastructure as a more effective means to capture hotel demand and this became a fundamental component of the corporate structure. As hotel portfolios became larger in the post-war period, infrastructure for generating hotel demand emerged more systematically. In essence, the demand generating infrastructure was the collection of sales and marketing executives and their support teams together with the systems and techniques used to generate demand, proactively. By 1960, it embraced all sales activities including: central reservations service and relations with visitor and convention bureaux. It also included marketing activities such as market research as well as advertising and press activities. This was paralleled by the emergence of the wholesale markets for hotels, which were both transient and packaged markets and provided high volumes of demand. They included companies with year-round demand from executives staying in hotels on business and using hotels for conferences. Wholesale leisure markets included domestic and inbound tour operators and leisure travel agencies. The high volume of demand in the wholesale markets needed hotel chains with high capacity to make the system of demand generation and demand processing effective.

The second function of the corporate structure is to achieve premium operating margin. The management of the two major operating costs, consumables and employees, dominate the effort. The larger the hotel portfolio, the more it buys consumables such as food, drinks, cleaning materials, furniture, fixtures and equipment in greater bulk and thus can buy at lower unit prices. In parallel, the larger the hotel portfolio the more people it employs. Growing hotel chains need a greater volume of employees with a wider range of skills and knowledge than unaffiliated hotels, thus as well as attracting new employees to the chain they also need to retain, train and promote employees from within the company. In short, whereas unaffiliated hotels provide jobs, chains offer careers. In turn, this enables them to attract higher quality employees, which is manifest, typically, in higher productivity and lower labour turnover than in unaffiliated hotels.

The third function of the corporate structure and a necessary requirement for growth is to attract competitive capital. Fundamental to this process is that the chain attracts premium demand and achieves premium operating margins. During the post-war period in the US, the affiliation between hotel chains and their hotels diversified. Hotel chains not only owned hotels, but also managed hotels for other hotel owners and entered into franchise agreements with hotel owner/operators. The different affiliations involve different types of capital, and produce different relationships between the chain and the hotels as well as between the chain and the capital providers. Each affiliation produces different risk profiles and delivers different returns on invested capital. Moreover, each affiliation requires a different corporate structure for the chain, complicated by the larger chains that were involved in more than one affiliation.

Owner/operator chains

Most of the US hotel chains such as Hilton and Sheraton, which were established before World War II, were based on the company owning or leasing as well as managing hotels. This was the classic formation of a hotel portfolio – an entrepreneur starting from one owned and managed hotel to which others were added as capital became available and the entrepreneurial drive to grow took hold.

Hilton Hotels were a prime example over this period, their resurgence at the end of the 1930s was maintained into the 1940s. Hilton Hotels Corporation (HHC) was listed on the New York Stock Exchange with a market capitalisation of $41 million in 1947. Then, in 1949 Hilton International was formed as a division of HHC when the Caribe Hilton in San Juan, Puerto Rico, was opened to service the growing demand from the US vacations and conference market. In the same year, HHC acquired the lease on the Waldorf=Astoria in New York City for $19 million. A measure of the severity of the Great Depression and World War II on grand hotels is that to acquire the Waldorf=Astoria, HHC paid only half of its construction cost almost 20 years earlier. Over that time all of the hotels that Hilton acquired were single, unaffiliated assets and all of the hotels in the portfolio were owned or leased by Hilton. The next and biggest development for HHC and indeed for any hotel company up to that time was the 1954 acquisition of Statler Hotels for $111 million, which set a new high for a hotel chain transaction. Like HHC's hotels, the Statler hotels were located in downtown areas of key cities, they were large and had a range of non-room facilities, but although the hotels were not identical to Hiltons, they bore sufficient family resemblance to be integrated.

Another example was Sheraton Hotels, which in 1946 merged with United States Realty, sold surplus real estate and used the funds to acquire more hotels. In the same year, Sheraton was listed on the New York Stock Exchange and the expansion of the brand continued apace. Prominent hotels were acquired in downtown New York City, Washington DC, Chicago and San Francisco. In the early 1950s, Sheraton acquired two short hotel chains in Canada and in 1958 it acquired the Eppley chain of 22 hotels in the US for $30 million. By 1956, Sheraton comprised 53 hotels, most of which had been acquired, but it had also started a $100m hotel construction programme. In 1957, the first new build Sheraton hotel, the 1000-room Philadelphia Sheraton was opened, more new hotels were added with more consistent specification so that by 1960 the chain had expanded to around 75 hotels with 15,000 rooms (source: Sheraton World Fiftieth Anniversary Issue, ITT Sheraton, 1987). The Sheraton brand was similar to the Hilton brand in terms of market positioning, the prices charged and in their locations. During the post-war period US chains such as Hilton and Sheraton enjoyed a virtuous circle. As their portfolios expanded so also did their corporate structures, which enabled them to outperform unaffiliated hotels and shorter chains and which in turn enabled them to access more capital to expand even further. At this time, the larger owner/operator chains had the most widespread corporate structures including the full range of the executive functions.

During the post-war period, new owner/operator entrepreneurs entered the hotel market and established chains that, like Hilton and Sheraton, were to become global brands. In 1952, Kemmons Wilson, a house-builder in Memphis, Tennessee opened the first Holiday Inn in Summer Avenue, Memphis, on the road to Nashville. Wilson related that he built his first hotel as a result of poor experiences when travelling with his wife and five children and staying in motels, which were idiosyncratic in terms of the facilities, services and products they sold. Despite their poor quality and poor cleanliness they charged $6 per night for the room and $2 per night for each child. To overcome these shortcomings the first Holiday Inn had 120 rooms all with two double beds, all were en suite, all were air-conditioned and all had radio, television and telephone. In addition, there was a restaurant, a swimming pool, free parking and dog kennels, but no conference facilities. The rooms were rented on a per room basis at $6 per night and kids under 12 years stayed free in their parents' room (Wilson and Kerr, 1996). In terms of the facilities, services and products that it sold, Holiday Inn was an improvement on other mid-market hotel offerings at the time as it also was in terms of the value it provided for customers. Other landmark owned and managed hotel chains and owner/manager entrepreneurs to emerge during the period included Travelodge, which was founded in 1945 and eventually became a significant economy brand in North America, Australia and Britain. Marriott Hot-Shoppes Inc. diversified into hotels in 1957 with the opening of the 365 room Twin Bridges Marriott Motor Hotel in Arlington, Virginia and eventually grew to be a major international multi-branded lodging company. In the same year, Jay Pritzker bought his first hotel the Hyatt House, near Los Angeles Airport and established Hyatt Corporation of America, which like Marriott also became an international multi-branded hotel company. Many other entrepreneurs also developed short chains over the period by acquiring and building hotels and included A.M. Sonnabend with Sonesta Hotels and P.R. Tisch with Loews Hotels.

Management contracting

The post-World War II period in the US was the time when savvier hotel chains realised that a critical factor in their growth was access to capital. The larger owner/operator chains such as Hilton and Sheraton used the public equity markets as their source during the 1940s and 1950s. However, for them to keep up with the opportunities for growth in the US hotel market would have required an unrealistically greater amount of equity to be invested in these companies and with the limitation that the public equity markets placed on the proportion of debt considered prudent for public companies the outcome would have been lower returns for their investors. Thus, additional and alternative sources of equity were needed to fund the growth and this required the development of a different relationship between the capital providers and the hotel chains.

Management contracting was one of these new relationships and was the second form of affiliation between a hotel chain and its hotels. Management contracting entailed the separation of hotel operation from hotel real estate ownership. Eyster defined a hotel management contract as:

> a written agreement between the owner and the operator of a hotel or motor inn by which the owner employs the operator as an agent (employee) to assume full responsibility for operating and managing the property. As an agent, the operator pays in the name of the owner, all operating expenses from the cash flow generated from the property, retains management fees and remits the remaining cash flow, if any to the owner. The owner supplies the lodging property, including any land, building,

furniture, fixtures, equipment and working capital and assumes full legal responsibility for the project.

(Eyster, 1988)

The modern era in management contracting emerged after World War II when Intercontinental Hotels entered into agreements to manage hotels in Latin America and as chains such as Hilton expanded outside the US, it sought to reduce its international risk by taking management contracts where it could on hotels owned by locals. The management contractor, the hotel chain, did not own the hotel, but as a precursor to the establishment of management contracting as a significant form of hotel affiliation the hotel chain needed to own a hotel brand and have a corporate structure able to generate premium demand and deliver high operating margins. In short, the management contracting hotel chain needed to be equipped with all of the corporate features needed to generate premium demand and premium operating margins and it needed to seek out potential hotel owners to develop hotels for the chain to manage.

The sources of capital to invest in hotel real estate are different from those financial institutions and private individuals who invest in the shares of publicly quoted hotel companies for whom return on investment includes dividend payments by the hotel company and any increase in value as the result of rises in the share price. Stock market investors can buy or sell their shares whenever they choose, which enabled them to be more opportunistic and short-term in their outlook. In contrast, the capital invested in hotel real estate comes from long-term investors such as high net worth individuals, long-term real estate owners and long-term institutional real estate investors such as insurance companies and pension funds for whom return on investment included free cash flow from the hotel and any capital appreciation of the real estate. The real estate investment is less liquid than the stock market investment and due to the higher risk and generally longer time of ownership seeks higher returns.

The performance of the owner/operator chains that became involved in management contracting improved because they did not need to raise capital in their own right to own hotels and they were able to concentrate on the capital-light activities of hotel operations and brand management. Thus, the hotel management companies had a lower risk profile because they were exposed primarily to reputational risk in the event of failure to deliver the required performance from the hotel, while the real estate owners had higher risk due to their investment in the hotels. The management contract between a hotel real estate owner and a hotel chain is based on two pillars, the first of which is that it is a long-term contract, typically for 20 years and often with negotiated extensions. The second pillar is the structure of the management fees paid to the hotel chain, which is designed to align the interests of the hotel owner and the hotel chain. There is a base element of the fee, which in the post-war period typically was set at around 3% of hotel turnover and is designed to reflect the demand generating capacity of the hotel chain. The greater the premium demand that the brand can attract the higher the value of its base fee. The other element of the management fee was typically, during the period, around 10% of the gross operating profit of the hotel to reflect the cost management effectiveness of the hotel chain. The higher the gross operating margin, the higher the fees earned by the hotel chain, while still leaving higher free cash flow available to the hotel owner.

Franchising

The third type of affiliation between a hotel chain and its hotels was franchising, which emerged during the post-war period in the US. Like management contracting, franchising involved the separation of risk between a hotel chain and a hotel asset owner. However, unlike management contracting, the franchisor, the hotel chain, neither owned the hotel nor managed the hotel. Franchising was designed to provide individual hotel owner/operators with access to the specifications of a brand, the rooms demand-generation capacity of a brand and access to preferential purchasing prices, but practically no involvement in the day-to-day management of the hotel. An important distinction between franchising and management contracting is that in franchising the prime responsibility of the hotel chain is to generate rooms demand, while the generation of local demand for the hotel restaurant, bar or function facilities was the responsibility of the franchisee. As with management contracting, a precursor for a hotel franchisor is that it owned a hotel brand including the comprehensive and coherent set of specifications and operating practices making it easier for customers to understand in advance the hospitality experience that could be expected and easier for the franchisees to achieve higher returns than in an unaffiliated hotel. Franchising facilitated a fast roll-out programme for the hotel chain since it involved replication of the brand at no capital cost and no hotel management risk. Unlike a management contractor, a franchisor did not need a full corporate structure in order to attract franchisees since they were not involved in managing the hotels, but they did need a demand-generating infrastructure and group purchasing arrangements. The first Holiday Inn was a refreshing success both for its owners and its customers. Then, in 1954, when it was only two years old, Holiday Inns of America began to franchise its hotel brand. Thereafter, expansion was fast. By 1958, 50 Holiday Inns had opened and by the end of the decade there were 100, which was unprecedented for a hotel chain at the time. Also in 1954, the first Howard Johnson Motor Lodge was franchised in Savannah, Georgia. By 1960, there were around 80 Howard Johnson Motor Lodges across 30 states and it competed with Holiday Inn in terms of its specifications and in the demand it sought to attract. Given the rate of growth of hotel franchisors during the 1950s, it did not take long for them to be able to offer to franchisees significant demand-generating infrastructure including sales, marketing and media activities; a central reservations system; technical support and additionally, a group purchasing agreement. The balance in the attraction of franchisees and customers tilted from the inherent features of the hotel to the effectiveness of the demand generating infrastructure, by which time alternative brands such as Ramada and Travelodge had become franchisors.

Franchising involves a different split of the risks and rewards between the parties involved than is the case in management contracting and this is reflected in the level and structure of the fees. The fees paid by franchisees are organised into several pots including an annual royalty fee, a reservations fee payable for each reservation generated by the chain and a marketing fee. Generally, the total franchise fees amount to between 4% and 7% of rooms turnover so the greater the capacity of the hotel chain to generate premium rooms demand, the higher the fees earned. Typically, franchise contracts are 20 years in duration often with renewal clauses. Income for the franchisor is the franchise fees from all of the hotels so that for a franchising hotel chain to become a significant economic size it needs to achieve a mass of hotels and this was reflected in their rate of portfolio growth during the period. By 1960, the two largest hotel brands in the US – Holiday Inn and Howard Johnson Motor Lodge – were involved in franchising and were also among the youngest hotel brands.

Consortia

Another affiliation that emerged was consortium membership. The most significant examples of the period were Best Western and Superior Motels. Best Western was established in the US in 1946 as a cooperative arrangement among independently owned and operated hoteliers who clubbed together to pool resources to generate more rooms demand and to negotiate discounts with suppliers to enable them to reduce their costs. The aim of the original members was to gain rooms demand generation and group purchasing benefits of the chains without conceding any control over the management of their hotels. Hotel consortia differ from other hotel affiliations in two critical ways. First, they are controlled by their members who consider themselves independent and want the consortium to have no more than arm's length involvement with the hotels. Second, whereas the other affiliations involve long-term relationships with their hotels, the hotel consortia membership can be renewed annually, although most members remain for longer periods.

The fee structure in hotel consortia reflects their limited corporate affiliation. Typically, membership fees are around 2% to 3% of rooms revenue, less than half the typical annual fee for a hotel franchise. Fees are payable monthly and are structured to include: a royalty fee, a reservation fee and a marketing fee. Best Western members were broadly mid-market in their positioning, but apart from the consortium signage and collateral such as brochures and toiletries there is no other standardisation of brand specifications or operating practices across the portfolio. The lower fees compared with franchisors means that consortia have more limited infrastructure to generate rooms demand and to negotiate group purchasing arrangements than franchisors. By 1960, Best Western had achieved a portfolio of 30,000 rooms and Superior Motels had reached 20,000 rooms. Whereas the chains control the hotels by virtue of their brand specifications and adherence to brand operating practices, the consortia do not. Whereas the chains are involved in long-term relationships with their hotels, the consortia can have short-term membership. Whereas the chains are businesses, the consortia are membership clubs. Taking these features together, hotel consortia are different in kind from hotel chains and accordingly, have been excluded from the analysis of hotel chains.

Hotel chains and branding

The second feature that differentiates a hotel chain from an unaffiliated hotel is brand. Hotel branding is not easy since hotel brands are inherently more complex and diverse than consumer goods brands, which were the original focus of the concept. Just as the manufacturing approach to hotel management is ineffective so too is the consumer goods approach to hotel branding. Branding only became a relevant concept for the hotel business when hotel chains began to grow significantly and that occurred during the post-war period in the US. The three central features of a hotel brand that were prominent during the post-war period were: the market level profile of the brand, the investment profile and the brand identity. They were geared to differentiating each brand from its competitors and to facilitating faster expansion.

The earliest initiative to differentiate hotels was hotel classification, which was grounded in the time when the industrial segment was the core of economic structure, when hotel demand was smaller and less diverse and when unaffiliated hotels were the dominant force in the hotel business. The classification of a hotel as a three-star did nothing for a hotel owner/operator to distinguish his from any other three-star hotel or from linking the investment in the hotel to the available demand. The relevance of classification declined when hotel chains gained the momentum in the business and hotel branding emerged as the concept congruent with the tertiary dominance in the structural balance of economies, congruent with the criteria used by customers to select a hotel and congruent with the needs of the growing hotel chains.

During the post-war period, the initial steps were taken in the systematic market level profiling of hotel brands. First, market levels are differentiated in terms of the facilities provided for customers to sleep – the substance of the built fabric of the hotel, the size of the bedrooms and the furniture, fixtures and equipment in the bedrooms. Market level retains the five-part structure of many hotel classification schemes, but whereas hotel classification schemes applied to the entire hotel uniformly, market level is only concerned with bedrooms. Second, hotel market levels are also differentiated in terms of the services that are provided for bedroom customers and included housekeeping, reception services, concierge, porterage and business support services. The higher the market level, the wider the range of services provided and the more staff that are employed by the hotel to deliver the services to customers. As hotel chains grew during the post-war period so hotel brands became more systematically differentiated in terms of market level, a process that was reinforced by the development of new-build branded hotels such as Holiday Inn that conformed to the specifications of the brand.

Deluxe hotels

During the post-war period in the US, hotel brands clustered around three market levels: up market, mid-market and economy, which accounted for the bulk of hotel demand. However, on a business wide basis deluxe hotels at the top of the market and budget hotels at the bottom of the market also existed, but only piecemeal within the chains, for instance, the Waldorf=Astoria and the Plaza hotels in New York City where deluxe hotels in the Hilton portfolio during the period. Deluxe hotels are located mainly in the most significant downtown locations of the most significant cities and charge the highest prices, invariably. Their hotel facilities are characterised by substantial built fabric, grand architecture, the largest bedrooms, the most luxurious and extensive furniture, fixtures and equipment, a significant number of suites and each of the bedrooms with a private bathroom. In terms of services, they have housekeeping not only to clean the rooms, but also to provide other bedroom services such as turndown, valeting and laundry. They provide 24-hour room service of meals and drinks and 24-hour reception services as well as additional services such as concierge, porterage and business support services.

Up-market hotels

Hilton, more generally, and Sheraton, are examples of up-market hotel brands during the post-war period whose hotels were then and still are located mainly in downtown areas of cities, but their room prices are lower than in similarly located deluxe hotels. The substance of their built fabric is less than in deluxe hotels and invariably their architecture is less elaborate. Their rooms are smaller than in deluxe hotels and their furniture, fixtures and fittings are less luxurious and less extensive. Typically, the proportion of suites in up-market hotels is less than in deluxe hotels and each bedroom has a private bathroom. Housekeeping staff clean the rooms, laundry facilities are available and additional services such as turndown or valeting are optional. They provided 24-hour room service of meals and drinks and 24-hour reception services and additional services such as concierge, porterage and business services are also available.

Mid-market hotels

Holiday Inn and Ramada are examples of mid-market hotel brands of the period still in operation in which a greater proportion of hotels than in deluxe or up-market are located in suburbs and in smaller cities and towns. Typically, their room prices are lower than in similarly located up-market hotels. Their built fabric is more utilitarian than up-market hotels, with less grand architecture, smaller rooms, less luxurious and less extensive furniture, fixtures and equipment, few if any suites and each bedroom has a private bathroom. Housekeeping staff clean the rooms, laundry facilities are available, but other room services such as turndown and valeting are absent. Room service is frequently provided for breakfast, but less frequently for other meals. They provide 24-hour reception service, but porterage is only available on request, concierge services are rare as are business support services.

Economy hotels

Travelodge and Econolodge are examples of economy hotel brands of the period still in operation in which a greater proportion of hotels are located in the suburbs, in smaller conurbations and on arterial roads than in the downtown areas of larger cities and their room prices are less than similarly located mid-market hotels. Their built fabric is more utilitarian than in mid-market hotels and their architecture is less elaborate with smaller rooms, more functional furniture, fixtures and equipment, no suites and each bedroom with a private bathroom. Room attendants cleaned the rooms, there is no room service of meals and drinks, 24-hour reception service is rare as are concierge, porterage and business services.

Budget hotels

Budget hotel brands did not operate during the post-war period, but Etap and Premier Classe are latter-day examples that invariably are located in suburban areas and on roadsides where their room rates are the lowest of any similarly located branded hotels. They are entry-level hotel brands. Their built fabric is no more than functionally sustainable and their architecture is determined by the low build cost. They have the smallest rooms with the least range and most utilitarian furniture, fixtures and equipment. There are no suites and some brands such as Formula 1 operate without en suite bathrooms. Housekeeping staff clean the rooms, but there is no room service of meals or drinks. Reception services are not 24-hour and there are no concierge, porterage or business support services.

Table 6.3: US Hotel Chain Market Level Profile 1960

Up-Market	Rooms	Mid-Market	Rooms	Economy	Rooms
Americana Hotels Inc	1,500	Affiliated National Hotels	1,000	Del E Webb Corp.	3,000
Bowman Biltmore	1,000	Alsonett Hotels	4,000	Dinkler Hotels Co.	2,000
Hilton Hotels Corp.	15,000	American Hotels Corp.	3,000	Dutch Inns	12,000
Hotel Corp. of America	8,000	Amfac	4,000	Econolodge	1,000
Hyatt	1,000	Associated Resort Hotels	1,500	Master Host	10,000
Knott	1,500	Boss Hotels Company	5,000	Morrisons Inc	1,000
Loews	5,000	Holiday Inn	100,000	Pick Hotels Corp.	6,500
Marriott	1,300	Howard Johnson	17,500	Travelodge	7,500
Sheraton	15,000	Outrigger	1,000	Treadway Inns	1,800
Westin	5,000	Quality Inns	17,000		
		Ramada Inns	4,000		
		Sahara-Nevada Corp.	2,500		
		The Downtowner Corp.	8,000		
Total	**54,300**		**168,500**		**44,800**

Source: Otus & Co Advisory Ltd

Table 6.3 provides an indicative market level profile of the more prominent hotel chains in the US in 1960 with room numbers for each chain an approximation based on available data. The chains in the table account for 90% of all chain rooms at the time. Many of the chains, notably in the up-market segment acquired most of their hotels with the result that the specifications of hotels in the chains was not rigid or precise. It was not until chains such as Holiday Inn emerged and hotel franchising was introduced that branded hotels were new build and conformed to detailed specifications so that hotel chains became more consistent and explicit in their market level profiles.

By 1960, the mid-market was by far the largest segment accounting for more than half of the chain room stock because this was the most common format for unaffiliated hotels that were acquired by chains, while up-market and economy brands accounted broadly for equal proportions of the rest.

The investment profile of hotel brands

During the post-war period, the investment profile of hotel brands was determined in the first instance by the capital cost of the hotels. The higher the market level of hotel brands, the higher the capital cost and this was reinforced when the pattern of non-room facilities was added. Broadly, up-market hotels provided a range of facilities including restaurants and bars as well as ballrooms, banqueting rooms and smaller private dining rooms targeted at social events such as weddings, celebrations and dinner dances. They provided comprehensive non-room facilities and their mainly downtown locations in cities encouraged them to attract local demand. Up-market hotels in resorts additionally provided indoor and outdoor leisure facilities for vacation customers. It was not until late in the 1950s that hotels were being constructed with facilities dedicated to the conference and convention market and they were mainly in up-market hotels. Many mid-market hotels provided a restaurant and bar and limited function facilities, while economy hotels tended to provide only limited non-room facilities. Up-market hotels were not only more capital-intensive than mid-market and economy hotels, but also their more extensive non room facilities added to the capital cost differential between up-market and mid-market hotels. In turn mid-market hotels were more capital-intensive than economy hotels and their more extensive non-room facilities added to the capital cost differential between mid-market and economy hotels.

The investment profile of hotel brands was also determined by the operating costs. The wider the range of non-room facilities, the higher the number of employees needed to deliver the services and thus, the higher the operating costs. Up-market hotels had higher operating costs than mid-market hotels, which in turn had higher costs than economy hotels, because of the declining patterns of non-room facilities. The higher the proportion of turnover derived from renting rooms, most typically during the post-war period in economy hotels, the higher the operating margins due to less use of consumables and the lower volume of employees needed to meet the customer demand to sleep. The corollary is that the greater the proportion of hotel turnover derived from non-room facilities, most typically during the post-war period in up-market hotels, the lower the operating margins, due to the greater use of consumables and the higher number of employees needed to meet the customer demand to eat and drink. .

Hotels are long-term assets, their useful life measured in decades and in some cases centuries, which means that the investment does not end once a hotel has been constructed. A five-year to seven-year maintenance refurbishment cycle is necessary to keep the facilities in acceptable condition meaning that during the standard management contract and franchise period there are three to four refurbishment cycles. In the longer term, redevelopment of facilities is also necessary to enable the hotel to remain relevant to contemporary demand. Adding private bathrooms, converting three single rooms into two double rooms, adding conference facilities, adding health clubs, replacing conference facilities with bedrooms and re-cladding the façade are all examples of major development capital expenditure that has occurred in chain hotels. The gist of hotel brand management is the tantalisingly difficult balancing between the level of investment and the pattern of demand, which are not constant. The creation of brand specifications, the proactive generation of demand and the roll-out of successful hotel brands during the post-war period was a major development in the professionalisation of the hotel business, which also increased the prospects of achieving professional returns on investment in branded hotel.

Brand identity

When the supply profile and investment profile of a hotel brand have been established it is brand identity that differentiates hotel brands with similar market level profiles and similar investment profiles. Hotel brand identity includes: the brand name, the brand signage, the brand collateral, the colour spectrum used as well as the specific style or form of services unique to the brand. Thus, a Hilton was differentiated from a Sheraton and a Holiday Inn from a Howard Johnson Motor Lodge. The more hotels there are in a portfolio and the longer that the brand has operated, then the fewer hotels in the portfolio are identical. The Hilton brand name has been attached to hotels since 1925 and has undergone many developments in its market level profile, investment profile and brand identity. Before the 1950s, all of its hotels were acquired unaffiliated hotels that were not created to a consistent market level profile, investment profile or brand identity. At the end of the post-war period, the hotels in the portfolio of larger chains were of different ages, had different architecture, had different interior design and were at different stages of the refurbishment cycle, yet the brand identity gave them a closer family resemblance. For these reasons it is not possible for hotel brands to conform to the consistency of consumer goods brands. Consumer product brands are hard brands since they can be manufactured in long batches to the same standardised specifications, but this is not possible in the case of hotels, which are softer brands. Brand identity is the basis on which some consistency of hotel brands can be achieved.

Hotel supply and demand performance in the US

The post-war period was a landmark period for the US hotel business in response to the shift in the structural balance of the US economy to service businesses. The number of hotel rooms escalated. Hotel chain expansion exploded and captured the momentum of growth in the hotel demand. During the post-war period hotel chains focused their attention on growing their share of business demand because of its strong growth and lower seasonal fluctuations. This strategy also led them to focus portfolio expansion on cities rather than resorts. Unaffiliated hotels were more dominant in resorts and focused on the highly seasonal vacation market. The success of the chain strategy is evident in their average annual supply growth of 12% against only 3% for the market as a whole. It was also evident in demand performance in which hotel chains in 1960 achieved room occupancy of 60% against only 45% for the market as a whole. Overall, in 1950, hotel chains accounted for only 8% of total hotel room stock, but 12% of hotel demand. By 1960, their share of supply grew to 21% and their share of demand climbed to 28%. The 15 years after World War II were when hotel chains reached the stage at which their superior supply and demand performance differentiated them from unaffiliated hotels and their momentum propelled them to become the dominant force in the US hotel business.

Table 6.4: Supply and Demand Performance: US 1950–1960

	Total Hotels			Chain Hotels			Chain Share	
	1950	1960	CAGR	1950	1960	CAGR	1950	1960
Total rooms	1,100,000	1,500,000	3%	90,000	310,000	13%	8%	21%
Room nights available m	402	549	3%	33	113	13%	8%	21%
Room occupancy %	41%	45%		60%	60%			
Room nights sold m	**165**	**247**	**4%**	**20**	**68**	**13%**	**12%**	**28%**
Domestic business	58	89	4%	9	29	13%	15%	33%
Domestic leisure	99	146	4%	10	31	12%	10%	21%
Foreign business	3	5	4%	1	4	21%	18%	83%
Foreign leisure	5	7	4%	0	3	24%	8%	46%
Supply ratio	7.2	8.3		0.6	1.7			
Secular growth in hotel room supply	60,000	200,000		25,000	210,000		42%	105%

Source: Otus & Co Advisory Ltd

In this chapter, data on employment for 1950 has been estimated by Otus from a variety of sources, and that for 1960 was drawn from the US Department of Labour.

7 European Economic Structures and Hotel Businesses: 1945–1960

Introduction

Europe was in a dire state in 1945 having endured a half century defined by two world wars, the Great Depression and ideological shifts. By 1950, the Soviet empire had stretched westwards. Bulgaria, Czechoslovakia, East Germany, Estonia, Hungary, Latvia, Lithuania, Poland and Romania as well as Albania and Yugoslavia had become communist. They all retrenched behind the Iron Curtain, their economic development ossified and so did their hotel businesses, which were minor. In contrast, West Germany and Italy were re-established as parliamentary democracies with supporting political institutions. Thus, all Western European countries were parliamentary democracies except for Spain and Portugal. The prime economic imperative was recovery from the war and this required dedicated focus on agriculture, construction and manufacturing, but the democracies were unable to achieve this on their own. The Marshall Plan, which operated between 1947 and 1953 and involved $13 billion, mostly made-up of credit, to buy goods from the US and to pay US shippers for their transport to Europe enabled the democracies to kick-start their economies. Sixteen countries benefited – Austria, Belgium, Britain, Denmark, France, Greece, Iceland, Ireland, Italy, Netherlands, Norway, Portugal, Sweden, Switzerland, Turkey and West Germany. The Marshall Plan capital was distributed on a per capita basis with former allies getting more than former Axis Powers. The initiative was successful. Between 1948 and 1952 European industrial production grew by 35% (*source*: www.wikipedia.com).

The European Coal and Steel Community (ECSC) was formed in 1951 by six countries – Belgium, France, Italy, Luxembourg, the Netherlands and West Germany – to oversee the more effective development of their coal and steel industries. It was a success that led in 1957 to these countries extending their economic cooperation with the Treaty of Rome, which established the European Economic Community (EEC). The EEC began to remove trade barriers among the six countries and created a common market in agricultural and industrial goods, which became the most significant economic development in Europe, ever. As the economies began to recover, the governments pursued explicit, long-term, big government macroeconomic policies that expanded citizen services and created welfare states in Europe, but left service businesses to market forces.

The traumas of the European economies at the end of World War II were reflected in the European hotel business. Conventional demand was absent and showed no likelihood of returning quickly when wartime specific demand was stopping. Urban and resort hotel supply had been depleted by bombing and business failures and there was no rush to construct new hotels because the hotel business, like other service businesses, was not an economic priority. Leisure demand into hotels would have to wait until civilian employment was re-established and the distortions of the war became a less vivid memory. As the economic ascent of the hotel business in the US accelerated strongly over the period, the European hotel businesses struggled to regain their pre-war levels.

British economic structure and hotel demand

Britain entered the post World War II period as victor, but with the loss of almost 25% of its wealth (source: http://uk.encarta.msn.com). The array of social issues needing to be resolved and the awful state of the economy produced a change in government as the war ended. Clement Attlee replaced Winston Churchill as Prime Minister and the new Labour government set about radically reorganising the economy. The Beveridge Report, published in 1942 established the blueprint for the introduction of the welfare state and the traditional modus operandi of industrial firms was upended by the most extensive programme of nationalisation ever undertaken in the country. Big government in Britain became even bigger. However, it did not produce a quick turn-around in economic performance, which was beyond fast solutions. Cash was an immediate problem and to increase liquidity, the Attlee government borrowed $3.75 billion from the US, C$1.25 billion from Canada and received $2.4 billion aid from the Marshall Plan. This enabled the post-war governments to pursue a policy of full employment, which they achieved generally with the aid of job creation in citizen services and the nationalised industries. In spite of policies to recover the economy, food and clothing rationing, introduced at the end of 1939, endured. At its height in 1947/48 rationing covered around 30% of all consumer spending and it lasted until late-1954 when meat was the last commodity to be de-rationed. An adult in 1948 had a weekly allowance of 13 ounces of meat, one and a half ounces of cheese, six ounces of butter, one ounce of cooking fat, two pints of milk and one egg (Sandbrook, 2005: 45) Thus, the austerity of the Great Depression and World War II continued until the mid-1950s.

After 10 years of post-war austerity the economy was enlivened in the second half of the 1950s, but not until the Suez crisis caused Britain to retreat from its position as a global military power (Sandbrook, 2005:27). The progress had been so noticeable that in 1957 the prime minister, Harold Macmillan delivered the political catchphrase of the late 1950s when he declared that, "most of our people never had it so good". During the post-war period, Britain achieved limited development in terms of the four factors that are necessary for progress in the structural development of an economy towards service businesses and this constrained the rate of growth in the volume of hotel demand, which started from a very low level. Civil and human rights were the main developments and came from the introduction of the welfare state. There was an increase in the proportion of women in the workforce, particularly in citizen services and there was a gradual increase in the number of women attending universities. The second factor, the development of the social sciences, was only slowly introduced into British universities during the period and their application to areas such as business was still minor (Sandbrook, 2005: 169). The third factor, access to personal credit, was mainly through hire-purchase schemes, which were tied to the purchase of generally small-ticket household appliances. The fourth factor, personal travel, was boosted by the extension of car ownership, but in Britain this was materially lower than in the US and was constrained in the first half of the period by petrol rationing. However, rail travel declined in response to the growth in car ownership and air travel remained minor. During the post-war period the structural development of the economy was determined by government policies and these centred on the expansion of citizen services and the restructuring of the industrial segment. It was a top-down approach, but corporate-focused market services such as banking, finance, distribution and professional services benefited. However, consumer-focused market services such as retailing and experience businesses such as hospitality and travel did not benefit as much and had to rely on bottom-up growth in customer demand, which was not determined by the government.

Otus estimates that in 1950, 28 million hotel room nights were sold in Britain; the level achieved in the first decade of the century. The austerity, rationing and the widespread programme of nationalisation limited the rate of hotel demand growth in the first 10 years after the war, but the improvements in the economy from 1955 accelerated hotel demand, which by 1960 reached 39 million room nights, comfortably above the pre-war level. Domestic business demand grew from 7 million room nights in 1950 to 11 million in 1960 and that the policies of the government and the developments in the structural balance of the economy produced different growth patterns across the economic segments. The pattern of employment per segment over the 1950s was as follows:

Table 7.1: Employment by Segment in Britain: 1950–1960 (m)

	Agriculture	Industry	Citizen Services	Service Businesses	Total
1950	1.4	10.3	5.2	6.0	22.9
1960	1.2	10.9	5.3	6.7	24.1

Table 7.2: Employment by Segment in Britain: 1950–1960 %

	Agriculture	Industry	Citizen Services	Service Businesses	Total
1950	6%	45%	23%	26%	100%
1960	5%	45%	22%	28%	100%

Source: Groningen Growth Centre

Agricultural demand into hotels

By 1950, British agriculture accounted for 6% of the workforce continuing the progressive decline despite food rationing. Otus estimates that only 2.3% of agricultural employees were business travellers, a total of 30,000, mostly originating demand and that they spent an average of eight nights in British hotels generating transient rooms demand of 0.2 million room nights for a 3% share of total domestic business demand. The small size of agricultural companies and limited geographic spread limited their hotel use. So also did food rationing until 1955. By 1960, agriculture accounted for 5% of the workforce due to the loss of 147,000 jobs. Otus estimates that in 1960, and in spite of the growing demand for food, the proportion of agriculture workers who were business travellers originating demand remained unchanged at 2.3%, but this entailed the reduction of 3,000 travellers to 27,000; they spent an average of eight nights in British hotels generating transient rooms demand of 0.2 million room nights down at a slower rate than employment for a 2% share of total domestic business demand as the other segments grew at a faster rate.

Industrial demand into hotels

The programme of nationalisation was passed through parliament as a priority. The Cable and Wireless Act of 1946 nationalised Cable and Wireless Ltd and transferred the control of telecommunications to the Post Office. In the same year, the Civil Aviation Act nationalised the airlines and the Coal Nationalisation Act, nationalised coal mining, which at the time employed over 700,000. These Acts were followed in 1947 by the Electricity Act nationalising electricity generation and distribution and the Transport Act, which consolidated the four railway companies into the state controlled British Railways. In 1948, the Gas Act nationalised the manufacture and distribution of gas and the Iron and Steel Act in 1949 established the Iron and Steel Corporation, which consolidated into national control 298 companies employing around 300,000 people. In 1950, 10.3 million Britons, 45% of the workforce were industrially employed.

Otus estimates that 2.7% of segment employees were business travellers amounting to 280,000. Those in the non-nationalised companies were involved primarily in originating demand, while the nationalised industries did not need many sales and marketing executives because volume and prices in their respective industries were controlled nationally. In contrast, 3.9% of US industrial employees were business travellers because they were not constrained by nationalisation. The British industrial business travellers spent an average of 11 nights in British hotels, compared with 29 in the US, which benefited from larger companies with a higher proportion of white-collar executives and wider geographic spread of their markets. In 1950, the segment in Britain generated mainly transient rooms demand of 3 million room nights for a 43% of total domestic business demand preserving its position as the largest segment for the hotel business.

The bombing damage during the war required extensive construction activities throughout most cities and towns where the building of houses, factories, offices and infrastructure were priorities. Manufacturing had to be converted from military to civilian production, a process limited by heavy government spending on defence, which accounted for a higher proportion of GDP than any country except the US and the Soviet Union (Sampson, 1962). The problematic state of the economy in 1945 produced a trading policy of limiting imports and growing exports. The export growth was achieved by Britain's traditional route of increasing sales to the empire and developing countries to the extent that between 1946 and 1951 total exports increased threefold. By 1960, only 16% of exports went to the six neighbouring EEC countries and the growth in exports over the period further limited the volume and growth of demand from manufacturing into British hotels (Sandbrook, 2005: 497).

In the 10 years to 1955, the heavily constrained domestic consumer goods markets caused Britain to fall further behind the US. During the period there was an average increase of 100,000 cars per year in Britain, but between 1955 and 1960, the number rose sharply to 500,000 per year. By 1960, 28% of households in the UK owned a car compared with 73% in the US (Marwick, 1982). In 1951, there were 764,000 television licences, by 1955 the number had increased to 4 million and jumped to 10 million by 1960. In 1955, 18% of households owned a washing machine. By 1960, the proportion had increased to 29% (Marwick, 1982). As the domestic consumer durables market grew strongly between 1955 and 1960, the problem for British manufacturing was that it was not tooled to meet the demand and consequently, the volume of imported consumer durables leapt. During the post-war period the investment in new manufacturing technology lagged that in the US, France, West Germany and Italy as did improvements in work practices. Indeed, restrictive work practices among heavily unionised workforces were a feature of the period as were price fixing agreements within industries that sought to replicate the market practice of the recently nationalised industries. Industrial companies were the largest employer, but whereas employment in manufacturing grew to meet the domestic demand, employment in mining fell by 10% over the period as new technology increased productivity.

By 1960, the volume of domestic business demand generated into British hotels by industrial companies continued to be constrained by the programme of nationalisation. By 1960, employment in the segment had risen to 10.9 million and Otus estimates that the growth in industrial demand was the prime driver of the increase to 3% of those who were business travellers, a total of 330,000, still mainly originating demand for non-nationalised companies. In contrast, industrial business travellers in the US amounted to 4.4% of employees. According to Otus, British business travellers spent an average of 13 nights in British hotels against 28 by the Americans. The British generated primarily transient rooms demand of 4 million hotel room nights up from 3 million in 1950 and its share of total domestic business demand fell to 40%, but it remained the largest segment for the hotel business. The hotel based conference market in Britain by 1960 remained minor with most industry-wide events held in London.

Citizen services demand into hotels

The welfare state was created from two Acts that became law in 1947. The National Health Service Act created the National Health Service, which established free access for all citizens to hospital and general practitioner services; and the National Insurance Act consolidated and extended all sickness, unemployment and old age benefits into one system for all citizens. Both of these initiatives created citizen services in health and welfare on a state controlled basis, without involvement from the private sector, but the welfare state did not end there. It stretched to public housing. A major problem for post-war Britain was the destruction by bombing of large tracts of urban housing. Moreover, much of the remaining housing stock was sub-standard: in 1951, 20% of households had to share a toilet (Sandbook, 2005: 98). The government solution was to establish more houses with modern amenities in urban and suburban areas. Critically, most new houses were council houses, owned by local authorities and rented to the majority of the population. This initiative generated few room nights for hotels since control was by local authorities. The Education Act of 1944 introduced compulsory education from ages 5 to 15 and the structure of state primary, secondary and tertiary education laid down in the Act lasted for a generation. The National Health Service became the largest single employer in the country. Welfare, social and housing services also employed high and growing numbers, as did education. National Service, which operated between 1949 and 1963, required all able-bodied 18-year-old men to enrol for a two-year period in the military.

In 1950, there were 5.2 million citizen service employees. Otus estimates that 9% were business travellers, significantly higher than all other segments because civil servants travelled on segment management particularly in the nationalised industries, health, education and welfare. They amounted to 470,000, but the frequency of travel was the lowest of any segment at only four nights in British hotels generating mostly transient rooms demand of 1.9 million room nights for a 26% share of total domestic business demand. During the 1950s, the citizen service workforce grew to 5.3 million, 10% of whom were business travellers. A total of 530,000 as civil servants travelled more and a greater proportion of professionals such as medics and academics attended meetings and conferences. In all, they spent an average of five nights in British hotels generating mainly transient rooms demand with a minor tranche of packaged conference demand for a total of 2.6 million room nights and a 25% share of total domestic business demand, down from 27% in 1950.

Service businesses demand into hotels

Service businesses were not a priority for the government at the start of the post-war period, but by 1950 the segment employed 6.0 million. Otus estimates that because of the high fragmentation of many service businesses, only 3.4% of the employees were business travellers, a total of 200,000, originating demand, executing contracts and servicing clients compared with 5.2% in the US due to larger companies with a higher proportion of white-collar and professional employees and more attendance at conferences. British segment travellers spent an average of 10 nights in British hotels compared with 25 in the US due to the larger geographic spread of the markets for service businesses. The British travellers generated mainly transient rooms demand of 2 million room nights for a 28% share of total domestic business demand. For the first 10 years of the period, segment growth was slow and tied to developments in the other segments, but during the last five years it accelerated and widened its range as consumer demand grew.

Financial services

Retail banking expanded over the period as more white-collar and professional workers opened bank accounts, but by 1960 this still represented only a small minority of the population. For most people, wages were paid weekly in cash and they did not have a bank account. Banks considered unsecured personal lending to be a high risk for many of their customers, thus, hire-purchase agreements backed by specialist finance houses were the most widespread form of personal credit, but also higher risk for the lenders, which was offset by higher interest rates to enable the purchase of small ticket household appliances and other consumer durables. In 1954, there was a relaxation of hire-purchase controls, which led the following year to an 8% surge in consumer spending, which then accelerated for the remainder of the decade as economic conditions eased, to the extent that over the decade as a whole there was a 20% increase in consumption per head (Sandbrook, 2005: 103). In 1956 alone, half of the televisions and one third of the vacuum cleaners were bought on hire purchase. Building societies, friendly societies and insurance companies also grew as savings increased, mostly among white-collar workers. In 1960, building societies provided 326,125 mortgages for the purchase of homes for a total value of £544 million (Porter, 1997: 115). This increased the proportion of households owning their home to 37% compared with 62% in the US. All of these developments were positive for the generation of demand into British hotels because service business executives needed to travel for a wider range of reasons than their counterparts in other segments.

Retailing

The rationing of food and clothing limited the development of retailing. For retailers, the main focus was on reducing operating costs rather than growing demand and this was achieved mainly by the introduction of self-service shops. Harris, Hyde and Smith estimate that whereas in 1947 there were only 10 self-service stores in the UK, the number exploded to 3,000 by 1956. After the end of rationing there was a surge of larger shops in larger population areas. By 1960, there were 357 supermarkets in Britain. Harris et al. estimated that chain stores such as, Boots, Burton, Co-operative, Marks & Spencer, WH Smith and Woolworth accounted for 28% of all retail sales (Harris et al., 1986). Commercial television was introduced to Britain in 1955 and exposed growing numbers of the population to mass advertising of consumer goods, but the only other television and radio broadcaster, the BBC, did not advertise. In 1956, £13 million was spent on television commercials, but by 1960 it had increased almost sixfold to

£76 million (Sandbrook, 2005: 363). All of these developments were positive for the generation of hotel demand because as market services expanded so did their corporate structures and a higher proportion of their executives needed to travel to originate demand, to execute contracts, to service clients and to manage the business.

Leisure activities

Over the period, leisure activities were mainly home-centred and included: television, radio, record playing, reading, knitting, gardening, pets and other home-based hobbies. As the prime focus of expenditure was on acquiring household goods, little cash was left for spending regularly in out-of-home experience businesses. Out-of-home leisure was dominated by informal activities such as angling, playing sports such as bowling, football, rugby, tennis and athletics, and attending clubs, societies and the church, as well as day trips in the car (Sandbrook, 2005: 122–123). As a result, it was not a good period for experience businesses. In 1946, the total cinema audience amounted to 1.6 billion, but the growth of television produced a slump and by 1960 they were down by more than two-thirds to 500 million. The fall in demand was reflected in the fall in supply, in 1950, there were 4,500 cinemas in Britain, but by 1960 the number was down to 2,950 (Docherty et al.. 1987). In 1960, British Rail reported a loss of £68 million, impacted among other things by the transfer of travel from rail to road due to the increased number of cars. In 1945, there were 72,960 pubs licensed in Britain, by 1960 the number had fallen to 69,184. At the same time the number of off-licences rose from 21,599 to 23,670 indicating a shift in drinking pattern from out-of-home drinking to in-home drinking *(source*: Liquor licensing statistics from the Home Office, quoted in the Monopolies Commission Report on the Supply of Beer 1969, p. 159) Like these facilities, the restaurants, cafes, variety theatres and amusement parks at the coastal resorts were fragmented and heavily seasonal businesses that did not add much to domestic business demand into British hotels.

By 1960, service business employment increased to 6.7 million, most of the growth coming from corporate-facing market service businesses rather than experience businesses. Otus estimates that the growth in the size and range of service businesses increased the proportion of business travellers originating demand, executing contracts and servicing clients. They were also involved in the development of new venues for service businesses and conference attendance emerged so that the proportion of segment employees who were business travellers increased to 4.7%, a total of 310,000, still far behind the 6% in the US. They spent an average of 11 nights in British hotels, half of that in the US, and generated mostly transient rooms demand of 3.5 million room nights for a 33% share of domestic business demand.

Domestic leisure demand into hotels

In spite of the austerity and rationing, domestic leisure demand recovery benefited from the full-employment policy of post-war governments coupled with the further extension of paid annual holiday leave to cover all full-time employ-ees. By 1950, summer holiday demand into coastal resorts was beginning to re-establish the momentum it had at the end of the 1930s and the annual summer holiday became a rare relief from the drudgery of life. Although most holiday accommodation was informal in guesthouses, in the homes of local residents, in holiday centres, caravan parks and campsites there was also a positive benefit for holiday hotels. The more that the structural balance of an economy moved towards citizen services and service businesses, the more white-collar and pro-fessional careers were created and the more these employees and their families took hotel-based holidays. However, weekend hotel stays, which had grown with the increase in car ownership, were constrained in the early years of the period by petrol rationing. In the early 1950s, only 1.5 million Britons took holidays abroad, by 1958 this had increased to 2 million and by the end of the period rose to 3.5 million diverting hotel based demand from domestic holidays (Sandbrook, 2005: 135). Nonetheless, the volume of domestic leisure demand grew from 18 million room nights in 1950 to 22 million in 1960. Between 1945 and 1955 there were more than 8 million births in Britain. The baby boomers accounted for 16% of the population in 1955, a lower proportion than in the US and there were only a few signs before the end of the 1950s that British baby boomers were a distinct generation. Their emergence was slower than in the US due to the less developed economy and they were only a market for hotels as members of families taking hotel-based holidays and that amounted to a small minority of the population.

Foreign visitors

The number of foreign visitors to Britain increased from 203,000 in 1946 to around 1 million in 1955. (Taylor, 2003:290), which is remarkable given the austerity and rationing. Two stage-managed events during the period provided short-term spikes in foreign hotel demand into London – the Olympic Games in 1948 and the Festival of Britain in 1951, but for most of the period there was little for foreign visitors to find attractive in the material conditions of the hotels or the meals. A further boost was given to this market as cross-Atlantic flights began to replace sea crossings. Flights were not only faster and more frequent, but also less expensive. Foreign business demand grew due to the high levels of imports, particularly from the EEC towards the end of the period, but this was a benefit only to London and the main industrial centres. Otus estimates that in 1950, foreign demand into British hotels accounted for three million room nights, 11% of the total, but by 1960 it had grown to 6 million room nights, 16% of total demand.

Hotel supply in Britain

At a constant 1945 supply ratio and with the recorded increase in population, Britain would have needed 315,000 hotel rooms in 1950. Otus estimates that in 1945 there were 300,000 hotel rooms in Britain. By 1950, this had increased only by 5,000 reflecting continuing urban hotel failures and the construction of small independently-owned hotels in coastal resorts to cater for the recovering holiday demand, producing a secular decline of 10,000 rooms. At a constant 1950 supply ratio and with the recorded increase in population, it would have needed 315,000 hotel rooms in 1960. The pace of supply growth accelerated during the 1950s with the net addition of 20,000 rooms to reach a total supply of 325,000, producing a secular growth of 10,000 rooms. The first new hotel built in London after the war, the Westbury, developed by the Knott Corporation of America, did not open until 1955. Similarly, there were no new hotels built in the large provincial cities in the first 10 years after the war. Hotel chains achieved average annual portfolio growth of only 2.3% during the 1950s expanding by 9,000 rooms to a total stock of 45,000 by 1960, much of which was by acquisition rather than new build. The hotel supply dynamic over the period reflected the stage in development of economic structure and over the 1950s hotel chains achieved 70% of the secular growth as concentration grew to 14%.

It was not only the volume of room stock that was depressed in 1945. The British hotel business was in a dire physical state after a 15-year period of underinvestment due to the ravages of the Great Depression and the war. The post-war period did not see an immediate return to normality in capital expenditure either. As Taylor says, "the hotels needed refurbishment, but the materials were in short supply. Permits were needed to buy all sorts of items and, to make matters worse, their cost was increased by Purchase Tax." (Taylor, 2003: 283). A measure of the extent of the degradation of British hotels at the time was the exceptional initiative agreed by the government, "to make a contribution to equipping and re-equipping dollar earning hotels for one year" to make the hotels of London more attractive to foreign visitors to the Festival of Britain in 1951 (Taylor, 2003: 289).

Hotel chains

Unlike the innovative and electric development of hotel chains in the US during the post-war period, the British chain developments were sluggish and without innovation. More emerged, but several of the established chains shortened their portfolios. As part of the nationalisation of the railways, the hotels operated by the four railway companies were consolidated to form British Transport Hotels (BTH). In 1947, BTH started life with 57 hotels, but poor trading triggered the sale of 18 of the worst performing and smaller hotels by the mid-1950s (Taylor, 2003: 286). The BTH hotels were predominantly up-market hotels in the main cities, but also included two of the most prominent golf resort hotels in the UK, Gleneagles and Turnbury. All of the BTH hotels were owned by British Railways and therefore by the state and continued to rely on the state-owned trains to deliver their customers. In the post-war period and thereafter, BTH management maintained the operating practices that evolved over the previous century and contributed no new thinking to the development and performance of hotel chains.

Trust Houses reached a peak of 219 hotels just before World War II. It lost hotels during the war and in the post-war period the focus was on portfolio restructuring. It sold hotels that were performing poorly due to their location, poor physical state and small size, but it remained a portfolio constructed by acquisition rather than new build. The brewers continued their haphazard involvement in hotels as an addendum to their brewing and pubs businesses and the pre-war decline of Gordon Hotels and Fredrick Hotels continued in the post-war period.

Two of the most significant British hotel businesses were formed during the post-war period. First, Grand Metropolitan Hotels (Grand Met) emerged from the hotel acquisitions made by Maxwell Joseph. During the 1950s, Joseph acquired a clutch of hotels mainly in central London and operating at the up-market and mid-market levels. They included the Mandeville, the Washington, the Green Park, the Clifton-Ford, Flemings, St Ermins and the Mount Royal. Grand Met was to grow in the hotel business both in Britain and abroad for the rest of the century, eventually owning the Intercontinental brand. The second major British hotel business to emerge during the post-war period was the result to the entrepreneurial initiatives of Charles Forte. Forte had been in the London restaurant market since the mid-1930s, but in 1958 he entered the hotel business with the acquisition of the Waldorf hotel in London's Aldwych from Frederick Hotels for £600,000 (Forte, 1986: 92). The hotel was constructed in 1908 at a cost of £400,000 and for Forte it heralded almost 40 years of expansion in the hotel business around the world and the creation of one of the largest hotel companies with a portfolio that reached 800 hotels at its peak.

With the exception of Trust Houses, all of the chains in Britain during the post-war period were short chains, which meant that their small corporate structures gave them limited performance advantages over unaffiliated hotels. Their capacity to generate premium demand was conditioned by their greater concentration in London and the larger provincial cities than in seasonal resorts, which were heavily dominated by unaffiliated hotels. Given that the chains were created predominantly through the acquisition of hotels there was not a systematic set of brand specifications to which the hotels in each portfolio had to conform and thus they were soft brands that bore only a passing family resemblance. The location profile of the chain hotels meant they attracted rooms customers from all demand sources: domestic and foreign, business and leisure, whereas the unaffiliated hotels in the resorts relied on domestic holiday demand. The small size of the chains also limited their capacity to create purchasing synergies in consumables, furniture, fixtures and fittings. Consequently, the operating cost structure of most chains during the period were little different from unaffiliated hotels and in terms of both demand generation and operating margins they were less effective than their counterparts in the US.

These were not the only ways in which British hotel chains were less developed than their equivalents in the US. Management contracting and franchising did not materialise during the post-war period in Britain. All of the hotel chains in Britain either owned or leased their hotels, which is indicative of less developed hotel capital markets. The acquisitions by British hotel chains were financed as property transactions. Max Joseph, according to Taylor, "was able to acquire the St. Ermins hotel for £500,000 and sell the freehold to the Church Commissioners for £625,000 and an agreed 40 year lease. The hotel included an office block, the rentals from which paid the interest on the £625,000 easily" (Taylor,

2003:326). On the face of it this was a slick transaction, but Joseph gave up long-term appreciation in the capital value of the asset for short-term cash flow improvement for the company. In 2000, the St Ermins hotel was sold to Jolly Hotels of Italy for £57 million representing an average annual growth in capital value of 11%, more than four times greater than inflation from the time it was acquired by Max Joseph. Similarly, Charles Forte's acquisition of the Waldorf hotel in London for £600,000 was funded by the sale of another central London restaurant and office property, the Monico building, for £500,000. The remainder of the purchase price was funded by debt. He then sold the hotel to Prudential Assurance and leased it back on a 99-year lease. (Forte, 1986:92) In 2007, the real estate of the Waldorf, which was by then managed by Hilton, was sold for £50 million representing an average annual growth in capital value of 10%, also well above inflationary growth since the Forte acquisition. The hotel chain developments in Britain during the post-war period were predominantly entrepreneurial or opportunistic property driven hotel acquisitions made by emerging corporate hoteliers such as Max Joseph and Charles Forte, which set the dominant trend in the capital structure of British hotel chains for the rest of the century. The prime advantage of the chains over unaffiliated hotels at the time was the access that the entrepreneurs had to the capital markets and it was this that enabled Grand Met and Forte to grow.

British hotel demand and supply performance

Otus estimates that room occupancy at the end of the War was only 20% as conventional rooms demand was absent, but given the patterns and volumes of hotel demand and supply growth in Britain it rose to 25% in 1950, still in the danger zone in which most hotels are not profitable.

Table 7.3: British hotels 1950–1960

	Total Hotels			Hotel Chains			Chain Share	
	1950	1960	CAGR	1950	1960	CAGR	1950	1960
Total rooms	305,000	325,000	0%	36,000	45,000	1%	12%	14%
Room nights available (m)	111	119	0%	13	16	1%	12%	14%
Room occupancy %	25%	28%		42%	55%			
Room nights sold (m)	28	33	1%	6	9	3%	20%	27%
Domestic business	7	11	2%	2	4	3%	34%	40%
Domestic leisure	18	22	1%	1	1	1%	6%	6%
Foreign business	1	3	4%	1	2	4%	56%	49%
Foreign leisure	2	3	3%	1	2	3%	69%	61%
Supply ratio	6.1	6.3		0.7	0.9			
Secular growth in hotel room supply	- 10,000	10,000		- 2,000	7,000		20%	70%

Source: Otus & Co Advisory Ltd

The position improved during the 1950s as the confluence of negative economic forces declined and by 1960, room occupancy had reached 33%, which was still not an effective performance and reflected the predominance of supply in resorts that were heavily seasonal with most of the hotels closing for the winter months and with little weekend rooms demand into urban hotels. The improvements in hotel supply and demand performance during the post-war period as well as the growth in concentration restarted the economic ascent of the British hotel business after the traumas of the Great Depression, World War II and austerity. However, because of the limited development in the structural balance of the British economy, it was not reforming and its position relative to the US declined on all counts.

French economic structure, hotel demand and hotel supply

In parallel with Britain, the French government of the Fourth Republic, which ruled from 1946 to 1958, reorganised the economy with a bout of nationalisation and the establishment of a welfare state, but the French economy grew faster and maintained the growth for longer than Britain. In 1945, France began "les trente gloreuses", 30 glorious years, during which time it produced average annual economic growth of 5%, almost double the rate of Britain (Prince, 1993: 290). France did not suffer bombing of its cities to anything like the same extent as Britain or Germany, which meant that fewer resources were needed for urgent construction and more resources were available for the development of the manufacturing base of the economy. The four factors that are indicative of the structural progress of an economy towards service businesses were less active in France than in Britain. Like Britain, most progress was made in human and civil rights as a result of the development of citizen services, which extended the rights of the population to health care, education and social security. However, women continued to be only a minor proportion of both the workforce and of enrolment in universities. Within the French universities there was a slower development of the social sciences than in the US or even in Britain. The access to personal credit was less than in Britain and lower levels of car ownership limited the frequency of personal leisure travel. The structural balance of the French economy is evident in the pattern of employment over the 1950s.

Table 7.4: Employment by Segment in France: 1950–1960 (m)

	Agriculture	Industry	Citizen Services	Service Businesses	Total
1950	4.8	6.9	4.4	3.8	19.9
1960	4.2	7.1	4.5	4.0	19.8

Source: Groningen Growth Centre

Table 7.5: Employment by Segment in France: 1950–1960 %

	Agriculture	Industry	Citizen Services	Service Businesses	Total
1950	24%	35%	22%	19%	100%
1960	21%	36%	23%	20%	100%

Source: Groningen Growth Centre

The French employment profile of very high employment in agriculture, low employment in service businesses and structural unemployment evidenced by falling total employment and rising population is not a context for strong domestic hotel demand. Otus estimates that in 1950, 18 million hotel room nights were sold in France compared with 28 million in Britain. The pattern of demand between the two countries was also different. Foreign demand, mostly holiday-makers, accounted for 47% of total hotel demand in 1950 rising to 49% in 1960. In contrast, foreign demand into Britain in 1960 amounted to only 16%. Accordingly, French domestic demand accounted for a lower proportion of total hotel demand reflecting the weaker economic structure.

Agricultural demand into hotels

Although there were some food shortages immediately after the war and limited rationing until 1949, agricultural production was enough to feed its population with much less rationing and fewer food imports than Britain. In 1950, French agriculture employed 4.8 million accounting for 24% of the workforce. By 1960, agricultural employment was reduced with the loss of half a million jobs and its share of the workforce declined to 22%, but this was still by far the highest of the major economies and acted as a drag on domestic business demand into hotels since agriculture generates the lowest domestic business demand of any segment into hotels due to the small size of farms with little corporate structure and only local arable farming markets. Otus estimates that in 1960, agricultural travellers were concerned with originating demand and generated 5% of the total French domestic business demand almost entirely transient rooms demand and down from 6% in 1950 as other segments developed more effectively.

Industrial demand into hotels

Three things differentiated the French industrial policy from the British equivalent and contributed to its superior performance over a longer period. First, the French programme of nationalisation was more extensive than the British. Like Britain, public utilities such as coal, gas and electricity as well as air transport were nationalised, but then so also were the four largest banks and Renault, the vehicle manufacturer. Second, and unlike Britain, the French government took stakes in key companies and industries as a precursor to the work of the Economic Planning Agency, which was responsible for state planning of the economy. The extent of the French government's control, intervention and planning of the economy meant that France became the most state controlled capitalist economy in the West. The third difference from Britain was that the state economic planning process involved the identification of investment priorities for industries and resulted in new technology in manufacturing and fuelled the greater growth achieved by the French economy than the British over the period. In 1945, industrial production in France was half of the pre-war level, but such was the success of nationalisation and state planning that by 1947 production was back to pre-war levels (Ardagh, 1973). The high birth rate and higher immigration increased the market size, while the growth in imports was lower than in Britain due to higher domestic agricultural output and a greater propensity of the French to buy consumer goods manufactured in France than of the British to buy products manufactured in Britain. Economic recovery was boosted by the Marshall Plan of which France, like Britain, was a beneficiary. However, unlike Britain, France was a founder member of the Common Market, which by the end of the 1950s brought greater rationality to continental production.

In 1950, secondary industries in France employed 35% of the workforce compared with 45% employed in Britain. By 1960, French industrial companies had increased their workforce by 190,000. Much of the growth came from manufacturing and construction since mining stocks were being depleted and public utilities were growing in line with the population. Whereas Britain experienced an explosion of demand for consumer goods in the second half of the decade the demand pattern in France was different. There was no explosion of growth and by the end of the decade ownership of consumer goods was at a much lower level than in Britain. At the end of the 1950s, 10% of French households owned a washing machine compared with 29% in Britain; 26% owned a television compared with 75% in Britain and 21% owned a car compared with 28% in Britain (Price, 1993: 292). The industrial growth increased domestic business demand into hotels, but the more limited growth in consumer durables produced less hotel demand from the French segment than from the British. In 1960 industrial travellers were concerned mainly with originating demand for their companies' products. Otus estimates that they generated more than half of the total French domestic business demand almost entirely transient.

Citizen services demand into hotels

The French organisation of welfare was different from Britain's. Whereas the British welfare system was managed by the central government, the French system was managed by the trade unions and employers. Contributions to the system were based on earnings and so were the benefits and as a result the system was more fragmented, often based around occupational groups. In addition to the expansion of social security and curative health care, the citizen services provision in France was extended in public housing, education and defence. At the end of the war, housing stock was old and lacked contemporary facilities just as it was in Britain, but at least in France most of the houses were still standing. In 1950, one third of households lacked running water (Price, 1993: 292). The government embarked on a spate of council house construction in some years building 400,000 new homes with modern facilities mainly in large suburban estates. Both of these developments paralleled the approach in Britain and had the same implication that although the material living conditions were improved, the renting rather than owning of the houses meant that the large majority of the French population, like their British counterparts, did not own an appreciating asset and had limited access to credit. Defence spending per capita in France was less than in Britain, but still high in comparison with other west European countries. In 1960, 4.5 million were employed in citizen services, up from 4.4 million in 1950. Otus estimates that the proportion of business travellers would have been smaller than in Britain and they would have spent fewer nights in hotels due to the heavily centralised digiriste system. In 1960, citizen services accounted for a quarter of total domestic business demand.

Service businesses demand into hotels

At the end of the War the service businesses were the smallest segment of the French economy in terms of employment and less diverse than in Britain and this was a further limitation on the volume and growth of domestic business demand into French hotels from the segment that typically generates the highest level of hotel demand. French banking and financial services were smaller than their British equivalents for three reasons. First, the French GDP in 1960 was one third smaller than the British. Second, the range of banking services available in France over the post-war period was narrower than in Britain because of the high level of nationalisation in French banking. Third, as was the case in Britain, few of the French had a bank account and they had less access to personal credit through schemes such as hire-purchase. More of the growth in French banking over the period came from business demand, which grew, but still remained smaller than its British equivalent. The retail business remained smaller and more fragmented than in Britain. At the end of the period there were significantly fewer households in France with a telephone than in Britain. Cinemas in France during the 1950s saw much less decline in attendance than in the US and Britain due to the lower level of television ownership. The restaurant and café business was almost totally fragmented. In 1960, 4 million were employed in service businesses, up from 3.8 million in 1950. Otus estimates that the proportion of business travellers from the segment would have been smaller than in Britain and they would have spent fewer nights in hotels due to the narrower range and smaller size of service businesses. Thus, in 1960 service businesses accounted for less than 20% of total domestic business demand.

Domestic leisure demand into hotels

Domestic holidays grew not only with the growth in paid annual leave, but also because in 1956 the annual average holiday entitlement was increased from two weeks to three weeks. Most of the summer holidays were taken in France and most holiday accommodation was informal in holiday camps, gîtes, homes and campsites rather than in hotels. Nonetheless, during the post-war period, domestic leisure demand into hotels grew and unlike Britain there was little seepage since only a minute proportion of the French took holidays abroad. Otus estimates that in 1950, domestic holiday demand accounted for 28% of French hotel demand falling to 27% in 1960 although the volume of demand rose from 5 million room nights to 7 million. There were over 8 million baby boomers born in France between 1945 and 1955, slightly more than in Britain and accounting for a higher proportion of the population. The increase in the birth rate accompanied by the acceleration of immigration from the colonies increased the population of France after 50 years of slow birth rate and high casualties in the two world wars. The baby boomers did not emerge as a distinctive generation during the 15 years after the war. Although they had greater access to health care, welfare and education than previous generations, the life experience of the French boomers was less different in other areas. Their experiences were a function of the lower levels of consumer products owned by the French as well as the smaller service business segment. There were fewer consumer products targeted on the boomers during the period and by 1960 they were barely a distinct market compared with the US or Britain. They experienced a narrower range of in-home entertainment and in particular they were less exposed to television programmes and advertisements dedicated to them. Apart from the annual holiday they had access to fewer organised our-of-home leisure activities.

Foreign demand into hotels

Foreign visitors to France were higher than in any other country. Otus estimates that in 1950, they spent 8.5 million room nights in French hotels and over the decade this demand grew to 12.5 million in 1960, double the number in British hotels. Mainly, this demand came from US and British holidaymakers, mostly during the summer months and they were accommodated mostly in hotels. Foreign business demand into hotels in 1950 was low, around only 4% of total demand, due to the low level of imports and the low level of investment by foreign companies in France, but benefited from demand from other EEC countries later in the period to close at 5% of total demand.

French hotel demand and supply performance

Otus estimates that in 1950, the volume and dynamics of hotel demand in France produced a supply ratio of 4.7 hotel rooms per 1,000 citizens compared with 6.1 in Britain and entailed a total hotel room stock in France of 195,000. During the 1950s there was a spate of hotel development in the country with the addition of 25,000 rooms driven mainly by foreign demand. At a constant 1950 supply ratio for the actual growth in population, France would have needed 215,000 rooms in 1960. Otus estimates that in 1960 room stock reached 220,000 producing secular growth of 5,000 rooms, but the supply ratio in 1960 of 4.8 still lagged the ratio of 6.3 achieved in Britain. Because most of the hotel construction during the 1950s was holiday related it was predominantly small, independently owned and highly seasonal. There were few significant hotel chains or hotel chain developments in France in the post-war period, which was little different from the pattern before the war. The chains that did exist were very short chains with little to differentiate their performance from unaffiliated hotels and the level of hotel concentration was lower than in the US and Britain. Otus estimates that the patterns of demand and supply over the period produced room occupancy of 25% in 1950 rising to 32% in 1960, still precarious, but the bulk of hoteliers lived in their hotel, which made it possible to endure poor performance. Thus, the French hotel business lagged its counterparts in the US and Britain on all fronts except in foreign holiday demand, but over the post-war period the economic ascent of the French hotel business was more noticeable than during the first half of the 20th century.

Table 7.6: French hotels 1950–1960

	Total Hotels 1950	Total Hotels 1960	CAGR % 1950 - 1960
Total rooms	195,000	220,000	1%
Room nights available m	71	81	1%
Room occupancy %	25%	32%	
Room nights sold m	18	26	4%
Domestic business room nights sold m	4	6	3%
Domestic leisure room nights sold m	5	7	3%
Foreign business room nights sold m	1	1	6%
Foreign leisure room nights sold m	8	11	4%
Concentration %	1%	2%	
Supply ratio	4.7	4.8	
Secular growth in hotel room supply	-15,000	5,000	

Source: Otus & Co Advisory Ltd

German economic structure, hotel demand and hotel supply

At the end of the World War II, German politics and its economy were more ravaged than in any other western European country as was its hotel business. For administrative purposes the country was divided into four sectors each controlled by one of the allied powers: Britain, France, the US and the USSR, whose initial economic plan was to restrict industrial production, but this resulted in hyperinflation, extensive black market operations, dysfunctional capital markets and shortages of food, clothes and industrial products. The problems came to a head in the severe winter of 1946/47 when shortages of coal produced cold homes and closed factories. The acute food shortages combined with the cold led to the death of many and the economy went into spasm. The Marshall Plan was extended to include Germany and it received $1.45 billion, but it was rejected by the USSR and in 1949 the Soviet zone became the communist controlled East Germany, the DDR, and the remainder of the country was established as West Germany, the Federal Republic of Germany, based on parliamentary democracy. Ludwig Erhard, the economy minister, was responsible for fixing the economic mess. This was a monumental task compared with the problems to be solved in Britain and France since the West German economy was not only in a much worse state, but also it had to rehabilitate itself politically from the Nazi period and to protect itself from the spread of communism from the east. Not surprisingly, Erhard's economic initiatives were different from those introduced into Britain and France. Politically, they succeeded in rehabilitating the country and in establishing West Germany as the buffer state against communism. In terms of economic recovery and growth the Erhard initiatives were miraculous. However, in terms of economic structure they anchored the balance of the West German economy in industrial activities and limited the development of service businesses.

The social market economy

Among the Erhard initiatives were the reconfirmation of private property rights, currency reforms were introduced to halt the hyperinflation and the Deutschmark was established in 1948. However, perhaps the most memorable of the Erhard initiatives was the introduction of the social market economy, which involved government intervention to maintain a balance between high economic growth, low inflation, low levels of unemployment, the extent of public services and social welfare provision. The social market economy was the framework that brought together the government, employers and trade unions in decision-making at a national level about matters such as wage rates, employment conditions, tax rates and price levels. Each company was required to have a supervisory board, which included trade union members. Three outcomes were that high employment security was introduced as the norm, extensive vocational training was made available and close relations between banks and industry became a standard. All of these initiatives together produced an exceptional turnaround in the economy. By 1951, pre-war levels of GDP were achieved and mostly with civilian production. Then, throughout the 1950s GDP grew at an average rate of more than 8% and reduced the unemployment rate from more than 10% to less than 3% (Glatzer , 1992: 145).

The emphasis in West Germany on growing industrial activities in the post-war period meant that the four factors necessary for the structural balance of an economy to make the transition to service businesses were constrained. Progress was made in the first factor, the growth in human and civil rights, in which West Germany achieved rehabilitation from its Nazi ideology. The West German civil code gave husbands the right to make final decisions in all areas of family life until 1959 and German husbands retained the right to contest a wife's decision to work outside of the home until 1965 (Loehlin, 1999). There was little progress with the second factor since there was little expansion in the teaching of the social sciences in universities. The main focus was on subjects from the natural and physical sciences and engineering that were required to provide pro-fessional employees to the burgeoning industrial activities. The third factor saw little progress either. There was a low level of ownership of appreciating assets and access to personal credit was very low. The fourth factor, personal travel made some progress, but the low levels of car ownership limited the volume and frequency of personal travel. Otus estimates that in 1950 West German hotels sold 15 million room nights of which 33% were from domestic business travel-lers, 59% from domestic leisure travellers and 8% from inbound foreign travel-lers. By 1960, demand grew to 22 million room nights of which 11% was from foreign travellers, 52% from domestic leisure demand and 37% from domestic business travellers. The pattern of segment employment over the 1950s was as shown in Figures 7.7 and 7.8.

Table 7.7: Employment by Segment in Germany: 1950–1960 (m)

	Agriculture	Industry	Citizen Services	Service Businesses	Total
1950	4.9	8.9	3.5	3.3	20.6
1960	3.8	12.1	4.6	5.0	25.5

Table 7.8: Employment by Segment in Germany: 1950–1960 %

	Agriculture	Industry	Citizen Services	Service Businesses	Total
1950	24%	43%	17%	16%	100%
1960	15%	47%	18%	20%	100%

Source: Groningen Growth Centre

Agriculture demand into hotels

After the war, there were 1.6 million farms most of which were small family concerns that were unable to operate effectively because of the economic spasm. Rationing throughout the country limited consumption to around 1,000 calo-ries per day, which was sustainable only in the short-term. The Erhard initia-tives turned agricultural production around dramatically enough for rationing to be ended in January 1950, five years before Britain. By 1960, agricultural employment was reduced with the loss of 1.1 million jobs and its share of the workforce declined to 15%, lower than France, but still well ahead of the 5% in Britain. But it acted as a drag on domestic business demand into hotels since agriculture generates the lowest domestic business demand of any segment into hotels. Otus estimates that in 1960 agricultural travellers were concerned with originating demand and generated 6% of the total German domestic business demand almost entirely transient rooms demand, down from 8% in 1950 as other segments developed more effectively.

Industrial demand into hotels

Notable among the post-war Erhard initiatives was the absence of a programme of industrial nationalisation of the type introduced by Britain and France. The opposition to nationalisation was reinforced after the creation of communist East Germany when West Germany established itself as a beacon of very successful market economic practice and East Germany languished along with the other communist states. Over the 1950s, secondary industries were the dominant segment of the economy and grew from 43% to 47% of the workforce. In 1950, West Germany accounted for 7% of world trade and by 1960 its share had risen to 20% (Mitchell, 1998). However, the West German success in exports was not matcvhed in domestic consumer durables markets, in which it lagged Britain and France. The lower level of ownership of consumer durables compared with the other major economies meant that a higher proportion of the industrial segment was involved in business-to-business activities that requires less business travel and hotel use than business to consumer activities. This was another factor in the lower volume and slower growth of domestic business demand into hotels generated by the German secondary industries. Otus estimates that in 1960 industrial travellers were concerned with originating demand and generated 61% of the total German domestic business demand almost entirely transient rooms demand, down from 65% in 1950.

Citizen services demand into hotels

An element of the Erhard initiatives was the extension of social welfare, which had existed in more limited forms in Germany since 1883. Like the French model, but unlike the British approach, benefits were earnings related and based on both employer and employee statutory contributions. Thus, expenditure on welfare and its growth was related to performance of the economy. Other elements of the West German post-war welfare system that differentiated it from Britain were that it was decentralised to the states, the Lander. Private, not-for-profit insurance funds managed the system and the involvement of the federal government was limited to regulatory control. Otus estimates that in 1960, citizen service travellers were concerned with management of the segment and generated 16% of the total German domestic business demand almost entirely transient rooms demand, up from 12% in 1950.

Service businesses demand into hotels

The pattern of ownership of consumer durables, which was a function of the low access to personal credit, also limited the size and growth of retailing over the period. The lower ownership of consumer durables meant less shopping. The low level of television ownership was accompanied by a very low level of television advertising and low stimulation of demand for consumer goods, which meant that the level of in-home entertainment was also lower than in Britain and France. Similar to Britain and France, few individuals had bank accounts, few owned appreciating assets and predominantly, wages were paid in cash. Consistent with its explicit commitment to the free market the government dismantled the three largest banks in the early 1950s and restricted them to regional coverage, in much the same way as the state-owned savings banks. Much of the business of West German banks in the 1950s was in the corporate market and with the re-emergence of the Mittelstand, the small and medium sized businesses, at that time the relationship between the regional banks and the local businesses was deeper, stronger and more enduring than in other countries.

Domestic leisure demand into hotels

Domestic leisure demand into German hotels was absent in 1945 and did not re-emerge in any measurable way until the 1950s as the population rebuilt its life. West Germans in full-time employment received holiday pay and most holidays were taken within the country during the summer months. Most were at inland resorts because there is only a short coastline on the Baltic. Camping and self-catering predominated and hotels were a minor feature of the domestic leisure market. Resort hotels were heavily seasonal, small, independently owned and operated, and performed poorly. Between 1945 and 1955 there were around 6 million births, the lowest number among the larger economies of Europe and the US. The economic context in which this generation was raised did not facilitate the development of a distinctive generation. Their life experiences were different from those in the US and Britain and they had less exposure to in-home entertainment or to the range of out-of home experiences. They were not seen as a distinctive market due to the lower levels of advertising and of the constrained market service and experience segments of the economy.

Foreign demand into hotels

Foreign demand into hotels in West Germany in the post-war period was at first dominated by the allied powers – the US, Britain and France, but this declined as West Germany became established. Thereafter, inbound foreign business demand grew as the export policy began to pay off. And in the last years of the period it was boosted by the reduction of trade barriers among EEC members. By 1960, it rose to 7% of total rooms demand and accounted for 1.6 million room nights. Foreign leisure demand into West German hotels in 1960 was less than one million and of only marginal significance as is invariably the case in economies with large secondary industries and mediocre summer weather. Holidaymakers do not travel to foreign countries to look at factories.

German hotel demand and supply performance

There was a higher proportion of urban room stock in Germany lost to bombing during the war than in any other country and business failures eliminated more hotels in the aftermath. Otus estimates that hotel room stock in West Germany amounted to 210,000 in 1950, a ratio of 4.2 hotel rooms per 1,000 West German citizens, lower than the 6.1 ratio in Britain and 4.7 in France. During the 1950s there was construction of new hotels in West Germany as the economy began its remarkable recovery so that by 1960, room stock had risen to 235,000, but the supply ratio remained unchanged as new room stock tracked the growth in population. Germany had very little history of hotel chain development and the few chains which did operate were very short. During the 1950s, Steigenberger, the largest chain, reopened the Frankfurter Hof which was bombed during the war and added another seven hotels. The demand and supply profiles produced unsustainably low total room occupancy of 20% in 1950. It rose to 26% in 1960, but this was still unsustainable without significant growth in demand or reduction in supply. The post-war recovery in the German hotel business was marginal compared with the economy as a whole because the segments that propelled economic growth were low yielding for the hotel business.

Table 7.9: German hotels 1950–1960

	Total Hotels 1950	Total Hotels 1960	CAGR % 1950 - 1960
Total rooms	210,000	235,000	1%
Room nights available (m)	77	86	1%
Room occupancy %	20%	26%	
Room nights sold (m)	15	22	4%
Domestic business	5	8	5%
Domestic leisure	9	12	3%
Foreign business	1	2	7%
Foreign leisure	0	1	7%
Supply ratio	4.2	4.2	

Source: Otus & Co Advisory Ltd

Hotel demand and supply in other European countries: 1945–1960

In the other continental countries, hotel demand was lower than in Britain and there were three distinct patterns. First, the pattern of recovery in the western Mediterranean countries: Spain, Italy, Greece and Portugal were broadly similar to that in France. Foreign gallivanters grew progressively and at a faster rate than domestic demand. Second, the pattern in the north European social market economies: the Benelux and the Nordic region, reflected that in West Germany in which there were low levels of foreign demand and most recovery relied on domestic demand, which was slow because the structural balance of the economies was in the industrial segment. Third, the depressed hotel demand in the USSR continued and the demand in the enlarged Soviet empire after World War II took on the depressed pattern of the USSR. Hotel demand was minor relative to the population and demand from outside of the Soviet empire was microscopic due to the severe controls imposed by the Soviet governments.

As the hotel demand patterns in the western Mediterranean countries reflected the pattern in France, so also did their supply pattern. Supply developments were focused heavily in summer resorts attracting northern European holidaymakers. The pattern during the post-war period was of small hotels owned and operated by local independent hoteliers with demand concentrated in the summer months. However, the rate of construction of new urban hotels was lower than in France since their economic structures were less developed. Similarly, as the pattern of hotel demand in northern European countries reflected the pattern in West Germany, so also did their hotel supply pattern. The Soviet empire produced little hotel development over the period since they had little need for hotels.

All references to employment in this chapter were drawn from the Groningen Growth and Development Centre of the University of Groningen, Netherlands.

8 The US Economic Structure and Hotel Business: 1960–1980

Introduction

The 1960s started with the idealism of President Kennedy (JFK) about the role of the US as the global champion of freedom, which translated into initiatives to limit the spread of communism. This in turn was manifest in the arms race, the space race and the Vietnam War, which in economic terms boosted the otherwise slowing industrial segment of the economy. The 1960s were also characterised by the Great Society reforms of President Johnson (LBJ) in response to the injustices highlighted by the Civil Rights Movement, which boosted the citizen services segment of the economy. In spite of these two emblematic developments of the 1960s, service businesses continued to grow in size and diversity as both corporates and consumers demanded more.

Economically, the 1970s were different for the US marked as they were by poor economic performance in 1970, 1974 and 1975. The international oil crisis hit the US hard. In 1970 it imported around one third of its oil at about $1.50 per barrel, by 1977 it was importing half of its oil at $32 a barrel (Evans, 1998:604) The international oil crisis contributed to the economic downturns and recession, but so also did the hangover from the cost of the Vietnam War, the space race, the arms race and the extension to citizen services required by the civil rights legislation. Incomes fell as the economy tightened. Unemployment rose, interest rates hit 20% and inflation moved sharply upwards. The 1970s were also different politically. The disgrace of Watergate, President Nixon's enforced resignation and the US failure in the Vietnam War set a gloomy political tone to sit beside the poor economic performance. Then there was the introspection of the Ford and Carter presidencies as they sought to recover some confidence and dignity in the US. In spite of these setbacks the structural development of the US economy continued over the 1970s. Notably, the two-decade period marked the entry of the baby boomers to adulthood and their establishment as an independent market. The civil rights legislation empowered black Americans to be participants in economic prosperity and other movements such as Women's Liberation and Gay Liberation created more independent markets for service businesses.

The progress in the structural balance of the economy over the 1960s grew domestic demand into US hotels. Although the economic performance of the 1970s was poorer than in the 1960s, citizen services and service businesses continued to expand and hotel demand benefited from secular growth from the baby boomers, black Americans, women and gays. The demand growth generated hotel supply growth and in particular the pace of expansion of hotel chains accelerated, adding 740,000 rooms over the period, an average annual growth of more than 6%. Thus, the period from 1960 to 1980 saw further economic ascent of the US hotel business.

US economic structure and hotel demand

At the start of the period, the US was achieving strong momentum in three of the four factors that produce the necessary conditions for service businesses to grow, but was out of step on the fourth. The social sciences in the US were more developed than in any other country. During the period, more social scientific research was undertaken than elsewhere and most of universities offered courses in pure and applied social sciences. The personal capital markets were also well developed. A higher proportion of US households than any other country owned their own homes. The US personal credit markets, with greater diversity and greater volume, were also more developed than elsewhere. Similarly, personal travel was more developed than elsewhere. There was more car ownership. The nationwide inter-state highway building programme continued throughout the 1960s and 1970s, while the airline business was expanding fast.

Civil rights

The one factor that held back the rate of structural development of the US economy was the unacceptably poor state of civil and human rights. In the early 1960s, after a century of freedom from slavery, black Americans in the US numbered 19 million and accounted for 10.5% of the population *(source*: US Census Bureau). However, they were still an underclass, denied rights that were commonplace among white Americans, particularly in the southern states. In the south, 10 million black Americans accounted for 21% of the population and endured the greatest explicit racism *(source*: US Census Bureau). Evans notes that on average:

> Investment in white school plant was four times higher, white teachers' salaries 30% higher... Segregating states spent $86 million on white colleges, five million on black ones. There was one accredited medical school for blacks, 29 for whites; one accredited black school for pharmacology, 40 for whites; one law school for blacks, 40 for whites. There was no engineering school for blacks, 36 for whites.

> (Evans, 1998: 459)

Discrimination also prevailed in other citizen services such as health, welfare and housing. Blacks accounted for much of the unemployment and the highest proportion of prison inmates. It was common for blacks not to vote and physical abuse was common when they did try. During the 100-year period from the abolition of slavery, racial segregation in social, cultural, political and economic life in the South was regarded by white supremacists as a natural state of affairs and the most extremist among them used clandestine associations such as the Klu Klux Klan to maintain and reinforce the racist and economic status quo irrespective of the illegality of the activities in which they engaged.

The economy of the South performed much worse than the economy of the North. It had consistently higher levels of unemployment, lower earnings, lower spending and lower growth rates. It was also structurally less developed, relying more heavily on agriculture and basic manufacturing than the North and it had fewer and less diverse service businesses. The civil rights gap between blacks and whites meant that blacks were excluded as a market for most goods and services available in the US. Their higher levels of poverty, poorer education, lower job security and lower career development were accompanied by extremely low levels of ownership of appreciating assets and extremely low access to credit. Primitive human and civil rights were the main impediments to the performance and the structural development of the economy of the southern states and this maintained a poverty gap not only between the blacks and whites of the South, but also between the segregated South and the less segregated and more structurally developed economy of the North. However, the groundswell of opposition to racial segregation among blacks and increasing numbers of more liberal northern whites gained momentum during the late 1950s and the early 1960s when the Civil Rights Movement became a national force as did its figurehead the Reverend Dr. Martin Luther King. The approach of the movement was the non-violent, public display of the injustice and moral degradation of racial segregation most memorably expressed in Martin Luther King's speech in Washington DC in August 1963:

> I have a dream that on the red hills of Georgia the sons of former slaves and the sons of former slave owners will be able to sit down together at the table of brotherhood. I have a dream that one day even the state of Mississippi, a state sweltering with the heat of injustice, sweltering with the heat of oppression, will be transformed into an oasis of freedom and justice. I have a dream that my four little children will one day live in a nation where they will not be judged by the colour of their skin but by the content of their character.

Thus, the Civil Rights Movement was brought to the centre stage of domestic politics. From the mid-1960s civil and human rights legislation, The Great Society reforms introduced by LBJ, changed the lives of Americans and provided a tangible and lasting boost to the economy. Improving citizen services, job security and career development enabled black Americans to participate in economic growth and as a result the performance and structure gap between the North and the South began to narrow.

Among the Great Society legislation introduced by LBJ to improve citizen services, three of the most significant were:

♦ The Civil Rights Act, 1964, which banned racial discrimination including discrimination in "public accommodations" such as hotels.

♦ The Voting Rights Act, 1965, which outlawed literacy tests as a qualification for registering to vote. The tests were used throughout much of the South to disqualify blacks from registering and their abolition enabled black Americans to have a greater influence on elections in the South.

♦ The Fair Housing Act, 1968, which outlawed discrimination on race, colour, religion or national origin in the rental or purchase of homes.

Once black Americans had won equitable civil rights and gained jobs, they became a market for consumer goods. The moral power of the civil rights movement translated into economic progress and was accompanied during the period by other mass movements that changed the civil and human rights landscape in the US. The Peace Movement was the groundswell that was influential in driving the Nixon administration to withdraw from Vietnam. The Women's Liberation Movement accelerated the closure of the gender gap in careers, in social activities and in economic value. Gay Liberation established that discrimination against gays and lesbians was socially, culturally, politically and economically unjust and unworkable. The economic momentum that stemmed from the extension of civil and human rights created secular growth in both domestic business and leisure demand into hotels. Otus estimates that over the two decades to 1980, domestic hotel room nights sold raced to 370 million, an average annual growth of 3%. Each of the main source markets grew during the period. Domestic business demand added 69 million room nights and domestic leisure added 82 million, foreign business demand increased by 24 million room nights and foreign leisure demand by 25 million.

The development in the pattern of employment in the economic segments over the period was as shown in Tables 8.1 and 8.2.

Table 8.1: Employment by segment in US: 1960 –1980 (millions)

	Agriculture	Industry	Citizen Services	Service Businesses	Total
1960	5.0	19.0	11.0	24.0	59.0
1970	4.0	22.0	17.0	32.0	75.0
1980	4.0	24.0	23.0	43.0	94.0

Table 8.2: Employment by segment in US: 1950–1960 (percentage)

	Agriculture	Industry	Citizen Services	Service Businesses	Total
1960	8%	32%	17%	40%	100%
1970	5%	30%	19%	42%	100%
1980	4%	26%	25%	45%	100%

Source: US Departmentof Labour

Agricultural demand into hotels

The patterns in the economic development of agriculture established in the previous decades of the 20th century – reduction in employment, growth in mecha-
nisation, growth in concentration, growth in output and growth in productivity
– continued between 1960 and 1980. In 1960, US agriculture employed 5 million, 8% of the workforce. Otus estimates that at the start of the period, 2.8%
of agricultural employees were business travellers who spent an average of 13
nights in US hotels generating mainly transient demand of 1.8 million room
nights and accounting for 2% of all domestic business demand. The 1960s was
the first decade that started with mechanised tractors outnumbering workhorses
on the 4 million farms in the US *(source:* W.J. White, The Economic History of
Tractors in the US, EH.net) and 20% of US grain was exported. Over the period,
employment in agriculture fell by 1% per year on average, causing a reduction
of one million jobs. By 1980, only 4% of the US workforce was employed in agriculture. The number of farms was reduced to 2.5 million as a result of mergers
and acquisitions *(source:* B. Gardner, University of Maryland, US Agriculture in
the 20th Century, EH.net). This bout of concentration produced an increase in
the proportion of white-collar and professional jobs in larger agricultural firms
that were producing higher output to feed the growing population. The period
was characterised by an increase in agricultural exports, which rose to one third
by 1980 as improving productivity made the US competitive in the international
markets, but it did little for the generation of additional domestic hotel demand.
There was also an increase in the number of conferences attended by employees from the segment. Otus estimates that by 1980, the changes in agriculture
produced a marginal increase in the proportion of agricultural employees who
were business travellers, up to 3%, a total of 120,000, originating demand and
beginning to attend conferences. They spent an average of 15 nights in US hotels
generating both transient rooms demand and increasingly packaged conference
demand of 1.7 million room nights, down a tad over the period and its share of
domestic demand fell to 1%, because the other sectors grew at a faster rate.

Industrial demand into hotels

In 1960, industrial companies in the US employed 19.2 million, 32% of the
workforce. Otus estimates that 4.4%, 850,000 of industrial employees were
business travellers originating demand, attending industry-wide conferences and
involved in company management. They spent an average of 28 nights in US hotels generating both transient rooms demand and packaged conference demand
of 24 million room nights, 32% of all domestic business demand. Four trends
in industrial activities over the period were important for hotel demand. First,
the growing population, with its rising demand for consumer goods produced
the growth in industrial employment to 24 million in 1980, but the segment
share of employment fell from 32% to 26% as citizen services and service businesses grew at a faster rate. Second, the ongoing trends in consolidation and
increases in productivity produced larger industrial companies with larger corporate structures and this was positive for the growth in industrially generated
hotel demand for rooms and for industry-wide conferences, conventions and

exhibitions. Third, the escalating cost of the Vietnam War, the arms race and the space race diverted manufacturing capacity to military production. The six moon landings cost around $25 billion (Evans, 1998: 555). Vietnam was the longest war in US history, lasting for 10 years to 1975 and estimated to have cost $125 billion (p. 522). The escalation of war production paralleled the arms race and the space race and also boosted employment in secondary industries at a time when the economy was moving naturally towards service businesses. An implication of this development was that it required fewer sales and marketing executives in the manufacturing companies involved since there was only one customer in the US, the government. Consequently, the proportion of employees who were business travellers and the number of nights military manufacturers spent in hotels was lower than for consumer goods manufacturers.

The fourth trend in the industrial segment that had implications for domestic business demand into hotels was the rise in imports. The diversion of manufacturing to military production opened the way to the import of consumer and other civilian goods to the US. Many consumer goods such as cameras, televisions and automobiles as well as heavy machinery and machine tools bought by Americans were increasingly manufactured in Japan, Germany and other industrial economies due to the higher quality and competitive prices compared with US manufactured goods. The trend to foreign goods became significant during the 1970s and further limited the rate of growth in domestic business demand into hotels from the industrial segment. Otus estimates that by 1980, the proportion of industrial employees who were business travellers, attending conferences and involved in company management, fell to 4% although the number of business travellers increased by 100,000 and they spent an average of 28 nights in US hotels generating both transient rooms demand and packaged conference demand of 27 million room nights, The industrial segment's share of all domestic business demand declined to 19% as it passed its peak of significance for the hotel business while the shares of citizen services and service businesses grew faster.

Citizen services demand into hotels

In 1960, there were 11.4 million citizen services employees. Otus estimates that 11.5% of them were business travellers involved in segment management and attending conferences who spent an average of 11 nights in US hotels generating both transient rooms demand and packaged conference demand of 14 million room nights and accounting for 19% of all domestic business demand. Employment in citizen services grew by an average of 2.8% per year more than double the rate of population growth adding 18 million jobs. By 1980, citizen services employed 23.4 million amounting to 25% of the US workforce. Early in his presidency LBJ bombarded the Congress with Great Society proposals. 'Through the first 10 months of 1964 an awesome 90 of his 115 legislative recommendations were signed into law' (Evans, 1998:: 516). The initiatives increased citizen services such as education, public housing, health care, urban renewal and legal aid. They increased the minimum wage and extended the distribution of food stamps and job training largely targeted at improving the lives of the poor and meant a significant improvement in the lives of black Americans. LBJ's expansion of Medicare and Medicaid was a major improvement to the health care of the old and the poor. During LBJ's Great Society initiative, citizen services spending increased from $67 billion in 1964 to $127 billion in 1968 (Evans, 1998: 516) and during the remainder of the period, the level of expenditure on citizen services grew as the provision of services was at least maintained. Hotel demand from citizen services was not uniform across the range of services. There were two camps. First, education and health were not only among the largest of the citizen services, but also generated the most hotel demand from two sources, professional employees – academics and medics, who travelled mostly to conferences and administrative executives who travelled as part of their jobs of managing the segment. In contrast, in other citizen services the dominant hotel demand was from administrative executives, since the volume of professional employees was much lower than in health and education. Otus estimates that by the end of the period in 1980, the proportion of employees who were business travellers, both in segment management and conference attendance increased to 12.5% and as the number of citizen service employees had grown, the number of business travellers rose to 2.9 million, up from 1.3 million at the start of the period. They spent an average of 12 nights in hotels to generate transient rooms demand and packaged conference demand of 35 million room nights to achieve a 25% share of domestic business demand.

Service businesses demand into hotels

The momentum of growth in service businesses during the post-war period continued between 1960 and 1980. In 1960, service businesses employed 23.7 million, 40% of the workforce. Otus estimates that 6%, 1.4 million of the segment employees, were business travellers involved in originating demand, executing contracts and servicing clients as well as attending conferences and travelling in the course of managing the company. They spent an average of 24 nights in US hotels generating transient rooms demand and packaged conference demand of 34 million room nights for a 46% share of domestic business demand. Over the period, the growth in the range of service businesses and in their size was beneficial for the hotel business. Employment in professional services grew by an average of 3.6% per year adding 3.9 million jobs to exceed 6% of the US workforce by 1980. By 1980, US service businesses employment grew to 42.8 million. Otus estimates that 7.4%, 3.2 million of the segment employees, were business travellers originating demand, executing contracts and servicing clients as well as attending conferences and travelling in the course of managing their companies. They spent an average of 25 nights in US hotels generating transient rooms demand and industry-wide conference demand as well as in the emerging trends of company specific conferences and conferences hosted by single companies for their clients. Thus, by the end of the period packaged conference demand from the segment had grown materially and with the transient rooms demand they generated 79 million room nights to achieve a 55% share of total domestic business demand and cement the segment's position as the most important for domestic business demand into US hotels.

The conference market

The movement in the structural balance of the economy towards service businesses and the expansion of service businesses nationally produced significant growth in conferences and meetings in hotels. First, industry-wide conventions and exhibitions that involved companies from across a sector with their clients and customers, expanded. Often, such events were annual occurrences that attracted progressively more attendees from across the country. They became showcase events for manufacturers, forums for professionals to keep up with developments in their fields and even organised gatherings of people involved in leisure activities.

However, the main development in the conference market during the two-decade period was the growth in company-specific conferences that involved employees from one company meeting to conduct business of the firm. The conferences included strategy meetings, training courses, sales promotion meetings and motivational sessions among others. They emerged more strongly among service businesses, they occurred more frequently than the industry-wide events and they were smaller. The most frequent hotel conferences were booked by expanding companies that had not yet acquired regional offices with their own conference and meeting space. The growth in conference demand impacted on hotels, on their management and on the relationship between hotels and their customers.

♦ First, conference hotels were larger than traditional hotels in order to accommodate the volume of conference demand. During the period there was a spate of large, up-market convention hotels constructed in major cities. Hilton, Sheraton and Marriott were at the forefront of this development in cities such as New York, Washington DC, Boston, Philadelphia and Atlanta.

♦ Second, conference hotels were more complex since they involved new activities for business customers in addition to the traditional hotel activities of sleeping, eating and drinking. For convention customers the hotel became their place of living and of work for the duration of the event.

♦ Third, conference hotels were more complex to manage since they involved the organisation of business events in addition to the standard hotel activities of organising for customers to sleep, eat and drink.

♦ Fourth, the development in mass conference demand changed the relationship between hotels and their business customers. Traditionally, hotel customers selected hotels at which they would stay in any location based on personal preferences related to the specific provision of facilities to sleep, eat and drink as well as the style and image of the hotel and the availability of rooms. The growth of the conference market entailed a shift in hotel selection criteria from personal preferences of transient customers to the corporate criteria of the businesses holding conferences and requiring the attendance of employees at the selected hotels to conduct business for which the corporation paid the bill. Thus, conference customers were sent to hotels rather than chose to go and this introduced a different dimension to the relationship between the hotel and its customers.

The conference market also enlarged the proportion of business customers who bought hotel packages that included not only the room and the meal, but also the price for the conference itself. Conference packages were discounted because of the large volumes of demand paying to use a wide range of hotel facilities – bedrooms, restaurants, conference rooms and bars – and they proved to be an efficient and lucrative market for hotels.

Domestic leisure demand into hotels

Otus estimates that between 1960 and 1980, domestic leisure demand retained its position as the largest hotel market in the US. In 1960, it amounted to 146 million room nights for a 59% share of all hotel room nights sold. As the citizen services and service business segments grew at faster rates than the other segments of the economy so the proportion of white-collar and professional employees grew at a faster rate than blue-collar and shop floor workers. Not only did this boost the volume of domestic business demand for hotels, but also boosted the volume of domestic leisure demand into hotels. Most US citizens took their vacations in the US and the growth was due to growth in the volume of traditional longer summer vacations as well as growth in the volume of short vacations of less than four nights. Domestic long vacation demand remained the largest market for unaffiliated hotels in resort locations, but the growth in weekend business was skewed more towards hotel chains and in cities. Leisure packages into hotels had become a tradition in earlier periods and continued during the two decades to 1980. The proportion of air and train travel for hotel customers increased, but automobile travel still remained strong. Just as convention hotels emerged strongly during the period in response to business customer demand, so hotel resorts grew to capture both conference and leisure customers. Hotels with extensive non-room facilities including restaurants and bars, but also retailing, theatres and both indoor and outdoor leisure facilities grew. Hotels in Las Vegas expanded to include not only casinos in addition to the traditional hotel facilities, but also an increasing range of other facilities, services and products designed to attract leisure customers. It was not only in Las Vegas that hotel resorts emerged. In 1968, Marriott acquired the Camelback Inn in Scottsdale, Arizona and Sheraton opened, among other hotel resorts, the Tucson El Conquistador Golf and Tennis Resort in Arizona. These hotels were large and included extensive indoor and outdoor leisure facilities often involving golf courses. By 1980, domestic leisure demand had grown to 228 million room nights, but its share had fallen to 51% as business demand grew at a faster rate.

Black Americans and baby boomers

During the 1970s, two new sources of hotel leisure demand emerged: black Americans and baby boomers. Historically, domestic leisure demand involved few black Americans staying in hotels, which in the south in the early 1960s were still segregated. Black American families on vacation in US hotels increased from a very low level over the period as educational attainment increased as did employment in white-collar and professional careers.

Second, baby boomers emerged as a leisure market for hotels as they pursued their careers. By the early1960s the baby boomer phase at universities had begun and by the end of the period in 1980 the boomer stage at universities had passed. This was a new period of mass college education of a generation that had grown up with widespread access to consumer goods and experiences targeted to them. It would prove to be like no other previous generation of students. During the 1960s and 1970s in the US, boomers were heavily involved in the mass movements of the day and demonstrations on university campuses became commonplace. As the 1970s progressed and the aims of the mass movements had been achieved the fashion of demonstrating declined. In parallel with campus demonstrations were the boomer lifestyle emblems of the period – the clothes, the hair and for many the living away from home in academic communities. The amalgam of all of the icons of student life and more were the hippies, a tiny, but visible and frequently reported minority of the student boomers who emerged sometimes to live in separate communes to illustrate the extent to which they had moved away from and rejected the conventional lifestyle of Middle America. Most of the student boomers graduated in the 1970s and sought challenging, white-collar careers. Most entered careers in service businesses and citizen services, because that was where most of the professional and white-collar careers were located. Fewer joined industrial companies where there was a narrower range of white-collar careers. Most graduating boomers were not attracted to military production and agriculture attracted fewest graduating boomers.

The experience of boomers as consumers was closely tied to brands and the emergence of boomers as hotel customers during the 1970s coincided with the strong growth in hotel brands. Customers with the life experiences, expectations and culture of the boomers were a new phenomenon for hotels. They entered the professional career market from the late 1960s and progressively became more regular hotel users both for business and leisure. As the frequency of their hotel use increased and the reasons for their use of hotels diversified so also did the diversity of their specific demand in hotels that changed the relationship between hotel customers and hotel employees. The historic social distance between hotel customers and employees, which defined the role of hotel workers as servants, began to fracture as increasing proportions of the population became hotel customers and the advances in human and civil rights created the objective context for more equitable relationships. The traditional role of the hotel employee taking orders from customers who were from a superior social class was changing. During the period, hotel employees began to be trained to act as salesmen actively persuading customers to buy more of the hotel facilities, services and products, a position that was attractive to hotel brands and improved the performance of branded hotels.

Foreign demand into hotels

Foreign visitor demand into the US also grew strongly over the period, but it was still the smallest source of demand. In 1960, 27 million room nights, 11% of hotel demand in the US was from foreign visitors. By 1980, the volume had increased to 76 million room nights and the share of the market increased to

17%. The two-decade period marked the completion of the transition from ocean liners as the main means of cross-Atlantic travel to air lines. The growth in capacity and speed as well in the reduction in fares of cross-Atlantic and cross-Pacific travel were the main factors in the growth in long-haul foreign leisure demand into the US. Short-haul demand from Canada and Mexico also grew. The growth in imports of consumer goods increased the volume of foreign business travellers as did the growth in the expansion of foreign companies, mostly manufacturers, in the US.

Hotel supply in the US

Otus estimates that in 1960 there were 1.5 million hotel rooms in the US producing a hotel supply ratio of 8.3. At a constant 1960 supply ratio and with the recorded increase in population, the US would have needed 2 million hotel rooms in 1980. However, Otus estimates that total US room stock climbed to 2.3 million generating secular growth of 300,000 rooms and a supply ratio of 10.1. The main hotel supply development over the period was the dramatic growth of hotel chains, which added 740,000 rooms, an annual average growth rate of 6% to reach 1,050,000. Unaffiliated hotels added only 60,000 rooms over the period to achieve only marginal growth. Listed in Table 8.3 are the 10 key hotel brands that operated throughout the period when they added 624,000 rooms accounting for 84% of all chain growth, emerging as the dominant force in the US hotel business.

Table 8.3: US Chain Rooms

	Market Level	1960	1970	CAGR % 1970/1960	1980	CAGR % 1980/1970
Hilton	Up-market	15,000	46,500	12.0%	71,800	4.4%
Hyatt	Up-market	1,000	10,800	26.9%	34,000	12.2%
Marriott	Up-market	1,300	7,600	19.3%	33,800	16.1%
Sheraton	Up-market	15,000	59,600	14.8%	108,000	6.1%
Westin	Up-market	5,000	20,000	14.9%	28,800	3.7%
Holiday Inn	Mid-market	100,000	182,500	6.2%	303,600	5.2%
Howard Johnson	Mid-market	17,500	39,500	8.5%	59,000	4.1%
Quality	Mid-market	17,000	30,700	6.1%	41,400	3.0%
Ramada	Mid-market	4,000	35,600	24.4%	94,100	10.2%
Travelodge	Economy	7,500	26,000	13.2%	32,000	2.1%
Total Rooms		183,300	458,800	9.6%	806,500	5.8%

All rooms estimates rounded to nearest 100

Source: 1970, 1980 Service World International; 1960 Otus estimates

Other chains that grew during the period included at the up-market level: Loews Hotels and Stouffer Hotels; at the mid-market level: Americana Hotels; at the economy level: Days Inns, Econolodge, Motel 6, Rodeway Inns and Super 8. The main departure from previous periods was that portfolio growth was mainly by new-build hotels, which enabled adherence to the specifications of each brand and for the first time most new hotels in the US were branded.

Hotel configurations

As well as differentiating brands in terms of market level, they also need to be differentiated in terms of hotel configuration, which refers to the provision of non-room facilities. It is a supply variable that operates independently from market level and there are five types of hotel configuration as Table 8.4 illustrates.

Table 8.4: Hotel Configuration Structure

Non-room facilities	Hotel resort	Full feature hotel	Basic feature hotel	Limited feature hotel	Rooms only hotel
Restaurants (min.)	1	1	1	1	0
Bars (min.)	1	1	1	optional	0
Conference rooms (min.)	1	1	optional	optional	0
Indoor health and fitness (min.)	1	either	optional	optional	0
Outdoor health and fitness (min.)	1	or	optional	optional	0
Retail outlets	optional	optional	0	0	0
Casino and other facilities	optional	0	0	0	0
Minimum number of non-rooms facilities	**5**	**4**	**2**	**1**	**0**

Source: Otus & Co Advisory Ltd

The MGM Grand, Las Vegas is an example of a modern hotel resort and is among the most complex of hotels not only because it has more than 5,000 rooms, but because of its configuration. It provides eight restaurants, seven bars, seven nightclubs, indoor and outdoor health and fitness facilities, a range of retail outlets, almost 900,000 square feet of conference and meetings space and an events facility that accommodates 16,800 people. It also has three theatres, 170,000 square feet of casino and employs almost 9,500 people. For a hotel to be a hotel resort it must have at least five of the facilities listed in the table – at least one restaurant, at least one bar, at least one conference room, indoor leisure facilities such as a health and fitness club and outdoor leisure facilities such as golf, tennis, swimming or other health and fitness facilities. Retail outlets and a casino are optional as are any other additional facilities such as nightclub, theatre or art gallery. The higher the market level of the facilities and services in hotel resorts, the wider the range of products sold in their restaurants, bars and retail outlets and the greatest number of employees.

Full-feature hotels such as most Hiltons and many modern Holiday Inns have at least four of the non-room facilities including at least one restaurant, at least one bar and at least one conference room and it must also have either an indoor or outdoor health and fitness facility. The largest full-feature hotels may include retail outlets, but other facilities are rare. The higher the market level of the facilities and services in full-feature hotels, the wider the range of products sold in the restaurants and bars requiring a significant number of employees.

Basic feature hotels are in the historic tradition that the function of hotels is to provide facilities for customers only to sleep, eat and drink. Branded basic feature hotels include many Howard Johnson Motor Inns and Quality Inns that have at least two of the non-room facilities – at least one restaurant and at least one bar. An optional facility is a multi-functional banqueting/meeting room, but any other non-room facilities are beyond the scope of basic feature hotels. The higher the market level of their facilities and services, the wider the range of products sold in the restaurants and bars and the higher the number of employees.

Limited feature hotels must have at least a restaurant, which is often designed as an all-day multi-hospitality area that incorporates a bar. Limited feature hotels provide only minor non-room facilities and thus a minor range of non-room services, because their prime demand is transient rooms demand rather than packaged demand that incorporates both rooms and non-room elements. Limited feature hotels do not seek local demand for their non-room facilities. A proportion of economy branded hotels in 1980 and more modern brands such as Holiday Inn Express are limited feature hotels. Accordingly, the range of products sold in the restaurant/bar of limited feature hotels is narrower than in resort, full feature and basic feature hotels and their staffing levels are lower. A typical 100-room limited-feature hotel employs typically around 20 full-time equivalent staff.

Many of the hotels in brands such as Travelodge in the US during the period were rooms-only hotels. They are the minimum hotels that have no non-room facilities and employ the fewest number of workers in each hotel.

Another way in which the five hotel configurations can be differentiated is in terms of the proportion of hotel turnover that is derived from renting bedrooms. Hotel resorts have the lowest proportion of turnover derived from renting bedrooms because they have the most extensive non-room facilities. Typically, and depending on the number of rooms and market level of the hotel, between 35% and 40% of turnover in hotel resorts is generated by renting bedrooms. In full-feature hotels depending on the number of bedrooms and market level, 40% to 55% of the turnover is generated from renting bedrooms. 55% to 65% of the turnover in basic feature hotels is generated from renting bedrooms, while more than 75% in limited feature hotels and the entire turnover in rooms only hotels is generated by renting bedrooms. Two other notable features of hotel configuration are first, that the greater the range of non-room facilities then the higher is the cost to build and second, that the higher the hotel configuration, then the lower is the operating margin. In comparison with the hotel bedrooms business, the non-room facilities involve higher volume and higher cost of consumables as well as more employees.

Hotel chains

The burst of hotel chain growth during the two-decade period produced growth across all hotel affiliations: owning, leasing, management contracting and franchising. During the period several of the larger chains operated multiple affiliations in their portfolios. The rate of portfolio expansion by the ten largest chains could not have been achieved if the companies had relied on generating capital to own the hotels. The addition to the Holiday Inn portfolio of 200,000 rooms in almost 1,000 hotels could only have been achieved by franchising since it allowed the brand to tap into the capital of a host of entrepreneurs, most of whom owned only one hotel. Marriott entered the hotel business in 1959 owning the hotels it developed. By 1961 it had sold and leased back its three hotels. Its first hotel management contract was negotiated in 1973 and by the end of the period in 1980 almost 70% of its room stock was in hotels with management contracts (Marriott and Brown, 2997: 181–189).Another feature of most of the ten largest US chains during the period was their international development, which involved up-market brands more than any others. In 1964, Hilton, whose international expansion started after World War II, created a separate division, Hilton International, which was responsible for all the hotels outside the US. By 1966, Hilton International had grown to 36 hotels with over 11,000 rooms, but the following year Hilton Hotels Corporation sold it to Trans World Corporation, the owner of Trans World Airways. This was a crucial step driven by the opportunity for Hilton Hotels Corporation to expand the business quickly and with lower risk in the US with a focus on management contracting and franchising rather than owning, leasing or contracting in a smaller, more widely dispersed and less profitable international business with lower medium-term growth prospects. Between 1966 and 1980 in the US, Hilton added 150 hotels with more than 48,000 rooms. In 1976, Hilton acquired the freehold of the Waldorf=Astoria, which it had leased since 1949, for $36 million of which $10 million was for furniture, fixtures and fittings. During the period, Hilton also embarked on a new dimension to its US business when in 1971 it acquired the International Leisure Company whose two main assets were the hotel resorts in Las Vegas that were to become the Las Vegas Hilton and the Flamingo Hilton. Thus, Hilton, unlike its competitor up-market brands, entered the hotel casino business with two large hotel resorts that enabled it to participate in one element of the growth in the domestic leisure market, which remained a part of Hilton Hotels Corporation until the 21st century.

During the period, Sheraton, which was acquired by ITT Corporation in 1968, Marriott, Westin and Hyatt all expanded into the international market. Westin had already expanded into Canada 1954 and Hyatt opened the Hyatt Regency in Hong Kong in 1969. In 1971, Sheraton opened its first hotel in Europe in Stockholm. Within the next two years it had opened the Conquistador in Guatemala City, the first Sheraton franchise outside of the US. It had also opened hotels in Brussels, London, Munich and Paris as well as Buenos Aires, Lima, Rio de Janeiro, Vancouver, Perth (Australia) and Hong Kong. Marriott's first venture into the international market did not occur until 1975 when it opened in Amsterdam in the Netherlands.

Mid-market chains such as Holiday Inn, Ramada and Quality, also made sorties into the international market in some unexpected ways. Holiday Inn, which by 1960 had already become established as the largest hotel chain in the US and was the definitive mid-market brand with the most developed franchise system, continued its powerful growth in the US. However, when it developed into Europe mid-way through the period it metamorphosed into an up-market brand because Holiday Inn had no brand infrastructure to generate demand in Europe in the way that it could in the US and to compensate it invested more in its hotel developments to elevate them to up-market specifications as a means of attracting customers. Moreover, many of the early Holiday Inns in Europe were owned by the brand because at the time hotel franchising did not exist in the region. At the economy level, Travelodge established itself in Australia and the Southern Pacific.

The growth in international exposure of up-market hotel chains attracted airlines that flew from the US to destinations around the world. Their passengers invariably needed to stay in hotels at the foreign destinations and it appeared as a neat piece of vertical integration for the airlines to have the hotels into which they could deliver their passengers. The hotel brands that were attractive to the airlines were the up-market ones that were mainly located in cities and which were full-feature hotels. It was this kind of hotel, in this kind of location and with these facilities that the airlines saw their passengers using most typically. PanAm owned Intercontinental Hotels since its inception, Hilton International was acquired by Trans World Corporation in 1967 and United Airlines bought Westin in 1970.

Supply and Demand Performance: US 1960–1980

Table 8.4: Supply and Demand Performance: US 1960–1980

	Total Hotels			Chain Hotels			Chain Share	
	1960	1980	CAGR	1960	1980	CAGR	1960	1980
Total rooms	1,500,000	2,300,000	2%	310,000	1,050,000	6%	21%	46%
Room nights available m	549	842	2%	113	384	6%	21%	46%
Room occupancy %	45%	53%		60%	60%			
Room nights sold m	**247**	**446**	**3%**	**68**	**231**	**6%**	**28%**	**52%**
Domestic business	74	143	3%	29	92	6%	39%	65%
Domestic leisure	146	228	2%	31	104	6%	21%	46%
Foreign business	12	36	5%	4	18	8%	33%	52%
Foreign leisure	15	40	5%	3	16	8%	23%	40%
Supply ratio	8.3	10.1		1.7	4.6			
Secular growth in hotel room supply	200,000	300,000		210,000	320,000		105%	107%

Source: Otus & Co Advisory Ltd

Otus estimates that total room occupancy rose above 50% for the first time in 1970 and continued to 53% in 1980 as more urban hotels were developed and the seasonality of demand was reduced.

The pace of hotel chain expansion was three times the average annual growth of the whole market. The weight of expansion by the chains was in urban and suburban markets, which were less seasonal than the resorts and with superior demand generation capability of the larger chains they were able to achieve higher room occupancy than the unaffiliated hotels or the market as a whole. Having established themselves with 46% of the total room stock and 52% of rooms demand, the chains were positioned to dominate the hotel market in the next economic period.

All references to employment in this chapter were drawn from www.bls.gov/ news.release/archieves/empsit_01092009.htm

9 The European Economies and Hotel Businesses 1960–1980

Introduction

In Britain during the 1960s and 1970s the key driver of economic structure was government policy, which is an indication of the extent of big government during the period. Throughout the 1970s, economic performance was very weak and economic policy concentrated on supporting secondary industries and expanding citizen services. The rate of growth in domestic business demand for hotels declined and the volume of domestic leisure demand into hotels fell as outbound packaged summer holidays to Mediterranean resorts grew apace. Disaster for the hotel business was averted by fast growth in leisure demand from foreign visitors. In hotel supply, the period was characterised by more government intervention than in any previous economic period, the reduction of hotels in coastal resorts, the expansion of hotels in cities and the on-going growth of hotel chains. Despite the challenges, the economic ascent of the hotel business in Britain continued during the two decades and at the end of the period total supply was up, and total demand was up, as was hotel concentration.

British economic structure and hotel demand

During the period there was progress in the four factors that are crucial to progression of the structural balance of an economy towards service businesses. The first factor was the extension of human and civil rights. During the 1960s and 1970s there was a range of laws, medical developments and social trends that expanded human rights, the most notable of which were:

♦ The first prescription of contraceptive pills in Britain in 1961.

♦ The Race Relations Act of 1965, which forbad discrimination in many contexts on the grounds of colour, race, ethnic origin or national origin.

♦ The decriminalisation of abortion by the Abortion Act in 1967.

♦ The easing of conditions for divorce by the Divorce Reform Act in 1969.

♦ The Equal Pay Act 1970, which required men and women to be paid the same rate for the same job.

♦ The Sex Discrimination Act of 1975, which made it a criminal offence to treat a woman less favourably than a man.

♦ The 1976 Race Relations Act, which extended the outlawing of discrimination to employment, council housing and financial services.

These developments gave women greater control of their lives at a time when drudgery was being taken out of housework, the numbers of women in further and higher education was increasing as was the number in the workforce. The developments also provided basic protection to ethnic minorities at a time when the number of immigrants to Britain was increasing. However, there was still one area of Britain that was stubbornly primitive in human and civil rights and that was Northern Ireland. Late in the 1960s the religious, social, cultural, economic and political differences between Catholics and Protestants came to a head and resulted in almost four decades of 'the troubles' in which institutionalised sectarian bigotry created a state of civil war. For the last four decades of the 20th century the Northern Ireland economy was heavily subsidised by the rest of Britain and the economic impact of "the troubles" was to abandon any prospect of development in its economic structure until the 21st century.

During this period, the second of the four factors, the extension of the social sciences, was achieved by the provision in universities and polytechnics of pure degrees in the social sciences and in the widespread expansion of vocational degrees that included applied social sciences. The third factor, the access to personal credit was increased as the rate of home ownership grew over the period. By 1980 around 60% of homes were owned and provided their owners with an appreciating asset. It signalled that they were in a career with a regular income. Homeowners not only held insurance policies, but also were most likely to participate in private pension plans and other forms of savings so that all of these together created a profile that lowered the risk for lenders. The fourth factor, personal travel, expanded materially over the period. Car ownership grew and the expansion of motorways made longer distance travel much easier and safer. Although the overall size of the rail system was reduced, the emphasis on inter-city travel increased the volume of passengers taking longer journeys, which also became faster. The growth in foreign holidays taken by Britons and the increase in overseas visitors into Britain required a marked increase in the volume of passengers on planes and at airports.

Although there was progress in the four factors necessary to advance the structural balance of the economy, the focus of economic policy on shoring-up secondary industries and expanding citizen services limited the progress of service businesses and the poor economic performance of the 1970s constrained the advance further. At the start of the period, the British economic structure was less developed than the American and the gap widened over the period. Three key factors contributed to the pattern of hotel demand over the period.

- First, British buyers of foreign package holidays increased and hotel based domestic holidays faded.

- Second, the decline in domestic summer holiday demand was less than the growth in domestic business demand so that total domestic demand rose over the period by three million room nights to 36 million and

- Third, the growth in foreign demand into British hotels was the highlight of the period. Otus estimates that room nights sold to foreign visitors in 1960 was six million, but rocketed to 30 million by 1980.

The pattern of employment in the economic segments over the period was as shown in Tables 9.1 and 9.2.

Table 9.1: Employment by Segment in Britain: 1960–1980 (m)

	Agriculture	Industry	Citizen Services	Service Businesses	Total
1960	1.2	10.9	5.3	6.7	24.1
1980	0.6	9.4	6.8	10.3	27.1

Table 9.2: Employment by Segment in Britain: 1950–1960 %

	Agriculture	Industry	Citizen Services	Service Businesses	Total
1960	5%	45%	22%	28%	100%
1980	2%	35%	25%	38%	100%

Source: 1960, Groningen Growth Centre; 1980, Office of National Statistics

Over the period, the rate of decline of employment in agriculture and industrial companies, the two segments that yield lower domestic business demand, had limited impact on hotel demand and was much more than offset by the strong growth in citizen services and service businesses, the two segments that yield higher domestic business demand.

Agricultural demand into hotels

By 1960, agriculture in Britain was already a marginal economic activity accounting for only 1.2 million employees, 5% of the workforce. Agriculture generated the lowest volume of hotel rooms demand of any economic segment because of the large number of small firms with little corporate infrastructure and the focus on local markets. Otus estimates that in 1960 2.3%, 27,000 of agricultural employees were business travellers, mostly originating demand. They spent an average of eight nights in British hotels generating mostly transient rooms demand of 220,000 room nights amounting to 1.5% of all domestic business demand. Over the following two decades, employment in agriculture fell by more than half a million and was paralleled by the progressive increase in agricultural imports. By 1980, agriculture employed only 640,000, 2.4% of the British workforce. There was some concentration among agricultural firms and there was more segment-wide use of hotels by agricultural associations, but these could not offset the reduction in hotel demand from the shrinkage of the segment. By 1980, the proportion of agricultural employees who were mainly demand-originating business travellers was up to 2.5%, amounting to 16,000, that the average number of nights spent in British hotels increased to nine and that the mostly transient rooms demand generated fell to 0.14 million room nights for a 1% share of total domestic business demand.

Industrial demand into hotels

In 1960, industrial employment was 10.9 million, 45% of the British workforce compared with only 32% in the US. 3% (330,000) of industrial employees were business travellers. British business travellers from the industrial segment were involved mostly in originating demand for non-nationalised companies. They spent an average of 13 nights in British hotels generating mostly transient rooms demand of 4.3 million room nights amounting to 40% of total domestic business demand and making the segment the largest for the hotel business. A central policy of the governments of the period was to support and develop secondary industries, but employment declined between 1960 and 1980 with the loss of 1.5 million jobs. Some reduction in industrial employment was the result of the increase in productivity, but other industrial businesses saw a stepped reduction in output and demand. Mining declined most with employment falling at an average of more than 4% per year and losing almost half a million jobs. The extent of the underperformance of British manufacturing is evident in comparison with Germany, France, Netherlands, Sweden, and Italy, which collectively achieved an average labour productivity of just 91% of the British average in 1950, but by 1980 their average performance exceeded that of Britain by almost 40% (Broadberry, 1997: 53–56). As the availability of consumer credit increased so imports of consumer goods increased. Between 1955 and 1980 imports as a percentage of British manufacturers sales increased from 8% to 30% (Williams et al., 1983: 118–119).

During the two-decade period big government initiatives were the fashion for managing the long-term development of the segment, none more so than the Ministry of Technology (MinTech) headed in the late 1960s by Anthony Wedgwood Benn. As Dominic Sandbrook noted, by 1969, MinTech had taken over, "responsibility for coal, electricity, oil and gas as well as the textile and chemical industries, regional policies and investment grants. By this point Benn commanded "the biggest state-directed complex of scientific and industrial power in Europe". His staff swelled from 8,000 to 39,000. He distributed £400 million a year on aircraft, electronics and defence technology. He administered 17 different government research establishments employing 22,000 scientists and engineers." In addition, "one of the chief responsibilities of MinTech was to encourage industrial mergers and acquisitions through the Industrial Reorganisation Corporation on the premise that enormous centralised companies had a better chance of competing in overseas markets" (Sandbrook, 2006: 310). The 1970s brought the fracturing of industrial relations due to the growth in wildcat and official strikes, rising inflation and rising unemployment after two decades of virtually full employment. Then the three-day week was enforced from 1 January to 7 March 1974, when, as a result of the oil crisis and the work to rule by the British miners, most industrial and commercial firms were limited to three consecutive working days of electricity. During the 1970s there was also another spate of nationalisation, undertaken this time to save failing companies and retain the levels of employment. They included: the aero-engine producer, Rolls Royce; the water companies in England and Wales; British Leyland Motor Corporation, the vehicle manufacturer; British Aerospace the defence manufacturer and British shipbuilders, which combined the four main shipbuilding companies in the country. By 1980, industrial employment fell to 9.4 million, a 35% share of the total workforce, down from 45% in 1960. Otus estimates that by 1980, the proportion of industrial employees who were business travellers increased to 4.0% due to the growth in concentration among non-nationalised industrial firms, which increased the number of executives travelling on company management activities, the increased involvement in demand origination and some increase in attendance at hotel based conferences and meetings. Despite the decline in employment in the segment the estimated number of business travellers rose by 50,000 to 377,000. The average number of nights that industrial business travellers spent in British hotels increased to 16, still mainly transient rooms demand, but with the addition of some packaged conference demand, which together generated 6 million room nights, up from 4 million in 1960. The industrial segment share of total domestic business demand fell to 27% from 40% at the start of the period and it lost its lead position as the producer of most domestic business hotel room nights as citizen services and service businesses grew at faster rates.

Citizen services demand into hotels

In 1960, citizen services employed 5.3 million, 22% of the British workforce. Otus estimates that 10%, 530,000 of citizen services employees were business travellers who spent an average of five nights in British hotels generating mainly transient rooms demand of 2.7 million room nights amounting to 25% of total domestic business demand. Over the two decades, employment in citizen services grew by more than 2% per year adding 1.8 million jobs. As Sandbrook said, "spending on health, education, research, transport, social security and housing went up by an annual average of more than 6% between 1964 and 1970. In its commitment to social services and public welfare, the Wilson government put together a record unmatched by any subsequent administration" (Sandbrook, 2006: 740). During the 1970s citizen services continued to expand, the prime driver of which was increased expenditure on education and health, while the sustained growth in unemployment required expansion of social services.

Higher education expanded over the period. The late 1960s and early 1970s saw the introduction of polytechnics, which taught undergraduates and postgraduates as well as providing sub-degree courses such as Higher National Diplomas. The rate of growth in higher education over the two-decade period is evident in the increase from 25,000 graduating students in 1960 to 65,000 in 1980, an average annual growth of 5% (source: www.data-archive.ac.uk). Over this period the main development in undergraduate degrees was the growth of vocational degrees designed to prepare graduates for white-collar careers in growing businesses and professions. One measure of this development was the growth in degrees in hotel and catering management. In 1965, the first two undergraduate degrees in Britain in hotel and catering management started at the universities of Strathclyde and Surrey. By 1980, there were further degrees in this field at the polytechnics of Huddersfield, Sheffield, Oxford and Manchester. Like health, higher education was a more significant user of hotels than other citizen services because professionals, the academics, were beginning to attend hotel-based conferences and administrative executives were involved in transient use of hotels as part of their management of the segment and nationalised industries. By 1980, citizen services employment had increased to 6.8 million, an average annual growth of 1.3% against only 0.6% for the economy as a whole. Otus estimates that the proportion of citizen services employees who were business travellers increased to 12.5% to produce 0.9 million travellers, up from 0.5 million in 1960 They spent an average of seven nights in British hotels generating both transient rooms demand and packaged conference demand of 6 million room nights, up from 2.7 million in 1960 to account for 27% of all domestic business demand.

Sservice businesses demand into hotels

In 1960, service businesses employed 6.7 million, 28% of the British workforce. Otus estimates that 4.7%, 310,000 of service business employees were business travellers They spent an average of 11 nights in British hotels generating demand of 3.5 million room nights for a 33% share of domestic business demand. Two government interventions had significant impacts on service businesses during the period, one was positive and one was negative. First, early in the period, retailers received a boost from the Conservative administration with the 1964 Resale Prices Act. The Act moved control of retail prices from the producer to the retailer. It provided flexibility to retailers in establishing selling prices and increased competition among retailers. Before the Resale Prices Act, retailers were predominantly small businesses without differentiation by price or brand. As a result of the Act, retailers had to identify the prices at which they could attract a market as well as the volume of products that they could sell in their neighbourhood. In short, they now had to manage yield rather than only the volume of goods sold. Thus, retailing became a more professional activity requiring explicit involvement in marketing, sales promotion, merchandising and advertising. The Act boosted innovations in retailing and promoted the growth of retail chains at the expense of corner shops. The professionalisation of retailing was positive for hotel demand because it generated bigger retailers with bigger corporate structures and more travelling executives. In contrast, the second and negative government intervention was introduced in 1966 by the Labour administration. Selective Employment Tax (SET) was introduced as a 7% levy placed exclusively on service businesses to limit their growth in employment and to promote employment in secondary industries. Within most service businesses the tax was passed on to customers making it more expensive to buy services and less expensive to buy products. The tax failed in its aim because of the inherent poor productivity and weak competitiveness of British manufacturers at a time when there was natural growth in demand for service businesses. In the 1971 budget, the Heath Conservative administration announced the scrapping of SET and that purchase tax was to be replaced in 1973 by a uniformly applied Value Added Tax (VAT) on most goods and services.

Despite government initiatives to slow the development of service businesses and the poor performance of the British economy during the 1970s, service business employment over the two-decade period grew at an average annual rate of 1% against 0.3% for the economy as a whole. Over the period the growth was not uniform across all service businesses. Banking and financial services grew the fastest with employment up by an average of 3.4% per year adding almost 900,000 jobs. There were three main reasons: first, there was a surge in the numbers of Britons opening bank accounts because of the increase among white-collar and professional employees of monthly payment of salaries directly into their bank accounts rather than the payment of weekly wages in cash. There was a surge in the number of undergraduates opening bank accounts into which were deposited their university grant cheques. Second, in 1966, eight years after the introduction of credit cards into the US, Barclays Bank introduced the first British credit card, Barclaycard. It was followed in 1972 by the introduction of Access as the second British credit card. Third, the growth in home ownership involved the subscription to insurance policies and increasingly white-collar and professional careers involved pension schemes and superannuation schemes, which added further to employment in the financial services sector. All of these developments were positive for the growth in domestic business demand into hotels.

Retailing and wholesaling also experienced significant growth and added almost 600,000 jobs. For most of the population, the 1960s and 1970s produced a progressive change in lifestyle, which was a continuation of the trend established during the post-war period facilitated by the growth in ownership of household appliances. Leisure time in the home became more plentiful for women who had appliances such as vacuum cleaners, washing machines and tumble driers and for those who moved from coal fires to gas or electric heating. Leisure time was also increased by refrigerators, and freezers, which enabled weekly supermarket shopping rather than daily corner shopping. Retailing also benefited from the coming of age of the baby boomers. By 1960, the oldest boomers had reached 15 years of age and some were already leaving school. Boomers were a prime market for the fashion of swinging London, the rock and pop music of the Beatles, the Rolling Stones, the Kinks and the other bands that achieved international acclaim. Throughout the period, retail chains expanded, they enlarged their corporate structures and a high proportion of their executives were involved in business travel and hotel stays. Other service businesses that grew during the period included broadcasting and communications. Television and radio growth exploded. Colour television demand increased from around 1 million sets in 1970 to more than 11 million by 1980 (Briggs, 1995). Commercial radio stations were established and grew and this in turn produced an expansion in advertising. Professional services also expanded during the period primarily to service the corporate markets. As was the case in financial services and retailing the other expanding service businesses generated increasing levels of domestic business demand into hotels.

Experience businesses

In contrast, the period was not strong for experience businesses. The predominant location of leisure activities was the home. During the 1960s and 1970s the main in-home leisure activity that filled much of the time saved by household appliances was watching television and for most of the period there were only two television channels, yet 97% of adults were estimated to watch at least 12 hours of television per week (Sandbrook, 2006: 376) The growth of home-based leisure activities limited the growth in out-of-home leisure activities. Attendance at football matches peaked in the late 1940s. It declined to 28 million in the mid-1960s and did not exceed that total by 1980 (source: http://www.european-football-statistics.co.uk). As a result, the quality of sports stadiums declined. There was also a sharp reduction in attendance at cinemas from 500 million in 1960 to 100 million in 1980, which reduced the number of cinemas. Their physical state also declined (source: Social Trends 30, Office of National Statistics). Following the trend established in the post-war period, another British leisure institution that saw change in the pattern of usage over the two decades was the pub. Whereas between 1966 and 1986 the number of pubs in Britain rose modestly from 75,283 to 80,364, the number of off-licences increased from 30,138 to 49,347, a growth of almost four times as many per year as pubs and an illustration of the shift in drinks consumption to the home (Monopolies and Mergers Commission, 1989). During the 1960s and 1970s, leisure lifestyle for many British families dichotomised. Predominantly, the increased leisure time throughout the year was spent privately at home, while the main out-of-home leisure activity was the annual family summer holiday. Transport saw a marginal reduction in manpower losing 58,000 jobs due to the introduction of new rail technology such as the more manpower efficient diesel and electric trains that replaced steam trains. It was also reduced by the Beeching cuts in the rail network, which saw the scrapping of more than 4000 miles of railway line and the closing of around 2300 stations(source: Beeching Report, 1963). In parallel, during the twenty-year period around 2000 miles of less manpower-intense motorways were built.

The baby boomers

The main alternative to the in-home family lifestyle was that created by the baby boomers. They avoided National Service, which ended as the oldest boomers were becoming 18 years old, but they were the beneficiaries of the spread of university and polytechnic attendance and a significant proportion of them lived away from home in halls of residence and apartments with other students. In their academic communities more students experienced a greater lifestyle freedom based around learning and enjoyment than any previous generation. British undergraduate baby boomers did not participate in mass movements to the same extent as their counterparts in the US since they had fewer issues to protest against. Civil rights in Britain were more developed, Britain did not enter the Vietnam War and homosexuality was decriminalised much earlier and with much less fuss than in the US. Undergraduate boomers were confident in their capabilities and prospects. They were hedonistic in their social lives and they engaged in mass conspicuous consumption. Importantly, boomers were a target market for out-of home leisure activities such as discos and pubs. They bought more experience services and spent more of their leisure time outside of the home than their families who bought more consumer goods and pursued more in-home leisure activities creating a lifestyle based on private inconspicuous consumption. These lifestyle differences with their parents were key factors in the prominence of the generation gap that became explicit during the 1960s. However, during the 1960s, boomers were not a market for hotels since it was not until the 1970s that they entered the career market. It was the first decade of the significantly increased number of graduates and by 1980 37% of them were women. The boomers career demand was for white-collar and professional careers and for most graduates the opportunities were in the citizen services and service business segments. Otus estimates that in 1980 the proportion of service business employees who were business travellers increased to 7.2% entailing 740,000 business travellers, up from 331,000 million in 1960. They were involved in originating demand, executing contracts and servicing clients. They were also involved in travel related to company management and increasingly the attendance at conferences. They spent an average of 14 nights in British hotels generating both transient and packaged conference demand of 10.4 million room nights for a 46% share of total domestic business demand and establishing the segment as the largest generator of hotel demand.

Domestic leisure demand into hotels

The largest market for British hotels in 1960 was domestic leisure demand which accounted for 22 million room nights, 57% of total hotel demand. Domestic leisure demand in the 1960s was still dominated by summer holidays to coastal and country resorts. For the year 1964, the British Travel Association recorded hotel room occupancy data for 200 "good class" hotels of only 47.5% ranging from 20% in January to 78% in August (, Caterer and Hotelkeeper, 1978). This pattern indicated the high exposure to the summer holiday market, which at the time was predominantly domestic. At this time also, most coastal and country resort hotels closed for the winter months, because there was no demand. Thus, the low occupancy in January was almost entirely generated by business demand and almost all in urban areas. The swinging sixties and permissiveness, which were mainly the preserve of the baby boomers, was not reflected in demand for hotels. By 1980, the eldest boomers were 35 years old and the youngest, 25 years old. During this period they were at the early stage of the family life cycle and those in white-collar careers were in the process of buying homes and personal consumer goods. However, they were a significant buyer of foreign, hotel-based summer holidays, but hardly bought hotel room nights in Britain for leisure purposes. In 1962, Britons spent £430 million on holidays at home, but only £220 million abroad. Between 1970 and 1980, the number of outbound holidays of four nights or more from Britain, mostly to the Mediterranean, increased from

5.75 million to 12 million and expenditure on these holidays increased from £470 million to £3,510 million. The strong growth in outbound foreign, hotel-based packaged holidays established a major trend that has continued since. In parallel, the number of holidays of four or more nights taken in Britain by Britons fell marginally from 34.5 million to 30.5 million, but the major loss was in hotel-based holidays since camping, caravanning and self-catering grew. By 1980, per capita spending grew to £66 for domestic holidays, but rose to £292 on foreign holidays, a high proportion of which were hotel based. By the end of the period, domestic leisure demand had fallen by one third to 13 million room nights accounting for only 20% of total hotel demand. This was the most significant downward shift in peacetime hotel demand in Britain during any economic period *(source*: The British National Travel Survey, The British Tourist Authority, 1996).

Three developments in demand prevented a disaster for British hotel business.

♦   First, the growth in domestic business demand reinforced the shift in hotel demand away from coastal resorts to urban centres.

♦   Second, the emergence of domestic short breaks introduced a new market to the British hotel business and further offset the loss of demand from long holidays. Packaged short breaks typically involved two nights at the weekend in a hotel on a dinner, bed and breakfast basis and often included Inter-City rail travel to and from the destination. The packaged short break market into hotels came to life in 1964 when Grand Metropolitan established Stardust Mini Holidays to generate demand for short breaks from the provinces into its London hotels. "In the first year the company spent £1,000 and sold 325 packages. Ten years later Grand Metropolitan were spending £1,000,000 and moving over 150,000 people from all over the country" (Taylor, 2003: 304). Derek Taylor led the only initiative in which a British hotel company identified a new hotel market early, established the infrastructure to attract the demand and set a long-term positive trend that was adopted by almost every other hotel chain. In the period to 1980, short breaks were mainly city based and London was the main beneficiary. Coastal resorts were no more than a fringe market for packaged short breaks and so their introduction accelerated the locational shift in hotel demand towards urban centres.

♦   The third and most significant development that boosted hotel demand in Britain during the period was the stellar growth of foreign demand into the country and, like other sources of demand, foreign visitors rarely travelled to coastal resorts.

Thus, each of the growing hotel markets in Britain overcame the loss of domestic summer holiday demand into hotels, but exacerbated the decline of coastal resorts. The coastal resorts lost their traditional market and gained only a tiny fraction of the emerging demand. Their decline was inevitable and many hotels in the resorts closed never to open again.

Foreign leisure demand

In 1964, the International Passenger Survey (IPS) reported that 3.3 million foreign visitors arrived in Britain and spent £190 million. By 1970, the number of visitors doubled to 6.7 million and their spending rose to £432 million. Then, in the decade to 1980 the number of foreign visitors doubled again to 12.5 million and their spending zoomed to £2800 million (source: International Passenger Survey). Of the four categories of foreign visitors tracked by the IPS, the important categories for the hotel business were business travellers and holidaymakers, significant proportions of whom stayed overnight in hotels. The least important categories were those visiting friends and relatives and miscellaneous, very few of whom stayed in hotels. In 1970, 1.2 million foreign business travellers arrived in Britain; almost 70% came from western continental countries and almost 20% from North America. By 1980, the number of foreign business travellers more than doubled to 2.6 million of which 1.4 million came from the European Economic Community (EEC). The main drivers of the growth in foreign business travellers were the growth in imports and the growing trading ties with the EEC following Britain's membership in 1971. The growth in foreign business travellers was good news for the hotel business, particularly in London and the main provincial cities. However, not all foreign business arrivals stayed in hotels and indeed a feature of the period was the growing number of day visits from the continent as the volume and frequency of air travel improved. The length of stay of foreign business travellers also declined over the period as business trips became more routinised. In 1960, foreign business travellers accounted for 7% of total hotel demand, almost 3 million room nights, but despite the trend to shorter trips, hotel demand by 1980 had risen to 8 million and a 12% share of total demand.

At the start of the period there were less than 1 million foreign holiday arrivals, but by the end of the period this had rocketed to 5.5 million. A defining feature of these travellers was that they used serviced accommodation during their stays. Although hotels were their main form of accommodation, a small minority also used quasi hotels such as bed and breakfasts. The length of stay over the period declined, particularly for long-haul visitors due to the increase in the volume of Europe-wide package holidays in which very few nights were spent in any country. Foreign leisure demand was not attracted to Britain by the promise of warm and dry summer weather. Rather, history, heritage and culture were prime drivers of this market and were centred in cities rather than coastal resorts. At the time, a typical British tour included London, Stratford-on-Avon, York and Edinburgh. In 1960, foreign holidaymakers accounted for only 8% of total hotel demand, more than 3 million room nights. By 1980, it had risen dramatically to 23 million room nights and a share of one-third of all hotel demand.

It was during this period in Britain that the wholesale markets for hotel rooms emerged on the back of inbound packaged holidays, domestic short breaks, regular business demand from larger companies and government agencies as well as growth in conferences. Tour operators seeking to organise inbound package holidays, specialist travel agencies such as Stardust Mini Holidays and Super Breaks organising short-break packages into hotels and travel managers such as

Hogg Robinson and Expotel servicing the travel and hotel needs of companies and government agencies as well as conference organisers arranging hotel based conferences all emerged in Britain during this period. For the wholesaling of hotel demand to be successful it needs wholesaling of hotel supply and this entails a significant presence of hotel chains. However, at this time the chains were still too small to accommodate the majority of wholesale demand. Thus, there was a mismatch. Independent hotels were less attractive to wholesalers because their venue size was too small, most failed to provide en suite bathrooms, they were insufficiently safe and they were frequently in locations that the wholesale markets did not want to be.

Developments in hotel supply in Britain

Otus estimates that in 1960 there were 325,000 hotel rooms in Britain. At a constant 1960 supply ratio and with the recorded increase in population, Britain would have needed only 350,000 hotel rooms in 1980. By 1980, room stock had increased to 385,000, producing secular growth of 35,000 rooms derived from growth in domestic business demand and growth in foreign visitors. The average annual growth of 1% in room supply over the period conceals the sea changes that occurred in the location pattern of hotels, in the exits from the market and entrances to the market, in the physical state of the hotels and in the structure of the hotel business. As well as the shift in the pattern of hotel demand that impacted on supply, there were three key influences on the changes in hotel supply during the period – the Tourism Development Act, 1969, the Fire Precautions Act, 1971 and the continuing growth of hotel chains. Otus estimates that at the start of the period there were only 45,000 chain hotel rooms in the country and hotel room concentration had reached only 14%. The growing demand at the start of the period triggered growth in hotel supply, but developments were still slow. In 1960, the Caterer and Hotelkeeper reported that, "The year opened with the biggest hotel building programme seen in London for over 30 years. At least five new hotels were on the stocks" (*source*: Caterer and Hotelkeeper, 1978).

In recognition of the changes in demand and the limited investment in hotels, the motoring organisations in 1965 reduced the number of five-star hotels in their hotel guide books. The Grand and Cavendish hotels in Eastbourne, the Royal Bath and Branksome Towers in Bournemouth, the Majestic in Harrogate, the Palace in Torquay and Turnbury in Ayrshire were all downgraded to four stars (Automobile Association, 1965). All were in resorts and of the three remaining five-star hotels in the provinces, Gleneagles was in the countryside and the Carlton in Bournemouth and the Imperial in Torquay were in coastal resorts. All of the other five-star hotels were in London.

However, not all new city hotels built early in the period were driven by the growth in rooms demand. In Scotland, the licensing laws at the time prohibited pubs from opening on Sundays, but allowed hotels to open and to be the only source of alcoholic drinks. To take advantage of this situation companies such as Stakis and Scottish & Newcastle Brewers created hotels in city suburbs with few rooms – more than the minimum of four required under the Scottish law to be a hotel and rarely more than 20 – since rooms demand in these locations was minor. The raison d'être of these hotels was that they had multiple bars, indeed on Sundays almost all of their public areas were used for selling drinks. Examples in the Glasgow suburbs included the Burnside hotel, the Burnbrae hotel, the Tinto Firs hotel and the 16-room Redhurst hotel, which was the first hotel in which I was employed as an assistant hotel manager, by Stakis, during a summer break from university.

Hotel developments in the 1960s

By 1960, there had been significant changes to the roster of hotel companies listed on the London Stock Exchange. Of the 56 hotel companies listed in 1939, concentration, bombing, insolvency and taking private had removed 34, mostly single hotels, by 1960. New quoted hotel chains had also become established by 1960 including Clydesdale and County Hotels with eight hotels in Scotland and Eglington Hotels with seven. Most of the supply activity of the key hotel chains during the 1960s was in building and acquiring city hotels. London saw most developments and hotel chains were the most active in building and acquiring hotels mainly at the up-market and mid-market levels. Among the more notable activities in London were the following:

♦ In 1963, Trust Houses acquired the 450-room and 140-apartment Grosvenor House hotel for £6.75 million, then in 1966 it opened the new 230-room Cavendish hotel in Jermyn Street and in 1969 it acquired the 500-room Kensington Close hotel for £4.7 million.

♦ In 1961 Grand Metropolitan was floated on the London Stock Exchange and the following year bought the 265-room Piccadilly hotel for £1.81 million In 1964 it opened the 300-room Europa hotel in Grosvenor Square and the following year acquired Gordon Hotels, which included the 290-room Mayfair Hotel in London. In 1969, Grand Met opened the 437-room Britannia hotel in Grosvenor Square and by the end of the decade it owned 22 hotels in London making it the largest chain in the capital.

♦ In 1962, Forte was floated on the London Stock Exchange and in 1964 opened the 440-room London Airport Hotel, then in 1967 acquired the Frederick Hotels portfolio of eight hotels for £2.75 million including the 370-room Russell Hotel in London.

Other highlights of the decade in London included the 1965 opening of by Oddenino's of the £5 million, 500-room Royal Garden Hotel and in 1967, the Rank Organisation opened the Royal Lancaster with 392 rooms. Centre Hotels was established by Henry Edwards with, 300 rooms at Heathrow Airport as well as the 310-room Bloomsbury Centre and the 330-room Regent Centre.

Foreign hotel companies also penetrated the London market. In 1961, the Hotel Corporation of America's Carlton Tower opened with 318 rooms and in 1963, the £8 million London Hilton opened in Park Lane with 512 rooms.

The provinces saw new hotel building and acquisitions, including:

♦ Early in the 1960s, Trust Houses introduced Post House hotels, the first mid-market hotel brand in Britain with modern en suite bedrooms as well as restaurant, bar and conference facilities, it was the British equivalent of Holiday Inn that had opened 10 years earlier in the US. Post House became a highlight of the decade as it emerged in Chester, Lincoln, Nottingham, Plymouth, Southampton, Leeds, Swindon and Coventry. Trust Houses also opened, among others, the 117-room Dragon Hotel, Swansea in 1961, the first hotel built in Wales since World War II. In 1969, the company acquired the 175-room Imperial hotel, Torquay for £1.25 million, one of the few in coastal resorts that it added during the decade.

♦ In 1961 Grand Met acquired the six Eglinton hotels in Scotland.

♦ Forte opened the Excelsior hotel at Manchester Airport.

♦ In 1965 Ind Coope, the brewer, in a major diversion in its hotel business, opened the 265 room Piccadilly hotel in Manchester.

Hotel developments in the 1970s

Otus estimates that in 1970, hotel room stock in Britain had risen to 345,000 producing a supply ratio of 6.3, unchanged from 1960. By 1970, 16 of the 25 largest hotel chains were publicly quoted; the total chain room stock had risen to 95,000 and concentration had grown to 26%. The 1970s proved to be a much more important decade for hotel supply than the 1960s due to fiscal and demand changes. The period was also notable for the first systematic attempts to estimate the size of hotel room stock in Britain (NEDO, 1972, 1976). In a heroic initiative at a time when industry-wide hotel supply and demand data were absent, the Hotels and Catering Economic Development Committee (H&CEDC) chose a very loose definition of hotel as "an establishment of a permanent nature, of four or more bedrooms, offering bed and breakfast on a short-term contract and providing certain minimum standards" (NEDO, 1976: 1). Thus, they included not only licensed and unlicensed hotels, but also guest houses and their equivalents.

Four features of the hotel and guest house stock in 1974 that the H&CEDC reported provide insights into the state of supply at the time.

♦ First, it reported that, "almost three-quarters of the nation's hotels were built before 1920" (NEDO, 1976) , that is, at the time of its publication three-quarters of the hotels were more than 55 years old. Modern buildings constructed after 1960 accounted for only 8% of the total. Hotels and guest houses were not only old, but also too many lacked modern facilities such as bedrooms with en suite bathrooms. In 1975, 25% of the 138 hotels recommended by the Egon Ronay Organisation in London had rooms without en suite bathrooms (Egon Ronay, 1975).

♦   Second, 48% of all hotel and guest house bedrooms were in coastal re-
     sorts and a further 9% were in the countryside leaving only a minority of
     room stock in urban areas (NEDO, 1976: 1).

♦   Third, "61% had 10 or fewer bedrooms and 90% had 25 or less". In the
     mid-1970s, hotels and guest houses in Britain were predominantly very
     small businesses.

♦   They were even smaller businesses due to the fourth feature that 36%
     closed for three months or more and 44% closed for at least a month, il-
     lustrating that hotel demand and supply were heavily seasonal.

The H&CEDC estimated that there were 497,502 bedrooms in 33,659 hotels
and guest houses in 1974 in Britain. Guest houses were predominantly unlicensed and thus not permitted to sell alcoholic drinks on site, they were among
the smallest venues, located predominantly in coastal and rural areas, and they
were among the oldest properties with the fewest facilities and were entirely independent ventures. Another distinction between hotels and guest houses was that
under the Innkeepers Liability Act 1956, guest houses were private hotels. They
were not open to the public. They were considered as extensions to the home of
the owner and the renting of bedrooms was at the discretion of the owner. They
were open only to resident customers who had to book in advance and agree
to the terms of price, duration and any other social conditions of the owner. Licensed hotels were inns at law. They were open to the public and explicitly they
were businesses. To remove the guest house element from the calculation and estimate the volume of hotels alone, Otus has included all licensed hotels and one
third of the unlicensed hotels selected to reflect the lower exposure of hotels to
the coastal and the rural areas, to reflect their lower exposure to smaller venues
and to private hotels, while simultaneously reflecting their greater exposure to
urban centres, to larger venues and to inns at law as Tables 9.3–9.6 detail.

The exclusion of guest houses means that Otus estimates around 375,000 hotel
rooms in Britain in 1974. In this analysis there were 60,000 hotel rooms in London against more than 67,000 rooms in hotels and guest houses. For the emerging international conference market London was still an inefficient city with too
many small hotels. In 1971, the 13,000 delegates and guests for the American
Bar Association conference required 70 London hotels to accommodate them
(Caterer and Hotelkeeper , 1978).

Table 9.3: Licensed Hotels Rooms, 1974

	4 to 10	11 to 15	16 to 25	26 to 50	51 to 100	Over 100	Total
Seaside	12,131	14,743	22,351	33,216	25,856	8,938	117,235
Countryside	12,225	5,443	5,677	5,157	2,710	1,126	32,338
Small towns	17,186	8,468	10,062	14,182	13,611	7,453	70,962
Large towns	2,825	2,955	2,661	9,268	15,775	56,834	90,318
Total	44,367	31,609	40,751	61,823	57,952	74,351	310,853

Source: Hotel & Catering EDC, Hotel Prospects to 1985

Table 9.4: Unlicensed Hotels and Guest Houses Rooms, 1974

	4 to 10	11 to 15	16 to 25	26 to 50	51 to 100	Over 100	Total
Seaside	71,834	33,051	12,508	4,905	854	244	123,396
Countryside	5,996	1,990	439	209	80	0	8,714
Large towns	9,503	11,706	3,716	3,600	1,729	1,717	31,971
Total	87,333	46,747	16,663	8,714	2,663	1,961	164,081

Source: Hotel & Catering EDC, Hotel Prospects to 1985

Table 9.5: Unlicensed Hotels Rooms, 1974

	4 to 10	11 to 15	16 to 25	26 to 50	51 to 100	Over 100	Total
Seaside	18,000	9,000	6,250	2,450	600	100	36,400
Countryside	1,800	1,000	200	100	0	0	3,100
Small towns	4,150	2,950	850	300	200	200	8,650
Large towns	2,850	5,850	1,850	2,150	1,200	1,350	15,250
Total	26,800	18,800	9,150	5,000	2,000	1,650	63,400

Source: Otus & Co Advisory Ltd

Table 9.6: Total Hotels Rooms, 1974

	4 to 10	11 to 15	16 to 25	26 to 50	51 to 100	Over 100	Total
Seaside	30,131	23,743	28,601	35,666	26,456	9,038	36,400
Countryside	14,025	6,443	5,877	5,257	2,710	1,126	3,100
Small towns	21,336	11,418	10,912	14,482	13,811	7,653	8,650
Large towns	5,675	8,805	4,511	11,418	16,975	58,184	15,250
Total	71,167	50,409	49,901	66,823	59,952	76,001	63,400

Source: Hotel & Catering EDC, Hotel Prospects to 1985 and Otus & Co

The Hotel Development Incentive scheme

In its earlier publication, Hotel Prospects to 1980, the H&CEDC estimated that in 1970 in Britain there were 35,200 hotels and guest houses with 450,000 rooms. In the first four years of the 1970s almost 55,000 new hotel and guest house rooms were added, of which 20,000 were in London (NEDO, 1976: 15, 17). The driver of this powerful supply growth was the Hotel Development Incentive scheme (HDI) introduced as part of the Tourism Development Act of 1969. Broadly, the HDI scheme made grants available, equal to 20% of the expenditure or £1,000 per bedroom, up to a maximum of £100,000 for new hotels and extensions, whichever was less. Eligible grants required work to begin after 31 March 1969 and the end date for completion was 31st March 1973. By the closing date, applications had been received for 66,400 bedrooms. The total investment of public money in grants under the HDI scheme was reported in the House of Commons as £60 million and was unprecedented in British history (*source*: Hansard, 13 June 1974 vol 874 c639W). The Act was the most significant initiative by any British government in hotels and tourism and was introduced because of the growth in foreign and domestic tourism in Britain, which had gathered pace in the 1960s and was expected to accelerate in the 1970s. A critical impediment to the growing demand was the lack of appropriate hotels and it was this imbalance that the HDI was created to redress. The act specified that eligible hotels had to comply with the following five requirements:

◆ That it has not less than 10 (or, if it is in Greater London, 25) letting bedrooms and that the sleeping accommodation offered at the hotel consists wholly or mainly of letting bedrooms;

◆ That breakfast and an evening meal are provided at reasonable times on the premises for persons staying at the hotel;

◆ That there is on the premises a lounge (whether a room or part of a room) for the common use at all reasonable times of persons staying at the hotel;

◆ That hotel services appropriate to the establishment (but including in every case the cleaning of rooms and making of beds) are provided for persons staying at the hotel;

◆ That the accommodation is in a building or buildings of a permanent nature.

(*source*: Tourism Development Act 1969)

A typical 100-room mid-market hotel, achieving the maximum grant would, depending on location, have 15% to 20% of its build cost subsidised. Typically, the mid-market HDI hotels had small rooms and there was a high proportion of single rooms per hotel to maximise the grant. The design of the hotels was invariably utilitarian to minimise the build cost and maximise the speed of construction. Most of the hotels built with the aid of public money were in urban areas rather than in coastal and country resorts because that is where much of the growing foreign demand, domestic business demand and domestic short-break demand were focused. Another attraction of the urban market, particularly to the hotel chains, was that it was a year-round market rather than the heavily seasonal market in the resorts that required closure of the hotels for part of the year. The burst of hotel expansion between 1970 and 1973 produced the sharpest ever rise in hotel supply in such a concentrated period. Alas, the new room stock came on the market when the British and other western economies were confronting harsh conditions. In Britain, the oil crisis, the three-day week, hyper wage inflation, fast growing unemployment and industrial unrest on top of the growth in urban hotel supply caused hotel performance to plummet.

The Fire Precautions Act 1971

As the HDI scheme produced new room stock, the Fire Precautions Act 1971 (FPA) was instrumental in removing unsafe and obsolete hotels. A fire at the 14th century, 38-room Rose and Crown Hotel, Saffron Walden on Boxing Day 1969, where 11 people died, was one of a number of hotel fires which gave added impetus to the passing of the FPA. In 1972, hotels and boarding houses that provided sleeping accommodation for more than six people were the first premises required to have a fire certificate under the Act because their very old average age and the low level of modern facilities, particularly in coastal resorts and in the countryside, put them among the least safe properties. When the FPA was passed there was a major task for the fire authorities to survey the 35,000 hotels and guest houses in Britain, to identify the investment required for each venue to comply with the FPA and then to monitor the compliance with the Act. The proliferation of independent hoteliers and guest house owners squealed about the cost of compliance with the Act and its threat to their livelihood so that in 1973 a bill passed through parliament enabling local authorities to make loans available to small hoteliers for structural alterations required under the FPA. By 31st December 1977, it was announced in parliament that the fire authorities in England and Wales had issued fire certificates in respect of 15,871 hotels and boarding houses; 6,059 premises had been inspected and issued with a notice of steps to be taken for the purpose of certification and 6,560 applications remained to be dealt with *(source:* http://hansard.millbanksystems.com). Given the 35,000 hotels and guest houses estimated by the H&CEDC to be in existence when the FPA was enacted in 1971, the position at the end of 1977 implies that there was a net reduction of around 5,000 hotels and guest houses since the introduction of the Act.

The FPA alone was not responsible for these closures, which were also forced by the accelerating domestic summer holiday exodus from Britain to the Mediterranean. Just as their market was deserting them, old and obsolete hotels and guest houses in resorts were required to invest in structural changes, in equipment and in facilities to comply with the FPA .The powerful combined force of the cost of compliance with the FPA and the deserting demand produced the closure of more guest houses and hotels in resorts than at any other period. The 1970s was a remarkable decade of change for hotel supply in Britain. It produced the biggest locational shift ever in the British hotel business as resort hotels closed and urban hotels were built and expanded. It also witnessed the biggest ever increase in the levels of life safety in British hotels. In short, during the 1970s, old, clapped-out hotels and guest houses in resorts were replaced by modern hotels with more extensive and safer facilities in urban areas.

Hotel chains in the 1970s

As independent hoteliers and guest house owners were the most severely impacted by the HDI, the FPA and the changes in demand, the main beneficiaries were the hotel chains. The HDI was a magnet for the chains pursuing year-round demand in urban centres. The lower average age of their hotels and safer facilities meant that the average cost per hotel of compliance with the FPA was lower for the chains. The chains also suffered less from the exodus of holidaymakers to the Mediterranean since their exposure to coastal resorts was lower. The chains also benefited from the accelerating growth of inbound foreign visitors to British cities. The favourable trading conditions for the chains increased their development activities and the 1970s started with the largest corporate development yet seen in the British hospitality business. Trust Houses merged with Forte in May

1970 to create Trust Houses Forte (THF) with assets of £120 million. It had 215 hotels in Britain and more in other countries (Forte, 1986: 134). At the time of the merger, Trust Houses owned 20% of Travelodge International in the US and Travelodge Australia and within three years THF had acquired the remaining 80% of the Travelodge shares for $28 million. In addition to hotels, THF included restaurants, entertainment centres, industrial and airport catering, travel agencies and Lillywhites, a sports retailer. In spite of the Post House developments and its clutch of up-market and deluxe hotels in Britain, the Trust House portfolio was still dominated by its legacy of small, old, basic-feature provincial hotels at the mid-market and below and this enabled it, with 20,200 rooms, to dominate the hotel chain market in Britain. THF had double the number of British rooms of Grand Met, the second largest chain, but despite its dominance of the hotel chain market, THF accounted for less than 6% of all hotel rooms in the country. In 1977, THF spent £27.6 million to acquire the Strand Hotels portfolio of 35 hotels in Britain and Ireland. Both Trust Houses and Forte had begun independently to acquire foreign hotels before the merger, notably, Forte's acquisition of the George V, the Plaza Athénée and the Tremoille hotels in Paris. After the merger, THF continued its international accumulation of prominent hotels during the period by acquiring such hotels as the King Edward in Toronto, as well as the Plaza Athenee, the Pierre and Westbury hotels in New York.

London was the main focus of development activity for the chains during the 1970s and included the following:

♦ In 1971, THF opened the 600-room London Heathrow Post House; in 1973, the 149-room Gatwick Post House started trading; other THF initiatives in the capital included the 1976 acquisition of the 285-room Westbury hotel, while the 1977 acquisition of Strand Hotels included four London hotels with 3,000 rooms.

♦ In 1974, Grand Met put several hotels on the market including Max Joseph's first hotel acquired in 1946, the 167-room Mandeville where only half of the rooms had an en suite bathroom. Grand Met's interest was to be more up-market in London and in 1977 it bought the 425-room London International Hotel from Trafalgar House.

Other notable initiatives in London by British companies included the 1973 construction by Strand Hotels of the 835-room Tower hotel at Tower Bridge for £8 million. The hotel traded poorly in its early years and in 1977 Strand sold the hotel to EMI for only £6.5 million. In 1973, the Rank Organisation acquired Oddenino Hotels – the Royal Garden, Atheneum, and White House with a total of 915 rooms for £34 million. In 1976 Trafalgar House bought the 120-room Ritz Hotel for £2.7 million and in 1977, Coral Leisure acquired Centre Hotels for £15 million.

Foreign hotel chains in Britain

Foreign companies were also active in the British hotel market.

♦ Early in the 1970s, the Holiday Inn brand entered the British market in a two-pronged initiative. Holiday Inns Inc., the brand owner, developed hotels at Heathrow airport and other cities and Commonwealth Holiday Inns of Canada (CHIC) opened the Holiday Inns at Swiss Cottage and Marble Arch, and expanded into cities such as Plymouth and Slough. These were the first franchised hotels in Britain and both Holiday Inns Inc. and CHIC metamorphosed the Holiday Inn brand from its positioning in the mid-market in North America to be an up-market brand in Europe.

♦ Another foreign mid-market brand that was a competitor to Post House entered the British market in 1973. Novotel arrived from France and opened new hotels in Coventry, Nottingham and Bradford.

♦ The 500-room Churchill hotel in Portman Square, London was opened in 1970 by Loew's Hotels of the US at a cost of £5 million. In the same year, Four Seasons opened the 228-room Inn on the Park in Park Lane.

♦ In 1972, Intercontinental Hotels, in a joint venture with BOAC, opened the 300-room Portman hotel for £3 million.

♦ In 1773, the 850 room London Tara was opened by Aer Lingus, the 611-room Kensington Hilton became the second Hilton in the capital and Penta Hotels opened the 914-room Penta hotel in Cromwell Road.

♦ In 1975, the 546-room Intercontinental, Hyde Park Corner, opened at a cost of £15 million and a Middle-Eastern investment group bought the Dorchester for £9 million.In 1977, Sheraton Hotels acquired the Skyline Park Tower, Knightsbridge and the Skyline at Heathrow Airport. The 318-room Carlton Tower was sold for £14 million to Proteus, but Lex continued to manage the hotel making it an early example of management contracting in Britain.

British chains in the provinces

The British chains were also active in the provinces:

♦ The most systematic development was by THF's Post House brand, which took advantage of the HDI and expanded to 30 hotels by 1980, the fastest growth of any brand in Britain up to that time. All of the hotels were owned or leased, but unlike the growth of Holiday Inn in North America this was modest since it did not involve franchising. The development of Post House did not deter THF from other provincial developments such as the 320-room Excelsior hotel at Glasgow airport in 1971 and the 157 room St George's hotel in Liverpool, the first new one in the city for 60 years.

♦ In the 1970s Grand Met extended its acquisitions to other business sectors, but Berni Inns, the brewer Truman Hanbury and Buxton and the larger brewer Watney Mann added over 50 provincial hotels to its portfolio.

During the 1970s, some of the national brewers came alive to the attraction of hotels. Most had pubs with bedrooms, which were unbranded and uncoordinated as hotel businesses. Some had more significant hotels, while some others actively developed and acquired hotels to create hotel brands:

♦ Allied Brewers collected the larger hotels from its various regional brewers to form Embassy Hotels, while still retaining pubs with bedrooms in its various regional breweries.

♦ In 1972 Bass Charington acquired Esso Motor Hotels, which gave it exposure to the mid-market in Britain and a foothold on the continent. Later in the decade, Bass branded its hotels as Crest Hotels, which was a mid-market brand, but with looser brand specifications than Post House.

♦ Scottish & Newcastle created Thistle Hotels as its main hotel brand to which it added by acquiring single hotels and short portfolios.

Other regional brewers such as Vaux established the Swallow Hotels brand in 1972. Courage, the London-based brewer, established Anchor Hotels and Greenall Whitley also entered the hotel business.

The structure of hotel portfolios

A feature of hotel chain expansion in the 1970s was the emergence of conglomerates among the leading hotel chains. When THF was formed in 1970, the hotels division was only one of seven divisions. Grand Met diversified into brewing, restaurants, contract catering and bingo. The hotel interests of Allied Brewers, Bass, and the other brewers during the period were minor parts of their brewing, drinks distribution and pubs business. The hotels division was only one of 14 divisions in the Rank Organisation and Ladbroke entered the hotel business from its bases in the betting industry and the property business. The conglomerates were attracted to the hotel business because of its growth prospects, but the hotel business was not large enough on its own for major companies to be focused solely on that activity. Otus estimates that by 1980, hotel chains had grown their British portfolios to 110,000 rooms, up from 45,000 in 1960 and concentration rose to 29%. The accelerating growth of hotel chains during this period was more about growing market share than it was about shaping their portfolios. Apart from favouring urban centres over coastal and countryside locations, the chains did little to structure their brands. Of course, Post House was the principal exception as to a lesser extent was Crest. Most of the rest of the portfolios were clustered around the mid-market and up-market levels. Many of the deluxe hotels in the country were affiliated to chains, but they accounted for a tiny proportion of rooms and were located mostly in London. Hotels below the mid-market level were predominantly small, old, legacy coaching inns in the portfolios of THF and the pubs with bedrooms portfolios of the brewers. The dominant configuration of chain hotels during the period was basic feature hotels with rooms, restaurant and bar with little more than a function room for local social events. As the conference market grew, so, more full-feature hotels emerged particularly in London and the key provincial cities. Hotel resorts with bedrooms, restaurants, bars and conference facilities as well as indoor and outdoor leisure facilities remained a rarity as did limited-feature and room-only hotels. Invariably, chains in Britain during the period owned or leased their hotels. Management contracting and franchising were rare and were introduced later in the period. The reliance on ownership and management of hotels constrained the rate of growth of chains in Britain compared with the US where management contracting and franchising had become commonplace.

Hotel demand and supply performance in Britain

Otus estimates that in 1980, after a decade of exceptional entrances to and exits from the hotel market, total room stock in Britain reached 385,000, a net increase of 40,000 rooms since 1970, but this involved the removal of 30,000 redundant hotel rooms from the market and the creation of 70,000 new rooms. The supply ratio in 1980 rose to 6.9, up from 6.3 in 1960. The very low room occupancy in Britain in 1960 reflected the heavy exposure of hotels to the summer holiday market with its heavy seasonality and winter closures. The improved occupancy by 1980 reflected the growth in domestic business demand and domestic short-break demand and importantly, the growth in foreign demand into the country.

Table 9.10: British Hotel Supply and Demand Performance 1960–1980

	Total Hotels			Chain Hotels			Chain Share	
	1960	1980	CAGR	1960	1980	CAGR	1960	1980
Total rooms	325,000	385,000	1%	45,000	110,000	5%	14%	29%
Room nights available m	119	141	1%	16	40	5%	14%	29%
Room occupancy %	33%	47%	2%	55%	59%	0%		
Room nights sold m	39	66	3%	9	24	5%	23%	36%
Domestic business	11	23	4%	4.3	9.5	4%	40%	42%
Domestic leisure	22	13	-3%	1.4	1.4	0%	6%	11%
Foreign business	3	8	5%	1.4	4.3	6%	46%	54%
Foreign leisure	3	23	10%	1.9	8.6	8%	61%	38%
Supply ratio	6.3	6.9	0%	0.9	2.0	4%		
Secular growth in hotel room supply	10,000	35,000		7,000	60,000		70%	171%

Source: Otus & Co Advisory Ltd

Between 1960 and 1980, the momentum of growth in the British hotel business shifted from unaffiliated hotels to hotel chains. Hotel chain room stock produced an average annual growth of 5% adding 65,000 rooms against the loss of 5000 unaffiliated rooms. Chain room occupancy was higher than the market as a, whole due to their greater share of the growth markets, their greater presence in the key growth locations and their greater investment in sales and marketing activities, particularly with the wholesale markets. Unaffiliated hotels had none of these benefits and their performance suffered. Between 1960 and 1980 the economic ascent of the hotel business in Britain owed a debt to government intervention in the management of hotel supply, which was a factor in the growth of hotel chains. It also relied on the stellar growth in foreign demand into the country, without which the British hotel business would have declined.

Continental European economies

As the most significant structural development in the western continental economies during the post-war period was the creation of the Common Market among France, Germany, Italy, the Netherlands, Belgium and Luxemburg, so during the 1960s and 1970s the most significant economic development was its expansion from six to nine states in 1973 with the inclusion of Britain, Denmark and Ireland. The major EEC initiative of the period was the Common Agricultural Policy (CAP) that provided subsidies to member states to retain and grow their agricultural output and it inhibited the structural development of the economies. Importantly, also at this stage of development of the Common Market was a laissez-faire approach to most service businesses. During the 1960s and 1970s, the original Common Market members produced higher economic growth than was achieved by other western European economies because their agriculture and industrial segments were growing fast and this was a key motive in the application of other states to join.

The four factors that provide the impetus for the structural development of an economy to service businesses progressed differently in the original Common Market members than in the US and Britain. Most progress was made in civil and human rights, manifest in the expansion of citizen services. However, there was less progress in the social sciences. Pure and applied social sciences were less available in continental universities than they were in the US and Britain. Access to personal credit was also less than in the US and Britain due to the lower levels of home ownership and lower levels of ownership of other appreciating assets such as insurance policies, private pension schemes and other saving schemes. Similarly, there was less expansion of domestic holiday travel and travel to other out-of-home leisure events.

In the 1960s and 1970s a distinction emerged in the structural balance of western European economies that was different from previous developments in economic structure. There was a regional basis to this distinction since it was prevalent in the western Mediterranean economies – France, Italy, Spain, Greece and Portugal, but not in the north western European economies – Britain, Germany, Benelux and Scandinavia. The structural development of the north western economies conformed to the classic progress of domestic economic activities from agriculture to secondary industries and on to citizen services at which stage, by the 1960s, they hit a blockage because their economic policies did not see beyond citizen services, unlike the US, which continued its development so that its structural balance moved towards service businesses. The variant that was experienced by the western Mediterranean economies was determined in the first instance by climate. These countries became increasingly popular destinations for summer holidays from northern Europe. As foreign holiday demand increased so also did investment in coastal resorts with the development of hotels, restaurants, bars, retail outlets and venues for other leisure activities as well as travel and transport infrastructure. Two critical features of these developments were first that they were uncoupled from the domestic economies in which they were housed and second, that with the exception of France, the economies were less structurally developed than any of the northern source countries of the holidaymakers. They were more heavily grounded in agriculture than the northern economies. Their secondary industries were less developed as were their citizen services and the proportion of their populations who were holidaymakers were smaller. This was the first example of the structural development of economies being propelled by foreign holidaymakers rather than the economic activities of their own citizens. As a result, the western Mediterranean economies developed an experience business segment too big for the structure, content and performance of the rest of their economies because they provided services that were not demanded by their own citizens.

The growth in holiday demand from the northern economies to the Mediterranean was powerful. The attraction was not only the climate. Mass market foreign holidays during the 1960s and 1970s became fashionable, even exotic and they were competitively priced against domestic holidays in the northern economies. The competitive pricing was due largely to the expansion of tour operators, particularly in Britain, selling packaged holidays that included the price of the flight, transfer from the destination airport to the hotel as well as the price for the hotel and the meals. For most of the holiday demand in the northern economies during the 1960s and 1970s, the Mediterranean package holiday was not only their first visit to a foreign country, but also their first flight and their first stay in a hotel. The attraction was so great that that it increased in spite of political aberration in the region: Spain remained under fascist control until 1975, Greece was controlled by a military junta from 1967 to 1974 and Portugal was a dictatorship until a democratic constitution was introduced in 1976. Unlike the economic developments that occurred during the period in Western Europe, there was no structural progression in the Soviet economies. Economic structure continued to be determined by communist ideology, it continued to ossify around state directed and unproductive agriculture and secondary industries, its hotel business remained minor and it continued to deliver poorer economic performance than the western democracies.

The most significant event during the period for hotel chains in continental Europe was the establishment in 1967 of a 62-room Novotel near the airport in Lille in Northwest France by Paul Dubrule and Gerard Pelison. The Novotel was a mid-market hotel that was the first hotel built in Lille for 50 years and doubled the number of bathrooms in Lille hotels (Accor, 2007: 16). During the period to 1980, Novotel expanded quickly to reach more than 120 hotels in several countries. Mercure, its mid-market conversion brand had grown to 32 hotels and there were 26 Ibis hotels, its economy brand. Novotel–SIEH quickly became the largest hotel chain in France and expanded internationally to other European countries, the US and the Middle East. It was the most systematic hotel chain initiative ever in Europe and by the end of the period in 1980 its story was only beginning. Other than this development there was little other innovation of note in the hotel businesses of France and Germany.

References to employment in this chapter were drawn from the Groningen Growth and Development Centre of the University of Groningen, Netherlands for 1960 and The Office of National Statistics for 1980.

10 The US Hotel Business: 1980–2008

Introduction

In 1980, the US elected Ronald Regan as President and the country began its move from the introspection and economic weakness of the 1970s. The period to 2008 was characterised by development towards even greater emphasis on service businesses, but it was not all plain sailing. There was a recession in 1981/82 before the Regan economic policies started to pay dividends. Military spending rose as ever more sophisticated weapons were created and used in Gulf Wars I and II as well as Afghanistan and Iraq. Spending on homeland security was increased following the atrocities of 9/11 and the growth of international terrorism by Islamic fundamentalists. Growth in service businesses was spearheaded by financial and professional services, but the widening diversity of the sector saw the emergence of experience businesses such as hospitality, travel and recreation more substantially than in any other country and its establishment as a discreet segment. The economic ascent of the hotel business during the period reinforced the position of the US as the world leader in the field with a supply ratio of 15.5 compared with only 8.4 for Britain.

Developments in the US economic structure and hotel demand

In 1980, the US economy was already more developed as a service business economy than Britain's and only a small proportion of the US population took holidays abroad leaving more taking hotel-based holidays in the US. Otus estimates that in 2008, total room nights sold in the US rose above one billion, an increase of 590 million representing an average annual growth of 3%. Over the period, the structure of the hotel business developed too as hotel chains grew to capture 75% of total demand, a strong annual average growth of 4.4%, whereas unaffiliated hotels demand grew only marginally. During the period, all four factors that are indicative of the shifting structural balance of an economy to service business developed significantly. Human and civil rights legislation expanded as it did in most western economies. Applied social sciences became a more significant component of vocational degrees than in any other country and the social sciences became part of the high school curriculum. The expansion of ownership of appreciating assets such as homes, insurance policies, pension schemes and other saving mechanisms was faster than in any other significant economy and this made personal credit more easily available than in any other economy. Domestic business and personal travel expanded strongly. Over the 28-year period to 2008, domestic business demand into US hotels grew from 143 million room nights to 322 million, an average annual growth of 3%. Domestic leisure demand added 270 million room nights to 499 million, including both summer holiday hotel stays and short stays benefiting from the low proportion of US citizens travelling outside the country on vacation. In 2007, only 64 million US residents travelled abroad, equivalent to the volume from Germany, which had a population only 27% of that in the US and a much less structurally developed economy (source: US Office of Travel and Tourism Industries). Over the period, the growth of foreign visitors to the US grew to 56 million (UNWTO, 2008) and accounted for 22% of all hotel room nights sold in the US (source: The American Hotel & Lodging Association (AHLA), Lodging Industry Profile, 2008).

The momentum in the development of the economic structure of the US created a wider range of service businesses and a greater number of larger service businesses. Tables 10.1 and 10.2 illustrate that over the 28-year period to 2008, the proportion of employment in agriculture and secondary industries, the two segments that yield lower domestic business demand into hotels, declined by 5 million and the proportion of employment in service businesses, the segment that yields the highest domestic business demand into hotels, grew by 32 million to account for more than half of all employees. Consequently, with the numbers in employment growing at a faster rate than the growth in population, unemployment was lower and more short-lived than in European countries.

Table 10.1: Employment by segment in US: 1980–2008 (millions)

	Agriculture	Industry	Citizen Services	Service Businesses	Total
1980	4	24	23	43	94
1990	4	24	29	56	113
2000	3	25	36	71	135
2008	3	21	41	75	140

Table 10.2: Employment by segment in US: 1980–2008 (percentage)

	Agriculture	Industry	Citizen Services	Service Businesses	Total
1980	4%	26%	25%	45%	100%
1990	3%	21%	26%	50%	100%
2000	2%	18%	27%	53%	100%
2008	2%	15%	30%	53%	100%

Source: US Departmentof Labour

Agricultural demand into hotels

In 1980, agriculture and fisheries employed 4 million, accounting for 4% of the US workforce compared with only 2% in Britain, illustrating the greater proportion of US agricultural output that was exported and the lower proportion that was imported. Otus estimates that in 1980, 3%, 120,000 of agricultural employees were business travellers who spent an average of 15 nights staying in US hotels on business to generate 1.7 million US hotel room nights for a 1% share of total domestic business demand. Over the period to 2008, employment in agriculture declined at an average annual rate of more than 1% and at the end of the period accounted for only 2% of the total workforce. There was further concentration among agricultural firms producing an increase in the proportion of professional and executive employees at the expense of blue-collar workers whose jobs were reduced by technology. At the end of 1998, the top 30 cattle operations had pen space to feed 5 million head of cattle, 20% more than the total cattle population of Britain at the time (source: Beef Today, Nov-Dec 1998). On the assumption that their sows each produced 20 pigs a year, the 50 largest pig farmers accounted for half of the pigs in the US (source: Successful Farming, October 1998). The creation of larger agricultural corporations required business travel from executives involved in the management of their companies. There was also a growth in the number of agricultural conferences in hotels, but the volume growth of agricultural demand into hotels was limited by the growth in agricultural exports, which generated hotel demand in the destination countries rather than in the US. Consequently, Otus estimates that by 2008, the proportion of agricultural business travellers originating demand, attending conferences and involved increasingly in the management of their companies increased to 3.5%, a total of 96,000 travellers, down from 120,000 in 1980. They spent an average of 17 nights in hotels on both transient rooms demand and packaged conference demand generating 1.6 million domestic hotel room nights, down from 1.7 million in 1980 and represented less than 1% of total domestic business demand.

Industral demand into hotels

In 1980, industrial employment was 24.3 million, 26% of the US workforce. Otus estimates that 4% of industrial employees were business travellers who spent an average of 28 nights in US hotels generating demand of 27 million room nights, 19% of total domestic business demand. Over the 28-year period to 2008, the industrial sectors – manufacturing, utilities, construction and mining – lost 2.9 million of their workforce so that, by the end of the period, the segment was reduced to 15% of the total workforce. The North American Free Trade Agreement (NAFTA) was established at the end of 1992 between the US, Canada and Mexico and coincided with the reduction in US jobs in agriculture and manufacturing at a time when they were increasing in Mexico. Demand for consumer durables increased over the period and led to a spurt of consolidation among manufacturers, which was positive for the hotel business. However, the growth in demand also led to further growth in imports as manufacturing costs were lower in developing economies, which acted as a constraint on the growth of domestic business demand into hotels. In 1980, spending on military production amounted to $45 billion rising to $124 billion in 1990 due to the development of more sophisticated weapons and after the fall of communism spending relaxed to $95 billion in 2000 (source: U.S. Office of Management and Budget, Historical Tables). Thereafter, Gulf War II and military action in Iraq and Afghanistan is estimated to have added a total military cost of around $125 billion per year (source: www.nationalpriorities.org). Military spending on production was only of marginal benefit to the US hotel business since, for the companies involved, there was only one client, the government. Over the period, utilities grew in line with population, construction grew as the economy and the population grew and mining declined. In each case, employment fell, but output grew as improved technology produced a decline in the proportion of blue-collar workers and an increase in the proportion of white-collar and professional employment.

Otus estimates that by 2008, the proportion of industrial business travellers increased to 5.5% due to the growth in size and geographic reach of industrial companies and the increase in the reasons for hotel use, which included: originating demand, travelling as part of the process of managing their companies and attending conferences. The number of industrial business travellers rose from one million to 1.2 million, and spent an average of 30 nights in US hotels to generate 35 million room nights, up from 27 million in 1980. As a result, the industrial segment share of total domestic business demand fell to 11% from 19% as citizen services and service businesses grew at a faster rate.

Citizen services demand into hotels

In 1980, citizen services in the US had a workforce of 23.5 million, a 25% share of the total workforce. Otus estimates that 12%, 2.9 million employees were business travellers. They spent an average of 12 nights in US hotels generating demand of 35 million room nights for a 25% share of the total domestic business demand. Over the 28-year period to 2008, the citizen services workforce grew to 41.3 million, ahead of the national average rate of employment growth with the addition of 18 million jobs. The growth in population and life expectancy were major contributing factors to the growth in citizen services, but there was also a faster growth in parts of the segment that were more positive for hotels. Higher education is a high yielding part of citizen services for hotel demand because of the incidence of professional and white-collar business travel and conference attendance. The National Centre for Educational Statistics reported that, "enrolment in degree awarding institutions increased by 16% between 1985 and 1995. Between 1995 and 2005, enrolment increased at a faster rate (23%) from 14.3 million to 17.5 million". Within higher education, the volume of MBA graduates between 1980 and 2002 grew by an annual average of 3.7% to 121,000 (source: www.census.gov). The growth in student numbers in higher education was supported by the growth in academic, executive, managerial and administrative staff, which grew between 1991 and 2005 by an annual average of 3.2%, double the rate of national employee growth.

Similarly, between 1990 and 2007 health service employment grew by an annual average rate of 3% to 15.4 million with the addition of 6 million employees ahead of the national average employment growth. The greater interaction between the US citizen services and the private sector than in European countries, the wider geographic spread and the larger number of conferences for the segment, all required more business travel by civil servants and professionals. Otus estimates that by 2008, the proportion of citizen service employees who were business travellers involved in segment management and attending conferences rose to 15%, 6.2 million and they spent an average of 13 nights in US hotels generating transient rooms demand and packaged conference demand of 81 million room nights giving a 25% share of total domestic business demand.

Market services demand into hotels

In 1980, service businesses in the US employed 42.8 million. Otus estimates that 7.4%, 3.15 million segment employees were business travellers. They spent an average of 25 nights in US hotels generating 79 million room nights for a 55% share of domestic business demand. Over the period, service business employment grew to 75 million, nearly twice the workforce of citizen services. There was growth in the size and range of service businesses to the extent that market services and experience businesses evolved as discreet segments. Market services was by far the larger of the two and was driven by financial services, professional services, real estate, retailing, and communications.

Employment in financial services grew by 3.2 million to 8.2 million, an average annual growth of 1.8%, marginally ahead of the national growth. However, the size of capital flows catapulted activity across the range of financial services so that it became the most significant sector for the hotel business. In 2002, private and mutual health insurance accounted for 33% of healthcare expenditure in the US compared with 12% in France and only 7% in Germany (source: OECD Health Data 2002). Residential mortgage debt outstanding grew by an annual average of 8% to $6.3 billion and consumer credit rose at a rate of 7.5% to $1.4 billion (source: US Statistical Abstracts, tables 811 and 815). In 2005, there were 111 million housing units in the US of which 33% were rented, 22% were owned and 45% were mortgaged (source: US Census Bureau, Selected Housing Characteristics: 2005). The sub-prime crisis in the US arose because mortgage providers sought to increase the proportion of citizens who were buying rather than renting their homes to the extent they provided mortgages to people with a poor credit rating and from whom the first spike in mortgage defaults arose. The growth of the stock market was also significant with the number of companies listed on NASDAQ increasing to 4,829 with the average addition of 100 companies per year and the value of shares traded over the same period rocketing from an annual 7 billion to 273 billion (source: US Statistical Abstracts, Table 833).

Professional and business services produced the fastest growing employment in market services. During the period from 1980 to 2008, employment in the sector grew by an annual average of 3.1% to reach 17.9 million and was a major source of domestic business demand into hotels over the period. Between 1990 and 1999 total advertising expenditure grew from $129 billion to $215 billion (*source*: US Statistical Abstracts, Table 937).

Experience businesses demand into hotels

A feature of this period for the US economy was the growth of experience businesses. Hospitality, travel, sport, recreation, private health, private education and the arts all came to greater economic prominence. In 1980, hospitality and leisure employment stood at 6.7 million, but by 2008 it had doubled with an annual average growth of 2.5%. The growth of hotel supply and demand contributed to the establishment of experience businesses as a discreet segment. The pattern was repeated in commercial restaurants of which there were 653,000 in 1997 representing an increase of 106,000 establishments from 1990, an average addition of more than 13,000 restaurants per year (*source*: US Statistical Abstracts, Table 1284). Motion picture screenings increased from 15 million to 37 million over the same period and in 1997 alone, 66% of the adult population went to the movies. The size and economic significance of the main spectator sports also increased. Between 1985 and 1999, attendance at major league baseball rose from 48 million to 71 million; the National Football League saw attendance grow from 14 million to 21 million; National Hockey League attendance grew from 12 million to 18 million and professional basketball attendance rose from 12 million in 1985 to 22 million in 1998 (US Statistical Abstracts, Table 1241). In total in 1997, 41% of US adults attended a sporting event. It was not only spectating sports that grew, but also participation in sports. The number of golf rounds played grew from 358 million in 1980 to 564 million in 1999 (*source*: US Statistical Abstracts, Table 1244). In 1997, 76% of US adults committed themselves to exercise programmes and 45% were involved in playing sport (*source*: US Statistical Abstracts, Table 1238). In 1997, amusement and theme parks were attended by 57% of the US adult population (*source*: US Statistical Abstracts, Table 1238).

Domestic air travel outlay grew from $50 billion in 1990 to $67 billion in 1999; outlay on private transportation, predominantly automobiles, grew from $517 billion to $805 billion and motor vehicle registration grew from 156 million to 216 million over the same period (*source*: US Statistical Abstracts, Table 1087). The momentum of growth in demand for experience businesses in the US over the period established some experience businesses as commonplace, whereas they were much rarer in other countries with less developed economic structures. Pet grooming salons are an example. The 2008 Yellow Pages recorded 638 pet grooming salons in Los Angeles. In contrast, in the less structurally developed British capital there were 323, while in the even less structurally developed French capital there were only 52, while in Germany with its greater emphasis on manufacturing, there were only two in Berlin. The great feature of experience businesses is that there is a vast untapped range of experiences that have yet to emerge as businesses in most economies. Experience businesses extend economic activities, generate employment, require investment and yield high volumes of business demand into hotels.

Otus estimates that by 2008, the proportion of service business employees who were business travellers increased to 9.2%, a total of 6.8 million. The three client-facing activities of originating demand, executing contracts and servicing clients continued to be at the core of segment business travel. A growth market over the period that came from service businesses predominantly was for longer hotel stays by executives in activities such as executing contracts, expanding their companies into new areas and working on secondment in regional offices. The hotel business response was to develop extended stay brands such as Residence Inns and Embassy Suites. Industry-wide conferences and conventions continued to grow in number and in size requiring mega centres such as the Las Vegas Convention Centre which can accommodate the International Electronics Show with 120,000 attendees or the World of Concrete with 100,000 attendees. The city has 100,000 hotel rooms in the largest hotel resorts on the planet. However, the volume and frequency of hotel based company specific conferences declined. As service businesses grew nationally they developed regional offices and an increasing proportion of individual company conferences and meetings were held in the offices rather than in hotels. The more that this practice spread, the more that packaged conference demand in hotels was transferred to transient rooms demand, which continued to grow. Business travellers from service businesses spent an average of 30 nights in US hotels generating more transient rooms demand than packaged conference demand. In 2008 service businesses generated 205 million room nights for a 64% share of total domestic business demand.

Domestic leisure demand into hotels

Otus estimates that domestic leisure demand into US hotels in 1980 stood at 228 million room nights. Throughout the 28-year period to 2008 there were three related developments that boosted leisure demand into hotels. First, the progressive growth in white-collar and professional careers provided a growing pool of customers whose lifestyles and earnings brought hotel-based vacation stays into greater prominence. Second, the growth of incentive travel, which was created to reward employees with a bonus that included travel and hotel stays, sometimes with their families, sometimes linked to motivational or strategic conferences created a strong market for hotels that was a mix of business and leisure demand. Third, the growth in ownership of appreciating assets as well as the growth in access to credit increased the use of hotels for long and short vacations In the US, in addition to the main annual vacation, a greater proportion of the population took multiple short holidays as well. Broadly, there were two types of hotel-based short vacations: private stays at hotels and attendance at a widening range of leisure based conventions and associations. This pattern increased throughout the period and was driven by the baby boomers, the oldest of whom were aged 35 in 1980 and reached 63 by 2008. Typically, this generation, many in dual-career families, reached the stage of maximum earnings and wealth during the period. Throughout their adult lives they benefited from the ownership of appreciating assets such as homes and savings. Moreover, as the period progressed, most boomers reached the stage at which their families became adult and left home. As a result, the necessary outgoings of the boomers declined leaving them with high levels of discretionary income, much of which was invested in financial instruments. Thus, the increasingly wealthy boomers were the mainstay of the growth in domestic leisure demand. Their short vacations were typically in domestic hotels or on short cruises, which also grew significantly. Increasingly over the period the long vacations of the boomers were to foreign, long-haul destinations. Domestic leisure demand into hotels in the US became more unpackaged as customers preferred to book their hotels and travel to suit their plans and preferences rather than to buy a package that limited their choices. This trend was stimulated by the emergence of online travel agencies and the convenience of booking hotels and travel online. Online agencies such as Expedia, Priceline and Travelocity became prominent in the field and enabled customers to book the major hotel and airline brands online. As a result, package tour operators in the US declined as facilitators of domestic leisure travel, but did retain some prominence in managing outbound vacations from the US to foreign destinations. However, this was still a small market relative to the total size of the US leisure travel market since by 2008 only 20–25% of the US citizens were estimated to own a passport. By 2008, domestic leisure demand into US hotels added 270 million room nights over the period.

Foreign demand into hotels

Otus estimates that in 1980 foreign demand into US hotels accounted for 76 million room nights, 17% of total demand. Over the period the market grew and by 2007 the American Hotel and Lodging Association estimated that foreign demand accounted for 22% of all room nights sold in US hotels (source: The American Hotels and Lodging Association, Lodging Industry Profile, 2008). This meant that foreign visitors accounted for 218 million room nights, an increase of 142 million over the period to 2007. In 2007, 57% of foreign visitors into the US came from Canada and Mexico, but their length of stay was shorter than visitors from overseas (source: US Office of Travel & Tourism Industries, 2008). The growth in imports over the period was a factor in the growth in foreign business demand into US hotels as was NAFTA. Foreign business demand in 1980 accounted for 36 million room nights and grew to 104 million by 2008, while foreign leisure demand of 40 million room nights in 1980 grew to 114 million in 2008.

Hotel supply in the US

Otus estimates that in 1980 there were 2.3 million hotel rooms in the US producing a hotel supply ratio of 10.1. At a constant 1980 supply ratio and the actual increase in the US population over the period to 2008, the economy would have needed 3.1 million hotel rooms in 2008. However, the growth in the range, size and significance of service businesses drove domestic demand and was supplemented by foreign demand to produce hotel room stock of 4.7 million, a supply ratio of 15.5 and secular growth of 2.3 million rooms, the greatest amount ever. Hotel chains took advantage of the demand growth to expand their portfolios by an annual average of 4% adding 2.2 million rooms to reach a total of 3.2 million in 2008 and account for 69% of all US hotel room stock. In contrast, unaffiliated hotels expanded marginally adding only 80,000 rooms over the same period. The growth in size and significance of hotel chains in the US between 1980 and 2008 is another compelling example of how the economic ascent of the hotel business is driven by progress in the structural balance of economies and that when the prime growth is in service businesses the secular growth is palpable. Only hotel chains are able to identify the mass movements in demand, to access the capital to build the room stock where it is needed and to capture premium growth in demand.

Hotel chains and multiple brands

In the first 10 years of its existence from 1993, Holiday Inn Express shot to 1,200 hotels to be the fastest growing hotel brand in history. The Marriott Corporation added nearly 400,000 rooms in the US alone, an annual average growth of almost 10% (*source*: http://investor.shareholder.com). However, this impressive growth does not tell the full story of the economic ascent of the hotel business in the US. Two other developments were important.

First, there was the adoption by the major chains of multiple brand strategies. In the US between 1980 and 2008, Marriott expanded from one hotel brand to nine, Hilton from one hotel brand to seven and Hyatt from one brand to six. In 1980, Sheraton and Westin were two independent hotel brands, but by 2008 they were joined by another seven brands in Starwood Hotels & Resorts. In 1989, Bass plc from Britain completed its acquisition of Holiday Inn and by 2008 it had morphed through the acquisition of the Intercontinental brand and the development of other brands to becoming Intercontinental Hotels Group with a total of seven hotel brands. In 1980, Ramada, Days Inns and Howard Johnson were all independent hotel brands, by 2008, they were joined by another nine brands, all of which had been acquired by Wyndham Worldwide. In 1980, Quality Inns and Rodeway were independent hotel brands, but by 2008 they were joined by another nine brands in Choice Hotels International. Radisson was a single brand in 1980, but by 2008 it was one of the five hotel brands of the Carlson Group of Companies. In 1980, Novotel of France added Sofitel to its brand portfolio and by 2008 it had been developed into Accor with nine hotel brands. Extended Stay, the smallest, youngest and least international of the largest chains in 2008 provided five extended stay hotel brands in the US and Canada.

The Marriott Corporation

The development of the Marriott Corporation over the period is indicative of these trends. At the start of the period in 1980, Marriott operated one brand, the up-market/full feature brand that has always been at the heart of its hotel portfolio. Then, in 1983, it opened its first Courtyard by Marriott, a mid-market/limited feature brand. In 1987, it acquired the Residence Inn brand, an up-market/limited feature/all-suite brand targeted on extended stay customers. In the same year it opened the first Fairfield Inn as its entry into the economy/limited feature category. In 1995, it acquired 49% of Ritz-Carlton, the deluxe/full feature and resort brand, and in 1998 took its ownership of the brand to 98%. In 1996, Marriott introduced Fairfield Suites in the economy/rooms only/all-suite category and the brand was renamed SpringHill Suites by Marriott in 1998. In 1997, there were three portfolio developments: Marriott acquired the Renaissance Hotel Group, which included the Renaissance brand, a parallel brand to the Marriott Hotels and Resorts brand and it also included the Ramada International brand, which was sold to Cendant in 2004 and the New World brand which was phased out. The first TownePlace Suites opened as Marriott's entry into the mid-market/rooms only/all-suite category The first Marriott Executive Residences was opened bringing Marriott into the up-market/rooms only/all-suite brand targeted on corporate customers staying for at least a month.

Marriott also initiated three new brands in partnership. In 2004, the first Bulgari Hotel opened as a deluxe brand developed in partnership with Bulgari, the jeweller. In 2007, the Edition brand was planned as an up-market boutique brand developed in partnership with Ian Shrager the boutique hotel specialist and Nickelodeon by Marriott was announced in partnership with the children's media and entertainment company, Nickelodeon, as an up-market/resort brand centred round family and fun. In 2008, the Marriott hotel brand matrix in the US was as shown in Table 10.3.

Table 10.3: Marriott Brand Matrix: USA 2008

	Resort	Full Feature	Basic Feature	Limited Feature	Rooms Only
Deluxe	Ritz-Carlton	Ritz-Carlton			
Up-market	Marriott, Renaissance, JW Marriott	Marriott, Renaissance, JW Marriott		Residence Inns	
Mid-market				Courtyard By Marriott	TownePlace Suites
Economy					Fairfield Inns, SpringHill Suites
Budget					

Source: Otus & Co Advisory Ltd

The Marriott growth in room stock and brand diversity was an example of the pattern of development of the major chains, but Marriott's portfolio management was as significant for the hotel categories that it avoided as much as it was for those in which it expanded. Notably, Marriott had no presence at any market level in basic feature hotels, which typically are hotels of less than 100 rooms that rely on local demand for the effective operation of their non-room facilities. They were the most dominant hotel configuration for the previous 200 years and in 2008, mid-market/basic feature remained the largest hotel category in the world. Marriott was also absent from budget hotels at all configurations, which were categories that chains in the US generally avoided as being insufficiently aspirational for domestic customers.

By 2008, Marriott's presence in categories in the mid-market and below was concentrated on brands with high rooms density, which relied little on non-room turnover. In contrast, its presence at the up-market and deluxe levels, with the exception of Residence Inns was in full feature and resort hotels in the Marriott Hotels and Resorts, JW Marriott and Ritz-Carlton brands that targeted packaged demand from conference and leisure customers to use the extensive non-room facilities in the hotels. The Marriott brands were also differentiated by typical length of stay at the hotels. Brands such as Residence Inns, SpringHill Suites and TownePlace Suites were targeted on demand of between a week and a month, while the other brands were focused on demand of less than a week. The Marriott brand profile like that of Hilton, Intercontinental, Wyndham, Choice and others had moved on from the idea of providing a universal hotel brand. They targeted specific markets by configuration of facilities, market level and length of stay reflecting the diversity of demand patterns that evolved in the US over the period. Moreover, there was sufficient demand in these categories to require significantly sized portfolios.

Shrinking markets and international expansion

However, it was not all about growth. The reduction in demand for company-specific conferences and the sharp decline in local demand for hotel restaurants, bars and health clubs were fundamental changes that had impacts on the US hotel business. Between 1993 and 2008, Holiday Inn, the iconic mid-market/full feature brand, shrank by 100,000 rooms in the US (*source*: www.ichhotels group.com and Paul Slattery et al. 1994) Intercontinental Hotels Group and its precursor companies sought to compensate by capturing transient rooms demand in its impressively growing Holiday Inn Express, mid-market/limited feature brand. Over the 15-year period to 2008, the Sheraton up-market/full feature brand declined by 14,000 rooms in the US and the Marriott Hotels brand, the iconic up-market/full feature brand had one less managed hotels in the US in 2008 than it had in 2000. However, over the eight years to 2008 it added 77 franchised hotels to the brand, a shift in portfolio balance that is indicative of a maturing market. Most of the growth in hotel brands over the past two decades has been in brands that rely less on non-room demand.

The second important development in the economic ascent of the hotel business over the period was the acceleration of international expansion. Of the 10 largest chains in the world in 2008, nine were weaned in the US. The only exception was Accor from France. Although Intercontinental Hotels Group was headquartered in Britain and listed on the London Stock Exchange, all its brands emanated from the US and had their major presence there. Table 10.4 shows the rate of global portfolio growth achieved by the major chains between 1980 and 2008.

Table 10.4: 10 Largest Global Chains Room Stock Growth: 1980 - 2008

	1980	2008		CAGR	Rooms Added
Marriott Corporation	33,800	533,000	Marriott International	10.4%	499,200
Novotel	35,200	465,000	Accor	9.7%	429,800
Hilton Corporation	71,800	496,000	Hilton Hotels Corporation	7.1%	424,200
Quality Inns International, Rodeway Inns	59,000	465,000	Choice Hotels International	7.7%	406,000
Howard Johnson, Ramada, Days Inns	197,000	593,000	Wyndham Worldwide	4.0%	396,000
Sheraton, Weston	136,800	285,000	Starwood Hotels & Resorts	2.7%	148,200
Holiday Inns Inc.	303,600	619,000	Intercontinental Hotels Group	2.6%	315,400
Radisson Hotel Corporation	11,400	147,000	Carlson Group of Companies	9.6%	135,600
Hyatt Corporation and International	47,000	114,000	Global Hyatt Corporation	3.2%	67,000
Total Rooms	**895,600**	**3,717,000**		**5.2%**	**2,821,400**

Sources: Service World International for 1980 and company websites

The way in which the major chains grew their portfolios differed over the period. Marriott added more rooms than any other and most of its portfolio growth was achieved organically. Similarly, Accor, Carlson, Choice, and Hyatt also achieved their growth mainly by organic developments. Intercontinental and Starwood were created by acquiring brands and creating brands. Hilton achieved much of its portfolio growth in the last 10 years of the period by the acquisition of Promus in the US, which provided its brand diversity and of Hilton Group from Britain, which provided its international thrust, while the acquisition of 12 hotel brands in the US was the basis of Wyndham Worldwide Hotel Group.

Table 10.5: 10 Largest Hotel Chains: World Presence 2008

	US		Europe		Elsewhere		World	
	Rooms	Share	Rooms	Share	Rooms	Share	Rooms	Share
Intercontinetal Hotels	420,000	9%	70,000	1%	129,000	17%	619,000	4%
Wyndham Worldwide	455,000	10%	26,500	1%	111,500	15%	593,000	4%
Hilton Hotels Corporation	378,000	8%	39,650	1%	78,350	10%	496,000	3%
Marriott International	428,000	9%	39,050	1%	65,950	9%	533,000	3%
Accor	100,000	2%	237,000	5%	128,000	17%	465,000	3%
Choice Hotels International	300,000	7%	42,250	1%	122,750	16%	465,000	3%
Starwood Hotels & Resorts	160,000	4%	40,150	1%	84,850	11%	285,000	2%
Carlson Group	80,000	2%	49,700	1%	17,300	2%	147,000	1%
Global Hyatt	78,000	2%	5,920	0%	30,080	4%	114,000	1%
Extended Stay	76,000	2%	0	0%	1,000	0%	77,000	0%
Totals	**2,475,000**	**54%**	**550,220**	**11%**	**768,780**	**12%**	**3,794,000**	**24%**

Source: Company Websites, Otus & Co Advisory Ltd

Table 10.5 provides a snapshot of the international profiles of the 10 largest hotel chains in the world. The first observation is their high penetration of the US market, 54% of all hotel rooms compared with only 11% in Europe and 12% in the rest of the world. For the major chains, the US was the anchor economy in which they had three times the number of rooms that they had in Europe illustrating that the major chains still have a long way to go in their international coverage.

Another measure of the immaturity of the major chains in the international market is the proportion of their rooms that are located in their home country. Table 10.6 illustrates the position at the end of 2008 when the range was from 99% for Extended Stay to only 26% for Accor. It is not unexpected that over the period to 2008, the US chains expanded in foreign countries at a slower pace than in the US. The foreign economies were less structurally developed than the US and their domestic hotel demand was less than the US. It was also more difficult to expand abroad because of different languages, laws and cultures as well as different capital markets. Over the period, the most effective strategy for the US hotel chains was to expand as vigorously as they could in the US where the demand and capital conditions were most advantageous.

Table 10.6: 10 Largest Hotel Chains: Home Country Exposure 2008

	World Rooms	Share	Home Country	Home Country Rooms	Exposure
Intercontinetal Hotels Group	619,000	4%	US	420,000	68%
Wyndham Worldwide	593,000	4%	US	455,000	77%
Hilton Hotels Corporation	496,000	3%	US	378,000	76%
Marriott International	533,000	3%	US	428,000	80%
Accor	465,000	3%	France	120,000	26%
Choice Hotels International	465,000	3%	US	300,000	65%
Starwood Hotels & Resorts	285,000	2%	US	160,000	56%
Carlson Group	147,000	1%	US	80,000	54%
Global Hyatt	114,000	1%	US	78,000	68%
Extended Stay	77,000	0%	US	76,000	99%
Totals	3,794,000	24%		2,495,000	66%

Source: Company websites, Otus & Co Advisory Ltd

US hotel demand and supply performance

The quality of industry-wide demand data improved during the period with the collection of statistics on hotel room occupancy, achieved room rate and revenue per available room (RevPAR) by Smith Travel Research. The 2008 total room occupancy of 60% shows that the rapid growth in supply was not out of kilter with the rise in demand. Indeed, 2008 not only had the highest total room nights sold in any year, but also the highest total room occupancy recorded for the market as a whole. The data illustrate improving effectiveness of hotel chain development and more effective capital markets. The period also continued the universal pattern of hotel chains outperforming unaffiliated hotels to account for 71% of supply, but 77% of demand volume.

Table 8.4: Supply and Demand Performance: US 1980–2008

	Total Hotels			Chain Hotels			Chain Share	
	1980	2008	CAGR	1980	2008	CAGR	1960	2008
Total rooms	2,300,000	4,700,000	2.5%	1,050,000	3,220,000	4.1%	46%	69%
Room nights available m	842	1,720	2.5%	384	1,179	4.1%	46%	69%
Room occupancy %	53%	60%		60%	66%			
Room nights sold m	**446**	**1,039**	**2.9%**	**231**	**778**	**4.4%**	**52%**	**75%**
Domestic business	143	322	2.9%	92	287	4.1%	65%	89%
Domestic leisure	228	499	2.6%	104	334	4.3%	46%	67%
Foreign business	36	104	3.8%	18	78	5.3%	52%	75%
Foreign leisure	40	114	3.7%	16	78	5.8%	40%	68%
Supply ratio	10.1	15.5		4.6	10.6			
Secular growth in hotel room supply	300,000	1,625,000		320,000	1,800,000		107%	111%

Source: Otus & Co Advisory Ltd

In this chapter, all data on employment has been drawn from www.bls.gov/news.release/archieves/empsit_01092009.html

11 The British Hotel Business: 1980–2008

Introduction

During the period from 1980 to 2008 the structural balance of the British economy changed more significantly than it had done during any period in the previous 100 years. The agriculture and industrial segments declined and citizen services continued to grow, but the definitive feature of the period was the growth in service businesses, which propelled the economic ascent of the British hotel business. Hotel demand grew strongly, but it was the rapid growth of hotel chains and the widening diversity of demand that had the biggest effects on the changes in the patterns of hotel supply.

The root of these changes was the shift in economic policy. When Margaret Thatcher came to power at the end of the 1970s the British economy was in a mess, having endured a decade of slow economic growth, industrial relations trauma, high inflation and high levels of unemployment. Manufacturing, parts of which were controlled by the government, and mining, which was nationalised, were declining. Citizen services had received almost half a century of high government investment and service businesses were not large enough nor growing fast enough to soak-up the rising volume of unemployed. The new government instituted wide-ranging changes to boost the economy including greater flexibility in the labour market, fewer restrictions on setting-up businesses and lighter regulatory control of financial services, which enabled the growth in home ownership, the extension of personal credit and the privatisation of businesses controlled by the government. In parallel, the Conservative administrations introduced fiscal and strategic initiatives to wean tracts of the population away from reliance on the government to resolve a wide spread of economic and social problems. In the Labour administrations of Tony Blair and Gordon Brown from 1997, the rate of government investment and growth of employment in citizen services accelerated again, but the growth momentum in service businesses was the main source of new jobs and the segment generated the highest rate of growth in hotel demand throughout the period.

Developments in British economic structure and hotel demand

Otus estimates that total hotel demand grew to 106 million room nights, up by 40 million, an annual average growth of 1.7%. Within this overall growth there was a material shift in the structure of the hotel business as hotel chains grew to capture 68% of demand, an annual average growth of 4%, whereas unaffiliated hotels demand shrank by 8 million.

During the period, the four factors that are indicative of the shifting structural balance of an economy to service business all progressed well. Human and civil rights legislation was expanded to enable the growing diversity of British society to be reflected in its institutions, in employment and in opportunities. The social sciences became commonplace in a wide range of undergraduate and postgraduate degrees and they entered the school curriculum. The expansion of ownership of appreciating assets such as homes, insurance policies, pension schemes and other saving mechanisms made the provision of personal credit more widespread. Business and personal travel expanded materially in terms of the numbers travelling, the frequency of travel and the distance travelled. The growth in travel to foreign countries accelerated in the period to 2006, the latest year for data, to 701 million nights, up from 228 in 1980 (source: International Passenger Survey, Travel Trends 2006, HMSO). Over the 28-year period to 2008, domestic business demand into hotels grew from 23 million room nights to 44 million, an average annual growth of 2.4% reinforcing its position as the largest source of demand into British hotels. Domestic leisure demand grew from 13 million room nights to 18 million, an average annual growth of 1.1%. Foreign demand continued its growth by an average of 1.4% per year to reach 45 million room nights.

Over the period, the rate of decline of employment in the agriculture and industry segments, the two segments that yield lower domestic business demand into hotels, hardly impacted on hotel demand, while the growth in domestic business demand was driven by growth in citizen services and service businesses, the two segments that naturally yield higher domestic business demand into hotels.

Table 11.1: Employment by Segment in Britain: 1980–2008 (m)

	Agriculture	Industry	Citizen Services	Service Businesses	Total
1980	0.6	9.4	9.8	10.3	30.2
1990	0.6	8.0	8.0	12.6	29.3
1997	0.6	6.5	9.3	13.3	29.7
2000	0.5	6.4	8.7	14.0	29.6
2008	0.5	5.6	10.0	15.6	31.7

Source: Office of National Statistics

Table 11.2: Employment by Segment in Britain: 1980–2008 %

	Agriculture	Industry	Citizen Services	Service Businesses	Total
1980	2%	35%	25%	38%	100%
1990	2%	27%	27%	43%	100%
1997	2%	23%	29%	46%	100%
2000	2%	22%	29%	47%	100%
2008	2%	18%	32%	49%	100%

Source: Office of National Statistics

Agricultural demand into hotels

In 1980, agriculture and fisheries employed 0.64 million, accounting for 2% of the British workforce. Otus estimates that by 1980, the proportion of agricultural employees who were business travellers was 2.5%, that the average number of nights they spent in British hotels increased to nine and that the demand generated fell to 0.14 million room nights for a 1% share of total domestic business demand. Over the period to 2008, employment in agriculture declined progressively at an average annual rate of 1% and at the end of the period accounted for only 1.5% of the total workforce. There was some consolidation among agricultural firms and there was continuing use of hotels through farming associations and conferences, but there was also continuing growth in agricultural productivity and in imports. By 2008, 2.8%, 13,000 agricultural employees were business travellers originating demand and attending conferences. They spent 10 nights in British hotels generating mostly transient rooms demand, but also packaged conference demand of 0.14 million room nights, down marginally from 1980, but the agricultural share of total domestic business demand fell to only a trace.

Industrial demand into hotels

In 1980, industrial companies employed 9.4 million, 35% of the British workforce. Otus estimates that 4.0% of the industrial employees were business travellers who spent an average of 16 nights in British hotels generating a total of 6 million room nights sold for a 27% share of total domestic business demand. Over the 28 year period to 2008, employment in the industrial sectors – manufacturing, utilities, construction and mining – declined by an average of 1.9% per year with the loss of 3.9 million jobs so that by the end of the period the segment accounted for 18% of the total workforce.

Of the significant changes in these sectors over the period three were notable. First, employment in manufacturing fell from 6.8 million in 1980 to 3.2 million in 2008. The momentum of decline in manufacturing that had been built up since the end of World War II on the back of low productivity, poor industrial relations, low levels of investment and poor quality of products was accelerated during the period by the removal of support by the government. Second, coal mining was decimated. Early in the period, the National Union of Mineworkers opposed the closure of unprofitable mines by the National Coal Board in spite of declining demand for coal and price competition from cleaner fuels. The industrial strife came to a head in the tense miners' strike, which lasted for almost a year until March 1985. The miners lost. Coal mining in Britain was privatised. Its work practices were transformed and by 2007, UK Coal plc, the dominant company in the industry employed only 3,100 *(source*: www.ukcoal. com). Third, the government pursued a programme of privatisation of industrial companies that it had taken into control in previous periods. Shipbuilding, British Leyland, the vehicle manufacturer, and utilities such as electricity, gas and water were all privatised. The utilities made the most successful transition and their performance and productivity improved materially, but with fewer employees. Without government subsidies, shipbuilding and British Leyland struggled to withstand foreign competition. Construction grew with the increase in private homes and service business real estate such as shops, offices, hospitality and travel. Although industrial employment fell by 40%, Otus estimates that the proportion of business travellers increased to 5.7%, but the total number of business travellers declined to 315,000, down only 16% since 1980 because the growth in the size of industrial companies increased the proportion of professional and white collar employees who travelled for a wider range of reasons. They were involved in originating demand, travelling within their company and also attending hotel-based conferences. In 2008, they spent an average of 19 nights in British hotels generating 6 million room nights from transient rooms demand and packaged conference demand in 2008, unchanged over the period for a 14% share of total domestic business demand, down from 27% at the start of the period as citizen services and service businesses grew at a faster rate.

Citizen services demand into hotels

In 1980, citizen services employed 6.8 million, 25% share of the total workforce. Otus estimates that 12.5%, 0.9 million citizen services employees, were business travellers who spent an average of seven nights in British hotels generating demand of 6 million room nights for 27% of all domestic business demand. Over the 28 year period to 2008, citizen services experienced two different phases of development. Under Conservative control between 1980 and 1997, citizen services added an average of 87,000 jobs per year, whereas the Labour administrations between 1997 and 2008, invested more heavily in citizen services and added an average of 156,000 jobs per year, almost double the rate during the Conservative administrations. By 2008, 12.5%, 1.26 million of citizen service employees, up from 850,000 in 1980, were business travellers. Their involvement in segment management increased, but travelling in the oversight of the nationalised industries declined due to the privatisations and the attendance at hotel-based conferences by medics, academics and civil servants increased. The segment travellers spent an average of nine nights in British hotels producing transient rooms demand and packaged conference demand of 11.3 million room nights, up from 6 million in 1980.

Service businesses demand into hotels

In 1980, service businesses employed 10.3 million and the segment was already the largest in the economy with 38% share of the total workforce. Otus estimates that 7.2% of service business employees were business travellers who spent an average of 14 nights in British hotels generating both transient rooms demand and packaged conference demand of 10.4 million room nights for a 46% share of total domestic business demand and establishing the segment as the largest generator of hotel demand. Over the 28-year period to 2008, service business employment grew to 15.6 million accounting for almost half of the workforce. At the start of the period, national unemployment was high and the agriculture and secondary segments were in decline. New demand had to be created as did new businesses to meet the emerging demand and only in so doing would new jobs be created.

Financial services growth

Two initiatives were put in place to kick-start this process and they benefited service businesses more than other segments. First, the encouragement to those at the early stage of their career to own homes as well as the opportunity for council house tenants to buy their home produced a significant multiplier effect, which generated jobs throughout the financial services sector and elsewhere. Jobs were created in mortgage providers. As a result, more professional and white collar jobs were created due to the increase in home buildings and contents insurance policies and in turn, many of these jobs included private pensions. The resulting increased income to financial service businesses accelerated stock market activity by insurance companies and pension funds. In 1986, the Big Bang, which modernised the stock market also accelerated share-buying activity by institutions. The growth, innovation and light regulation in financial services produced increasingly sophisticated international equity and debt instruments as well as derivatives, which involved trading within the financial services sector rather than serving corporate or personal clients, directly.

The credit crunch started in 2007 in the US and Britain where there were already around 70% of households owning their homes and lenders provided home mortgages to sub-prime buyers with dubious credit records and circumstances. The mortgage debt was packaged, syndicated and traded across international markets. Traders in debt instruments and derivatives dealt among themselves and the values attached to the instruments became increasingly detached from the reality of their sources. In 1980, financial and business services in Britain employed 5.6 million and by 2008 it had grown by an annual average of 2.9% adding 3.6 million jobs. In addition to the growth in financial services already discussed, the growth in ownership of appreciating assets such as homes, pension schemes, insurance policies and other saving schemes eased the availability of personal credit, most explicitly through the expansion of credit cards. The Office of National Statistics estimates that between 1991 and 1998 credit card transactions increased by 10% per year *(source*: www.statistics.gov.uk). By 2007, every British citizen, on average, carried 1.25 credit cards compared with the less structurally developed France and Germany where, on average, each citizen carried only 0.17 and 0.24 credit cards, respectively (*source*: www.pbs.org). Bank accounts became widespread among the population and most full-time employees had their salaries paid directly into their bank account.

The multiplier effect did not end there. Professional services such as accounting and the law grew as well as other market service businesses from home services to IT support. The new market service vibrancy in the economy with new and larger businesses also fed back into financial services since corporate banking expanded as the economy returned to growth and new businesses came into being so that, over the period, banks in Britain not only became larger, but also more diversified in both their corporate and personal banking activities.

Privatisations

The second parallel initiative to kick-start the economy during the period was the privatisation of government-controlled industries and service businesses. Three key experience businesses: British Airways (BA), British Airports Authority (BAA) and British Rail (BR) were important. The most significant for hotel demand were BA and BAA. However, the immediate change in these two privatised companies was the reduction in the numbers employed to enable the companies to be effective in the public markets. The effectiveness was also enhanced by the increase in flexibility of employment and operations to capture and process growing flight demand. The Air Transport White Paper records that in 1980, 35 million passengers passed through British airports and by 2008, the total increased to 250 million, an average annual growth of 7.3% (*source*: Air Transport White Paper, HMSO, 2003). In parallel, Oxford Economic Forecasting records that the volume of domestic business passengers passing through British airports in 1980 was 12.2 million rising to 35.5 million in 2005, an average annual growth of 4.6% (Oxford Economic Forecasting, 2006). Given that travel is a precursor to hotel demand then this growth in air travel reflected the growth in service businesses as a whole and the hotel business in particular. The initiatives in financial services and the privatisations contributed to growing demand and changes in the structure of other service businesses such as retailing and hospitality. Retailing grew materially during the period. The Retail Consortium estimates that in 2007, retail sales accounted for 8% of GDP and one third of consumer spending (*source*: www.brc.org.uk). In 2007, the consortium estimated that there were 298,000 shops in the country and that retailing employed 2.9 million, 11% of the British workforce.

Service business hotel demand drivers

The growth in service businesses was the main source of growth in domestic business travel over the period for three reasons. First, a higher proportion of executives in service businesses needed to travel and stay in hotels than those in any other segment, because they typically operate out of many more venues than the other segments. The comparison of a large manufacturer and large retailer in Britain serves as an illustration. At the end of 2007, Ford UK employed 13,000 in seven locations (*source*: www.ford.co.uk). Like other manufacturers, most business travellers at Ford, were sales and marketing executives located at their headquarters in Essex. In addition, purchasing executives travelled to suppliers. From time to time there was also travel by executives from the plants to the headquarters and by headquarters based executives to the plants. Only visits to and from the plants at Southampton, Bridgend and on Merseyside to the headquarters in Essex may have involved hotel stays due to the travel time required. Ford executives also attended conferences and meetings that could also have involved hotel stays. Applying to Ford the Otus estimate that in 2008, 5.7% of secondary executives were business travellers who spent an average of 19 nights in British hotels, then typically, 14,000 hotel nights per year were generated by Ford in Britain. In contrast, Boots the Chemist employed around 45,000 full-time equivalents in Britain, mostly in health and beauty shops, the largest component of the 2,620 locations in Britain where Boots traded (*source*: www.boots.com). Boots, like all retailing and hospitality chains, operated out of a mass of venues and required corporate executives from throughout the corporate structure to travel to the venues and to the corporate regions as part of the on-going process of managing the company. Boots executives were also involved in company conferences and meetings as well as industry-wide conferences and conventions. Applying to Boots, the Otus estimate that 12% of service business employees were business travellers who spent an average of 14 nights in British hotels then typically, 76,000 hotel room nights per year are generated by Boots in Britain, 5.5 times the hotel demand generated by Ford.

The second reason why there was such a sharp growth in service business demand into hotels was that many such as financial services, communications and professional services involve a high instance of executives travelling to originate demand, execute business for clients and to service clients.

Third, a further benefit that grew strongly for the first two decades of the period was conference and meetings demand in hotels mainly from service businesses. As occurred in the US in the 1960 to 1980 period, most of the growing service businesses in Britain did not have an office infrastructure throughout the country to accommodate meetings such as corporate meetings, training sessions or promotional meetings for which they used hotels. This meant that the benefit to hotels was not only in selling more rooms, but also in selling conference packages including bedrooms, meeting rooms, meals and snacks. In Britain, this market changed after the millennium. By that time, the rate of growth in hotel-based conferences and meetings had begun to decline because as service businesses grew nationally they created regional offices with meeting space so that company-specific conferences and meetings occurred on their own premises rather than in hotels. Hotels continued to benefit from the growing volumes of transient room demand, but progressively lost the non-rooms demand. This trend was structural and not cyclical and was reflected in the strong growth in limited feature hotels between 2000 and 2008 compared with minor additions to full-feature hotels.

Otus estimates that by 2008, the expanding diversity and size of service businesses propelled the proportion of service business employees who were business travellers to 12%, 1.9 million, up from 0.7 million in 1980. They were involved in originating demand, executing contracts and servicing clients. They were also involved in travel in the course of managing their companies, attending company-specific conferences and meetings, company/client conferences and in attending industry-wide conferences. They spent an average of 14 nights in British hotels, which generated both transient and packaged conference demand of 26 million room nights, up from 10.4 million in 1980 for a 60% share of total domestic business demand.

Domestic leisure demand into hotels

Otus estimates that in 1980, domestic leisure demand accounted for 13 million room nights into hotels in Britain. By 2008 this market had increased to only 18 million room nights, an average annual growth of 1%. There were complex trends involved in this development. First, the structural developments in the economy boosted the total volume of holiday demand from Britons, however, the holiday taking trends of the 1960 to 1980 period accelerated to 2008. Domestic long holidays declined from 36.5 million to 27.1 million in 2008, Britons made 45.3 million holiday visits abroad in 2006 compared with only 11.6 million in 1980 (source: The International Passenger Survey, Travel Trends, HMSO) Domestic short breaks increased progressively for the first two decades of the period, but as low cost airlines expanded their services to many more continental destinations within two hours' flying time so the proportion of short breaks taken by Britons on the continent increased. The main driver of British leisure demand into hotels in Britain and elsewhere during the period were the baby boomers. By the millennium, the boomers had reached peak earnings and by the end of the period the older boomers were heading for retirement healthier, wealthier and with more experience of service consumption and enjoyment than any other generation. Importantly, a greater proportion of them travelled on business than any previous generation and an even greater proportion of them and their families travelled for leisure more frequently and further than any previous generation.

The growth in the wholesale markets for short breaks was beneficial to the hotel chains in Britain since most operated their own short break programmes and also were involved in the short break programmes of wholesalers such as Superbreaks. From the early years of the 21st century as online travel agencies, such as Expedia and Priceline, became more active, they signed-up predominantly unaffiliated hotels throwing a lifeline to them by providing transient leisure demand for rooms that otherwise the hotels would never have attracted. Although hotel chains benefited from their involvement in the wholesale markets they benefited little from the development of online travel agencies. By 2008, hotel chains accounted for only half of the domestic leisure demand in Britain.

Foreign leisure demand into hotels

The International Passenger Survey estimates that in 1980, foreign visitors spent 146 million nights in Britain and Otus estimates that they accounted for 31 million hotel room nights, 46% of total hotel demand and that there were three times as many foreign leisure travellers as business travellers. By 2006, the latest figures available at the time of writing, the number of foreign holidaymakers to Britain had increased to 10.7 million room nights, up from 5.5 million in 1980, but the average length of stay declined due to the continuing growth in multi-country European tours and the growth in short breaks into Britain from western continental Europe. As a result of these trends, foreign leisure demand into hotels in 2008 increased to 32 million room nights, up from 23 million in 1980. In parallel, the number of foreign business visits increased to 9.0 million, up from 2.6 million in 1980, but the number of day visits from the western continent increased significantly over the period (*source*: The International Passenger Survey, Travel Trends, HMSO) By 2008, foreign business travellers accounted for 13 million hotel room nights, up from 8.0 million in 1980.

Hotel supply in Britain

Otus estimates that in 1980 there were 385,000 hotel rooms in Britain producing a supply ratio of 6.9. At a constant 1980 ratio and at the actual increase in the population over the period to 2008, the economy would have needed 420,000 hotel rooms in 2008. However, the growth in the range, size and significance of service businesses drove domestic demand and was supplemented by foreign demand to produce hotel room stock of 510,000, a supply ratio of 8.4, and secular growth of 90,000. The main hotel supply feature of the period was the growth in the significance of hotel chains, which expanded over at an average annual rate of 3.5% to reach a total of 291,200 rooms with a 57% share of total supply.

Hotel chains supply profile

In 1985, the analysis of hotel chain supply became more systematic with the first publication of the detailed portfolios of hotel chains in Britain and the development of analytical tools to interpret the data. In 1985, there were 119,000 chain hotel rooms in Britain in 1,248 hotels, which were affiliated to 93 companies with four hotels or more and they operated 116 hotel brands. The market level and hotel configuration matrix of these chains was as shown in Table 11.3.

Table 11.3: Chain Market Level/Hotel Configuration Matrix: Britain 1985

	Resort	Full Feature	Basic Feature	Limited Feature	Rooms Only	Total
Deluxe	0%	2%	0%			2%
Up-Market	1%	17%	9%			27%
Mid-Market	0%	19%	32%			51%
Economy	0%		10%	0%	0%	11%
Budget	1%		9%			9%
Total	2%	38%	59%	0%	0%	100%

Source: UK Hotel Groups Directory 1986 and Otus & Co Advisory Ltd

Of the 25 categories of hotel, the 1985 profile showed that chains in Britain were present in 15. Those hotel categories in the table with 0% have less than

0.5% of the room stock and the chains are absent from those categories with no entry. The market level profile was very narrowly focused with 78% of the rooms in up-market and mid-market hotels and the hotel configuration profile was narrower with 97% of the rooms in full feature and basic feature hotels. The three largest hotel categories – mid-market/basic feature, mid-market/full feature and up-market/full-feature – accounted for 68% of total chain room stock. The distribution of resort hotels throughout the market levels was due on the one hand to the continued, but dwindling presence of chains in hotel resorts in seaside towns, particularly at the economy and budget levels and on the other hand the emergence of brands at the up-market/resort category such as Whitbread's Country Club Hotels, which were located near large conurbations, had extensive indoor and outdoor leisure provision, notably golf courses and which focused on the conference market as well as short breaks.

Of the 22,000 rooms at the economy/basic feature and budget/basic feature categories in 1985, almost half were in rooms without en suite bathrooms, which was a legacy of old and under-invested hotels. The supply profile of chain hotels also reflected the sources of demand on which they relied. Basic feature hotels, which included the smallest chain hotels, operated with a restaurant and bar that relied on attracting local demand as well as resident customers and invariably also included a function room to attract local social functions such as weddings and rotary club lunches. In contrast, full-feature hotels included most of the modern and international hotel brands such as Hilton, Holiday Inn, Intercontinental and Posthouse, which created their portfolios with new-build hotels rather than acquisitions. In addition to these brands, full-feature hotels were also included in the portfolios of Edwardian, Crest, Mount Charlotte, Queens Moat Houses, Swallow and Thistle, which were developed mainly through acquisition and conversion rather than new build. The full-feature hotels were mainly located in urban centres and focused on business demand, both transient and conference as well as packaged short break leisure demand.

The emerging, but still embryonic, categories in 1985 were economy/limited feature and economy/rooms only. The 540 economy/limited feature rooms included one Ibis and three Travelodges, while the economy/rooms-only hotels with a total of only 70 rooms were in Little Chef Lodges, stand-alone bedroom blocks adjacent to three of Trust House Forte's Little Chef roadside restaurant brand.

Table 11.4: Chain Market Level/Hotel Configuration Matrix: London 1985

	Resort	Full Feature	Basic Feature	Limited Feature	Rooms Only	Total
Deluxe		5%	0%			5%
Up-Market		37%	3%			39%
Mid-Market	0%	25%	13%			37%
Economy		0%	12%	1%		13%
Budget			5%			5%
Total	0%	67%	32%	1%		100%

Source: UK Hotel Groups Directory 1986 and Otus & Co Advisory Ltd

The main location of chain rooms in Britain in 1985 was London where 53 hotel brands were present with 172 hotels and 41,100 rooms accounting for 45% of all rooms, whereas chains accounted for 35% of total British hotel rooms. The London market level and hotel configuration matrix for chain rooms in 1985 was as shown in Table 11.4. Given the growing volume of demand into London from across all demand sources – domestic and foreign, business and leisure – the range of categories was narrow. In 1985, chain rooms in London accounted for only 11 of the 25 hotel categories, a narrower range than in Britain as a whole. However, London did account for 81% of all chain deluxe rooms in the country and half of the up-market chain rooms. It also accounted for 75% of up-market/ full feature rooms indicating the extent to which the conference market was centred on London at the time. The 25 economy/basic feature hotels with 4,980 rooms included 610 rooms without en suite bathrooms and more significantly the 15 budget/basic feature hotels with 1,910 rooms included 1,750 without private bathrooms. The presence of hotel resorts and limited feature hotels were token and there were no rooms-only hotels. After London, the next largest hotel chain cities in Britain were Edinburgh, Birmingham and Manchester, which in 1985 accounted for 2,950, 2,810 and 1,850 chain rooms respectively.

In 1985, 93 companies operated portfolios of hotels in Britain. The 10 largest accounted for 64,800 rooms, more than half of all chain rooms and 16% of all hotel rooms in the country. The remaining 83 companies had an average of only 650 rooms each, thus for most of these there was little differentiation from unaffiliated hotels in terms of their capacity to generate premium demand, deliver higher operating margins or attract competitive capital to grow. All of the 10 largest were British and publicly quoted. In Britain as a whole there were 42 publicly quoted companies with 93,800 rooms and UK Hotels plc accounted for 80% of all chain rooms illustrating the importance of the public equity markets to the business at the time. Another feature of both the quoted and unquoted companies was that all but a few of the hotels were owned or leased by the companies. Management contracting and franchising were minor in Britain in 1985 and were the preserve of American brands.

Table 11.5: 10 Largest Holding Companies: Britain 1985

	Rooms	Share of Chain Rooms	Share of Total Rooms
Trust House Forte Plc	20,590	17%	5%
Ladbroke Group Plc	6,730	6%	2%
Bass Plc	6,210	5%	2%
Mount Charlotte Investments Plc	6,000	5%	1%
Queens Moat Houses Plc	5,950	5%	1%
Scottish & Newcastle Breweries Plc	4,670	4%	1%
Grand Metropolitan Plc	4,030	3%	1%
Allied Lyons Plc	3,690	3%	1%
Rank Organisation Plc	3,610	3%	1%
Vaux Breweries Plc	3,320	3%	1%
Total	**64,800**	**54%**	**16%**

Source: UK Hotel Groups Directory 1986

Of the 93 chains, 14 operated multiple brands and the remaining 79 chains operated only one hotel brand. Only 10 brands, accounting for 12% of chain rooms, were developed by building new hotels to explicit specifications and most of those were Posthouses and Holiday Inns, but also included: Four Seasons, Hilton, Ibis, Little Chef Lodges, Novotel, Ramada, Sheraton and Travelodge. The remaining brands accounting for 88% of the chain rooms were predominantly developed by acquiring existing hotels and thus their brand structures were loose and the hotels were old.

Hotel chain structure: 2008

In 2008, chain room stock in Britain reached 291,200, an average annual growth of 4.0% from 1985. However, it was not only the volume of hotel chain supply that grew, but also their diversity. In 2008, chains were represented in 21 of the 25 hotel categories, up from 15 in 1985 and indicative of a greater diversity of hotel demand.

Table 11.6: Chain Market Level/Hotel Configuration Matrix: Britain 2008, % Share

	Resort	Full Feature	Basic Feature	Limited Feature	Rooms Only	Total
Deluxe	0%	1%	0%		0%	2%
Up-Market	3%	22%	6%	0%	0%	31%
Mid-Market	1%	15%	14%	1%	0%	31%
Economy		1%	4%	14%	15%	35%
Budget			0%	0%	1%	1%
Total	4%	39%	25%	16%	17%	100%

Source: Otus & Co Advisory Ltd

The most significant development that changed the pattern of hotel supply was the astonishing average annual growth of 12% in the room stock of economy hotels, against the average annual growth of only 2% in mid-market hotels. The two largest hotel categories in 2008 were up-market/full feature and mid-market/full feature which accounted for 22% and 15% of chain room stock respectively. The average annual rate of growth in chain full-feature hotel room stock from 1985 to 2004 was a strong 4%. Thereafter, room stock growth in full-feature hotels was flat. This growth pattern in the non-rooms heavy hotels was driven by three factors. First, there was strong growth in conference and meetings demand, over the first half of the period, as the structural balance of the economy shifted towards service businesses. Broadly, in the second half of the period to 2008, the rate of growth in conference and meetings demand slowed as more service businesses developed national and regional office provision that they used for the meetings, reducing their hotel demand to overnight stays. This change in business demand into hotels was paralleled by the growth in online travel agencies generating transient rooms demand rather than packaged conference and meetings demand. Second, over the period, as national brands of restaurants, pubs and health clubs increased significantly across the larger conurbations so the local demand for hotel restaurants, bars and health clubs declined. Third, during much of the period from 1985, packaged short break demand into hotels increased and as a result so did the use of hotel restaurants, bars and health clubs over the weekends. However, since the millennium, as the use of online travel agencies to book unpackaged short breaks increased, so the use of hotel restaurants and bars at the weekends declined. Thus, the two non-rooms heavy hotel configurations: full feature and resorts lost non-rooms demand and their effectiveness was jeopardised. By 2008, in the up-market/full feature category there were four companies that accounted for more than half of the room stock in eight brands, as table 11.7 illustrates.

Table 11.7: Up-Market/Full Feature Brand Share %: 2008

Company	Brands	Rooms	Share of Category
Hilton Hotels Corporation	Hilton, Doubletree	13,520	22%
Marriott International	Marriott, Renaissence, JW Marriott	8,380	13%
Carlson Group of Companies	Radisson, Park Plaza	5,980	10%
Intercontinental Hotels Group	Intercontinental, Crowne Plaza	4,520	7%

Source: Otus & Co. Advisory Ltd

The remaining 48% of the category room stock was affiliated to another 53 brands, which had little or no power in the market and whose performance was at the mercy of the declining non-rooms demand. Similarly, in the mid-market/full feature category there were three companies with four brands that accounted for half of the room stock (see table 11.8).

Table 11.8: Mid-Market/Full Feature Brand Share %: 2008

Company	Brands	Rooms	Share of Category
Intercontinental Hotels Group	Holiday Inn	13,390	31%
Accor	Novotel, Mercure	6,460	15%
Wyndham Worldwide	Ramada	2,600	6%

Source: Otus & Co. Advisory Ltd

The remaining 48% of the category room stock was affiliated to another 39 minor brands. There is no evidence that the changes in the pattern of non-rooms demand or in the use of online travel agencies are temporary trends. Moreover, there have been few initiatives to reduce full feature room stock either by reconfiguring the hotels to have fewer non-rooms facilities or by converting entire hotels to other uses. The most vulnerable to the decline in non-rooms demand are the unaffiliated hotels and the shorter brands, particularly those with old hotels and those in sub-prime locations. Progressively, they are suffering declining performance and declining returns on investment, which can be expected to continue until a new equilibrium is established between the demand and supply of hotels in these categories.

In contrast, two categories grew prodigiously. First, the fastest growing category was economy/rooms only, which added 43,100 rooms, up from a mere 70 in 1985. Premier Inn, Travelodge and Holiday Inn Express accounted for 60%, 30% and 3% respectively of chain rooms in this category. The rest of the room stock was affiliated to 11 other brands with a total of 72 hotels and 3,100 rooms. In any analysis these brands are very small businesses with no pricing power in the country. Second, the economy/limited feature category added 41,600 rooms over the period, up from 540 rooms in 1985. The three major brands in the category: Premier Inn, Travelodge and Holiday Inn Express accounted for 30%, 24% and 24% respectively of chain rooms in this category. The rest of the room stock in the category was affiliated to 25 other brands with 122 hotels and 9,130 rooms, very small businesses with no pricing power. Hotels in the two main economy categories have been constructed at a faster rate than any other hotels in British history and Premier Inn and Travelodge have become the two largest hotel brands in the country. The quality and consistency of offering of brands within the two categories have enabled them to take demand away from unaffiliated economy hotels and quasi hotels such as bed and breakfasts, as well as transient rooms demand from mid-market and up-market hotels to produce consistently high levels of room occupancy and high levels of return on investment.

Three categories – economy/resort, budget/resort and budget/basic feature lost rooms over the period as demand moved away from them and chains withdrew from the categories. By 2008, these and deluxe/limited feature were the only categories in which the chains were not represented. Only 14 chain hotels with 935 rooms had less than 100% en suite bedrooms. Five of these were in Accor's Formula 1 brand in which rooms without private bathroom were a brand specification and their expansion in Britain has been halted. The other nine hotels with 535 rooms were affiliated to eight short chains. Well over a century after the first deluxe hotels were created with 100% en suite bedrooms and almost a century after Statler Hotels introduced the facility throughout its portfolio of mid-market hotels in the US, all chain hotels in Britain had still not achieved the standard. Moreover, it was still not uncommon for unaffiliated hotels to operate without 100% en suite bedrooms and it was typical for quasi hotels such as bed and breakfasts to have rooms without private bathrooms.

Hotel chains structure in London: 2008

Over the 23 years from 1985, hotel chains added 34,800 rooms in London an average annual growth of 3.5%, lagging the growth of the chains in the country as a whole. Even so, at the end of 2008, London accounted for 75,900 chain rooms reinforcing its position as the largest hotel city in Europe and with seven times the room stock of Manchester the next largest in Britain. Of the 53 brands operating in London in 1985, only 14 remained in 2008, but there were some surprising developments. The Intercontinental brand believed that it was better to exit three of its four hotels in London than to find ways to continue to operate in one of the most vibrant hotel markets in the world; Le Meridien suffered a rollercoaster of erratic expansion followed by erratic contraction to leave its London portfolio unchanged from 1985 and Sheraton resisted all opportunities for portfolio growth.

Table 11.9: Chain Market Level/Hotel Configuration Matrix: London 2008, % Share

	Resort	Full Feature	Basic Feature	Limited Feature	Rooms Only	Total
Deluxe		4%	0%		0%	5%
Up-Market		36%	10%	0%	1%	47%
Mid-Market	0%	10%	9%	1%	1%	21%
Economy		2%	4%	15%	3%	25%
Budget				1%	1%	1%
Total	0%	53%	24%	17%	5%	100%

Source: Otus & Co Advisory Ltd

In 2008, hotel chains in London were represented in 18 of the 25 hotel categories, up from 11 in 1985. More than half of the chain rooms were in full-feature hotels because of the significance of the packaged conference and packaged short break markets, particularly from foreign visitors. The non-rooms light categories accounted for more than half of the additional rooms over the period as experienced travellers to London used restaurants and bars outside of the hotels and the online travel agencies captured a growing share of the transient rooms demand.

Hotel chains structure: Britain 2008

By 1995, UK Hotels plc had increased to 62 companies and their room stock had increased to 124,600 accounting for 77% of all chain rooms. Over the next 13 years to 2008, there was a marked downward shift in the sentiment of stock market investors about the hotel business. They considered the quoted hotel companies to be top heavy with hotel real estate and therefore to have a high risk profile, to produce too low a rate of growth in earnings and to deliver too low a rate of return on invested capital. Consequently, by 2008, there had been a procession of quoted hotel companies that were taken private, that were acquired or had exited the hotel business. By 2008, UK Hotels plc had declined to only 19 companies and although their room stock had risen to 136,200, it accounted for only 47% of all chain rooms.

The valuation the stock market placed on public companies was invariably lower than the valuation achieved by private equity funds, real estate companies and high net worth individuals all of which attracted higher levels of debt and produced higher returns on invested equity. For most of the companies that retained their stock market listing it was a time of transformation in the affiliation between hotels and the brands. The number of leased, managed and franchised hotels increased sharply as major quoted hotel companies pursued programmes of sale and lease back, sale and management back and sale and franchise back to lighten their balance sheets and improve the rate of return on invested capital. Consequently, over the 13 years of the period to 2008, the stock market was not only closed for the provision of new equity for hotel companies, but also the shareholders of many public companies received special dividends, significantly from Intercontinental Hotels Group, which returned around £3 billion to shareholders from the sale of hotel real estate.

By the end of 2008 there were 146 companies with portfolios of hotels in Britain and the room stock of the 10 largest companies grew from 1985 at an average annual rate of 4.4% adding 111,000 rooms, ahead of the rate of growth of the chain market as a whole. They accounted for 60% of all chain rooms, 34% of total room stock and included a total of 39 hotel brands.

Table 11.10: 10 Largest Companies in the British Hotel Market: 2008

Brand	Rooms	Share of chain rooms	Share of total rooms
Whitbread Plc	39,040	13%	8%
Intercontinental Hotels Group Plc	34,790	12%	7%
Travelodge Ltd	23,370	8%	5%
Hilton Hotels Corporation	16,150	6%	3%
Accor SA	12,520	4%	2%
Wyndham Hotels Worldwide Inc	11,120	4%	2%
Carlson Group	10,480	4%	2%
Marriott International Inc	10,290	4%	2%
Thistle Hotels Ltd	8,820	3%	2%
The Alternative Hotel Group	7,420	3%	1%
Totals	**174,000**	**60%**	**34%**

Source: Otus & Co Advisory Ltd

The first observation is that none of the 10 largest hotel companies of 1985 survived intact. Second, whereas all of the 10 largest companies in 1985 were British, only three – Whitbread, InterContinental Hotels Group, and The Alternative Hotel Group – were British in 2008. Third, whereas all 10 companies in 1985 were publicly quoted, there were only six in 2008. Fourth, none of the companies were brewers and fifth, with the exceptions of Whitbread and Travelodge, the other eight companies operated multiple brands.

In 2008, there were 188 hotel brands operating in Britain. The two largest brands, Premier Inn, the fastest growing brand in British history and Travelodge, were economy brands as were Holiday Inn Express, the fifth largest and Ibis, the seventh largest brand. Holiday Inn and Hilton grew organically and by chain acquisition and Marriott grew organically to be significant brands in the country. The seven largest brands were more explicitly structured and homogenous in terms of their market level, hotel configuration and hotel age. The three other brands in the top 10 were more heterogeneous in terms of market level, hotel configuration and hotel age so that the hotels in the portfolios bore a more distant family resemblance. They were assembled mainly by the acquisition of hotels and short chains rather than by new development to explicit brand specifications. The remaining 118 brands accounted for 147,700 rooms, an average of only 830 rooms per brand. They were still sub-optimal and the portfolio management had been haphazard as had been their access to capital.

Table 11.11: 10 Largest Brands in the British Hotel Market 2008

Brand	Rooms	Share of chain rooms	Share of total rooms
Premier Inn	39,040	13%	8%
Travelodge	23,370	8%	5%
Holiday Inn	17,540	6%	3%
Hilton	15,380	5%	3%
Holiday Inn Express	12,030	4%	2%
Marriott Hotels	8,980	3%	2%
Ibis	6,990	2%	1%
Britannia	6,850	2%	1%
Ramada Hotels	6,840	2%	1%
Thistle	6,480	2%	1%
Totals	**143,500**	**49%**	**28%**

Source: Otus & Co Advisory Ltd

Of the 116 hotel brands operating in 1985, 88 were forfeited before 2008 and of the 188 brands that were operating in 2008, 160 had entered the market over the 23 years from 1985. Thus, over the period, there was a minimum turnover of 248 brands producing an average turnover of 11 brands per year. Annual brand turnover is the sum of the number of brands that enter the market and the number of brands that are forfeited. Of the 28 surviving brands, 12 outperformed the chains market in terms of portfolio growth and 16 underperformed of which six brands shrank their portfolios.

Table 11.12: Room Stock Growth of Surviving Brands 1985 to 2008

Out-Performing	CAGR	Under-Performing	CAGR	Shrinking	CAGR
Travelodge	20.9%	Edwardian Hotels	3.8%	De Vere	-0.5%
Marriott Hotels	17.3%	Hastings Hotel Group	3.5%	Le Meridien Hotels	-0.7%
Ramada Hotels	16.6%	Four Seasons Hotels	3.4%	Maybourne	-1.3%
Ibis	15.7%	Thistle Hotels	3.2%	Swallow Hotels	-3.1%
Hilton International	10.8%	English Lakes Hotels	2.5%	Intercontinental Hotels	-5.0%
Britannia Hotels	9.4%	Brend Hotel Group	1.5%	Orient-Express Hotels	-10.5%
Copthorne Hotels	8.3%	Imperial London Hotels	0.7%		
Holiday Inns	6.9%	Hatton Hotels	0.5%		
Novotel	6.7%	Nikko Hotels	0.0%		
Hyatt International	5.4%	Sheraton Hotels	0.0%		
Shire Hotels	5.1%				
Forestdale Hotels	4.9%				

Source: Otus & Co Advisory Ltd

The high average annual brand turnover between 1985 and 2008 and the high rate of addition of brands most of which have remained small are worrying signs. Most chains were unable to generate premium demand, to deliver higher operating margins and to attract effective capital to grow. It illustrates that for most hotel chains in Britain their strategic awareness was flawed, their portfolio management was poor and the capital markets made ineffective investment decisions about them.

British hotel supply and demand performance

Despite the limitations of the chains they still managed to widen the performance gap with unaffiliated hotels as is evident in Table 11.13. Not only was their rate of supply growth strongly positive, but also unaffiliated supply declined and was reflected in the increase in the supply ratio of the chains. Otus estimates that the chains enlarged their room occupa ncy premium over unaffiliated hotels and grew their penetration of each of the sources of rooms demand. In contrast, unaffiliated hotels retreated from each demand source and their supply shrank.

Table 11.13: British Hotel Supply and Demand Performance 1980–2008

	Total Hotels			Chain Hotels			Chain Share	
	1980	2008	CAGR	1980	2008	CAGR	1980	2008
Total rooms	385,000	510,000	1.0%	110,000	291,240	3.5%	29%	57%
Room nights available m	141	187	1.0%	40	107	3.5%	29%	57%
Room occupancy %	47%	57%		59%	68%			
Room nights sold m	66	106	1.7%	24	72	4.1%	36%	68%
Domestic business	23	44	2.4%	10	33	4.5%	42%	75%
Domestic leisure	13	18	1.1%	1	9	7.0%	11%	52%
Foreign business	8	13	1.7%	4	12	3.6%	54%	91%
Foreign leisure	23	32	1.3%	9	19	2.9%	38%	59%
Supply ratio	6.9	8.4		2.0	4.8			
Secular growth in hotel room supply	35,000	90,000		60,000	171,000		171%	190%

Source: Otus & Co Advisory Ltd

In this chapter, all data on employment was drawn from the Office of National Statistics.

Hotel chain supply data used here were drawn from: Paul Slattery and Angela Roper, The UK Hotels Groups Directory, Cassell, 1986; Paul Slattery et al, Quoted Hotel Companies, Kleinwort Benson Securities, annually 1986 to 1997 and The Otus Hotel Brands Database from 2000 onwards.

12 Continental European Hotel Businesses: 1980-2008

Introduction

In this chapter the two main economies of continental Europe, France and Germany are analysed separately and the position of the other economies are treated collectively. Not only are they smaller economies, but also they are very much smaller hotel economies. The exception is Spain which benefits from very high volumes of foreign leisure demand and thus, has one of the largest hotel supplies in Europe. The most significant economic development of the period was the break-up of the Soviet Empire and the collapse of communism in 1990. From then until 2008 hotel demand in this region rose, but the economies came from such a weakened and structurally primitive state that the growth in hotel demand and supply by 2008 still left them trailing far behind the western European economies.

France: 1980-2008

Developments in economic structure and hotel demand: France 1980-2008

Over the 28-year period to 2008, Otus estimates that hotel demand in France grew to 95 million room nights, up from 66 million, a 1.3% average annual growth. French domestic demand added 12 million room nights to reach 45 million, while Britain with a similar population added 26 million room nights to reach a total of 62 million, due to the faster development in the structural balance of the British economy and a greater proportion of its employment in service businesses. In contrast, foreign demand into French hotels added 17 million room nights to reach 50 million, while Britain added 14 million room nights to reach 45 million. Over the period there was also a shift in the structure of the hotel business as hotel chains grew to capture 66% of total demand, a strong annual average growth of 4.7%, whereas unaffiliated hotels demand shrank by 16 million room nights to end the period at 33 million. During the period, the four factors that are indicative of the shifting structural balance of an economy to service business experienced mixed developments. Human and civil rights legislation expanded as it did in most western economies. Undergraduate and postgraduate degrees in pure social sciences expanded more so than in applied social sciences and the social sciences became part of the secondary school curriculum. The expansion of ownership of appreciating assets such as homes, insurance policies, pension schemes and other saving mechanisms was slower than in the US and Britain and this limited the provision of personal credit. Business and personal travel expanded, but the proportion of French citizens travelling internationally and their frequency of international travel was less than for US and British citizens.

During the 1980s and 1990s, France suffered from high levels of unemployment, some years above 10%. To combat this, the first Aubry Act introduced on 1 January 2000 reduced the statutory working week to 35 hours and was successful in creating new jobs and containing the higher levels of unemployment. Tables 12.1 and 12.2 illustrate the encouragement that the Act gave to the total numbers employed. Over the 27-year period to 2007, the latest year for which employment data were available, employment in agriculture and industry, the two segments that yield lower domestic business demand into hotels, grew and the proportion employed was significantly higher than in the US and Britain. The proportion in service businesses, the segment that yields the highest domestic business demand into hotels, was lower than in the US and Britain.

Table 12.1: Employment by Segment in France: 1980–2007 (millions)

	Agriculture	Industry	Citizen Services	Service Businesses	Total
1980	1.9	7.6	6.5	6.0	22.0
1990	1.3	6.5	7.8	6.9	22.5
1996	1.3	5.6	8.7	7.0	22.6
2003	1.7	8.4	7.3	7.3	24.6
2007	1.5	8.5	7.8	7.8	25.6

Source: 1980 - 1990 Groningen, 2003 - 2007 INSEE

Table 12.2: Employment by Segment in France: 1980–2007 %

	Agriculture	Industry	Citizen Services	Service Businesses	Total
1980	8%	35%	29%	27%	100%
1990	6%	29%	35%	31%	100%
1996	6%	25%	39%	31%	100%
2003	7%	34%	30%	30%	100%
2007	6%	33%	30%	31%	100%

Source: 1980 - 1990 Groningen, 2003 - 2007 INSEE

Agricultural demand into hotels

In 1980, agriculture and fisheries employed 1.9 million accounting for 8% of the French workforce compared with only 2% in Britain, illustrating the greater significance that agriculture continued to have for the French economy. Otus estimates that 2.1% of French agricultural employees were business travellers, a lower proportion than in Britain due to the greater fragmentation of French agriculture and the much higher proportion of agricultural exports from France, which involves hotel stays in destination economies rather than in France. The French agricultural business travellers originating demand spent an average of seven nights in hotels and generated predominantly transient rooms demand of 0.28 million room nights for less than a 1% share of total domestic business demand. Over the period to 2007, employment in agriculture declined progressively at an average annual rate of less than 1% and at the end of the period accounted for 6% of the total workforce. There was some concentration among agricultural firms, but in terms of their generation of hotel room nights the benefits from concentration were more than offset by the growth in agricultural exports, which channelled agricultural business travellers away from France and into destination countries. Consequently, Otus estimates that by 2007, the proportion of agricultural employees who were business travellers rose to 2.3%, 35,000, marginally less than in 1980 and that predominantly they were active originating demand. They spent an average of eight nights in French hotels generating mostly transient rooms demand of 0.28 million room nights, unchanged from 1980 and accounting for 1% of total domestic business demand.

Industrial demand into hotels

In 1980, industrial employment was 7.6 million, 35% of the French workforce, a similar proportion as in Britain. Otus estimates that 5.1% of industrial employees were business travellers involved in originating demand, travelling in the course of managing their companies and in a minor way attending industry-wide conferences. They spent an average of 17 nights in French hotels and generated mainly transient rooms demand, but also some packaged conference demand of 6.6 million room nights for 39% share of total domestic business demand to be still the largest segment for the French hotel business. Over the 27-year period to 2007, employment in the industrial sectors – manufacturing, utilities, construction and mining – added 870,000 jobs so that, by the end of the period, the segment accounted for one third of the total workforce. Automotive manufacturing was one of the fastest growing parts of the segment with 31,000 jobs created between 1999 and 2001 alone (source: www.diplomatie.gouv.fr). By 2007, 5.1%, 430,000 industrial employees were business travellers originating demand, but also travelling as part of the management of expanding companies. Attendance at industry-wide industrial conferences held in French hotels was less frequent than in other major economies. French industrial travellers spend an average of 21 nights in French hotels generating mainly transient rooms demand of 9 million room nights retaining a 35% share of total domestic business demand, the highest of any segment.

Citizen services demand into hotels

In 1980, citizen services in France had a workforce of 6.5 million, a 30% share of the total workforce. Otus estimates that 11.5% of citizen services employees were business travellers involved in segment management and overseeing nationalised industries and businesses. They spent an average of eight nights in French hotels to generate 6 million room nights of demand. This pattern was different from the segment in Britain where a higher proportion of employees were business travellers because there was a greater incidence of civil servants, medics and academics attending conferences, which increased the proportion of employees who were business travellers, but their average length of stay was less than in France where the demand generated was almost entirely transient rather than packaged. In 1980, the French citizen services segment accounted for 35% of total domestic business demand compared with 27% in Britain. Over the 27-year period to 2007, the citizen services workforce grew to 7.8 million, ahead of the national average rate of employment growth with the addition of 1.3 million jobs. By 2007, 12.6%, 980,000 of citizen service employees were business travellers involved in segment management and overseeing nationalised industries and businesses, but with conference attendance increasing. They spent an average of eight nights in French hotels to generate both transient rooms demand and packaged conference demand of 7.8 million room nights for a 30% share of total domestic business demand.

Service businesses demand into hotels

In 1980, service businesses in France employed 6.0 million compared with 10.3 million in Britain. Otus estimates that 6.5% of French service business employees were business travellers, 390,000, a million less than in Britain. They were involved in originating demand, executing contracts and servicing clients, but the smaller size of French service businesses limited the numbers involved in company management and attending conferences. They spent an average of 11 nights in French hotels to generate both transient rooms demand and packaged conference demand of 4.3 million room nights for 25% of total domestic business demand. In the same year, the service business segment in Britain generated almost two and a half times the hotel demand because it was a larger segment with larger companies with executives who travelled for a broader range of reasons. Over the period, service business employment in France grew to 7.8 million, half the number employed in Britain.

There were two reasons that were significant in the lower hotel yield of French service businesses. First, many financial services businesses in France were smaller because over the period there was low growth in home ownership. In 2008, only 55% of French households owned their own home compared with around 70% in Britain and the US *(source:* www.demographia.com*)*. Following from this, the number of insurance policies, private pension schemes and other saving instruments were lower in France than in Britain and the US. Consequently, a lower proportion of the French population owned appreciating assets and a higher proportion only owned goods that depreciated in value. The low level of home ownership and other appreciating assets were reflected in the low access to personal credit in France. By 2007, there were only 9 million credit cards in circulation in France compared with 75 million in Britain, which had the same population *(source:* www.pbs.org). French banks had been willing to provide debit cards to their customers, but only 40 million were in circulation in 2007 compared with 60 million in Britain. France also sticks out in other service businesses. In 2002, private and mutual health insurance accounted for 12% of healthcare expenditure in France compared with 33% in the US *(source:* OECD, Health Data 2002).

Second, there were laws that inhibited the growth and performance of chains of service businesses in France. The Raffarin Law (1996) was designed to limit the rate of growth of supermarkets of more than 300 square metres to provide protection to corner shops. Then, the Gallard Law (1996) constrained the buying power of retail and hospitality chains by limiting the discounts that they were able to negotiate with suppliers to protect corner shops, independent hotels and independent restaurants against the growth of chains. Additionally, the law was designed to protect the pricing power of farmers and food and drink manufacturers. The Raffarin and Gallard Laws created a false market in retailing and hospitality as well as contributing to the slower growth and lower effectiveness of the retailing and hospitality business.

Otus estimates that in 2007, 8%, 620,000 of employees from service businesses were business travellers compared with 1.9 million in Britain. The French travellers continued to be engaged in originating demand, executing contracts and servicing clients and there had been an increase in the numbers involved in travel associated with managing their companies, but there were fewer involved in industry-wide conferences, single-company conferences and company/client conferences. The French travellers spent an average of 14 nights in French hotels to generate both transient rooms demand and packaged conference demand of 8.7 million room nights, which accounted for 34% of total domestic business demand against 60% in Britain.

Domestic leisure demand into hotels

The lower level of ownership of appreciating assets and the lower access to personal credit are indicative of economies with a high proportion of employment in the primary and secondary segments as has been the case in France. One implication of this was that a lower proportion of employees took hotel-based holidays and there was a low presence of holiday wholesalers such as tour operators and short break travel agencies. Three characteristics of French holiday demand reflect this context. First, Eurostat estimated that in 2004, British outbound holidaymakers took 19.1 million trips in which they stayed in a hotel or similar establishment for at least four nights, whereas the French took only 7.8 million equivalent trips *(source:* Eurostat, Panorama on Tourism 2006, European Union) Second, the corollary of this is that there was a higher volume of domestic holiday taking in France, particularly during the summer, but hotels were a relatively small part of the total, which included holidays in second homes, gîtes, campsites and other non-hotel accommodation. Third, the relatively low access to personal credit was an impediment to the development of hotel short breaks. This was reinforced by the lifestyle of French baby boomers, which had always been less experience-based than those in the US and Britain because of the less structurally developed French economy. During the period, the pattern of leisure demand into hotels was reflected in the pattern of hotel supply. The low level of short-break demand into hotels was also a factor in the regularly reported low levels of hotel demand at weekends in France. In 1980, domestic leisure demand accounted for 16 million room nights into hotels in France. It also estimates that by 2008, this market had increased to only 19 million room nights, an average annual growth of less than 1% to account for 20% of all room nights sold.

Foreign demand into hotels

Since World War II, France has been an attractive destination to foreign visitors who have accounted for a higher proportion of hotel demand than in the US or Britain. In 1990, The World Tourism Organization (UNWTO) estimated that 52.5 million foreign visitors stayed at least one night in France and it estimates that in 2008 the total increased to 81.9 million (UNWTO, 2008). Three notable features of these visitors are first that around two-thirds of them, 54 million in 2008, were leisure travellers and business travellers amounted to only 10 million. Second, the average length of stay of leisure travellers in hotels was low since some of the visitors from neighbouring countries drove through France to destinations in other countries. Third, most of the foreign visitors staying in provincial France for summer holidays did not stay in hotels. Otus estimates that in 1980, foreign leisure travellers stayed for 29 million hotel room nights and accounted for 44% of total demand. By 2008, foreign leisure demand into hotels in France increased to 43 million room nights and accounted for 45% of total demand having grown at an average annual rate of 1.4%. This compares with 32 million in Britain, which accounted for 30% of total hotel demand. In parallel, in 1980, foreign business travellers accounted for 4.0 million hotel room nights and that by 2008 this volume had doubled to 8.0 million. However, foreign business travellers in Britain accounted for 60% more room nights than in France, because France attracted a lower volume of international conferences and the level of foreign investment in France was lower in Britain, thus attracting fewer foreign executives. In total, foreign visitors accounted for 53% of hotel demand in 2008 compared with 42% in Britain.

Hotel supply in France: 1980–2008

Otus estimates that in 1980 there were 400,000 hotel rooms in France producing a hotel supply ratio of 7.4. At a constant 1980 supply ratio and with the actual increase in the population over the period to 2008, the economy would have needed 450,000 hotel rooms in 2008. However, the growth in foreign demand supplemented by the growth in domestic business demand produced hotel room stock of 540,000, a supply ratio of 8.9, and secular growth of 90,000. The main hotel supply feature of the period was the growth in the significance of hotel chains, whose room stock expanded at an average annual rate of 4.7% to reach a total of 270,000 rooms with a 50% share of total supply. However, the drivers of hotel chain growth in France were different from those in Britain and so also were the supply profiles in both countries. There was little historic detail available about hotel chain portfolios in France until the early 1990s. In 1993, publicly quoted hotel chains in France accounted for 115,000 rooms, three-quarters of all chain rooms. The three dominant chains were French: Accor, with 81,400 rooms; Société du Louvre, with 23,300 and Eurodisney with 5,200, while the other 10 foreign quoted brands including: Hilton, Holiday Inn, Intercontinental and Sheraton accounted for only 5,100 rooms (Slattery et al. 1993). Rooms in economy and budget hotels accounted for 60% of the quoted chain rooms in France in 1993. Up-market and deluxe hotels accounted for 14% with the remainder at the mid-market. The low level of exposure of the French economy to service businesses limited the demand for hotel-based conferences and a high proportion of foreign leisure demand was also predominantly transient rooms demand. Thus, the demand for full-feature hotels was minor compared with the US and Britain whose economies were more structurally developed and the growing service businesses used hotels more frequently for conferences. Moreover, the growth of short-holiday demand in the US and Britain was into hotels with significant non-room facilities.

Hotel chain supply profile: France 2008

By 2008, the non-room light categories: rooms only and limited feature, strengthened their domination of the market with 61% of chain supply, while economy and budget hotels accounted for 62% of chain supply. The hotel conundrum about France was that the country that gave the world haute cuisine and haute couture had a hotel business dominated by economy and budget hotels.

Table 12.3: Chain Market Level/Hotel Configuration Matrix: France 2008

	Resort	Full Feature	Basic Feature	Limited Feature	Rooms Only	Total
Deluxe	0%	1%	0%			1%
Up-Market	1%	7%	2%	0%	0%	11%
Mid-Market	1%	8%	9%	5%	3%	26%
Economy		1%	8%	18%	6%	33%
Budget			0%	2%	27%	29%
Total	3%	17%	20%	25%	36%	100%

Source: Otus & Co Advisory Ltd

Paris, like London, is a major hotel city, but whereas in 2007, Paris had 68,400 chain rooms, London had 75,900 and the supply profiles of the two cities were different. The three largest chain hotel categories in Paris were budget/room only, economy/limited feature and up-market/full feature, which together accounted for 43% of chain room stock. Paris was also different from the French provinces. In 2008, Paris accounted for 26% of chain rooms in France, but 60% of the upmarket/full-feature room stock. Paris was the most structurally developed city in the French economy benefiting from more conference demand from domestic and foreign businesses as well as from leisure travellers. Although Paris dominated the up-market/full-feature category in France with 11,580 chain rooms, it was minor compared with the 25,780 rooms in the category in London and the 59,950 up-market/full-feature rooms in Britain compared with only 21,800 in France. There was an even more dramatic difference between the two countries at the budget level. France had 76,370 chain affiliated budget hotel rooms while Britain had only 2,540. In contrast to Paris, the French provinces accounted for 74% of the chain room stock, but only 40% of the up-market/full-feature rooms yet 78% of the economy rooms and 87% of the budget rooms.

Of the 112 hotel brands with a presence in France in 2007, 48 were French and 64 were foreign brands. The French brands dominated with 74% of all branded rooms and the Accor brands dominated the French brands with 44% of all branded rooms in the country. No other hotel company had achieved such a large and dominating presence in any European country. The market level and hotel configuration profile of the Accor hotel brands in Europe was as shown in Table 12.4.

Table 12.4: Accor Hotel Brand Portfolio Matrix: Europe 2008

	Resort	Full Feature	Basic Feature	Limited Feature	Rooms Only
Deluxe	Sofitel	Sofitel	Sofitel		
Up-market	Pullman	Pullman	Pullman		Mercure
Mid-market	Mercure, Novotel	Mercure, Novotel	Mercure, Novotel	Suitehotel	Mercure
Economy		Ibis	All Seasons, Ibis, Mercure	All Seasons, Ibis, Mercure	All Seasons, Ibis
Budget					Etap, F1

Source: Otus & Co Advisory Ltd

Accor, which is one of the global major hotel companies, was represented with its brands in 25 European countries and its main categories were mid-market/full feature, economy/limited feature and mid-market/basic feature. The corollary of the Accor position was that foreign brand penetration of France was minor with only 72,000 rooms. Within this total, the other global major hotel companies: Carlson, Choice Hotels International, Global Hyatt, Hilton Hotels Corporation, Intercontinental Hotels Group, Marriott International, Starwood Hotels & Resorts and Wyndham Worldwide collectively accounted for only 26,250 rooms, which gave them less than 5% share of supply in one of the most significant hotel markets in the world.

Hotel replacement values

The difference in the hotel supply profiles of Britain and France is also reflected in the replacement value of the chain hotels. Tables 12.5 and 12.6 records the Otus estimated replacement value per room for hotels at each hotel category, which for the purpose of analysis, is assumed to be the same in Britain, France and Germany and is intended only to be indicative.

Table 12.5: Replacement Value/Room €m: 2008

	Resort	Full Feature	Basic Feature	Limited Feature	Rooms Only
Deluxe	0.750	0.700	0.650	0.600	0.550
Up-market	0.280	0.260	0.240	0.220	0.200
Mid-market	0.175	0.160	0.145	0.130	0.115
Economy	0.100	0.090	0.080	0.070	0.060
Budget	0.050	0.045	0.040	0.035	0.030

Source: Otus & Co Advisory Ltd

Table 12.6: Chain Hotel Replacement Value €m: France 2008

	Resort	Full Feature	Basic Feature	Limited Feature	Rooms Only	Total
Deluxe	615	1,000	155			1,770
Up-market	960	4,860	1,280	180	220	7,500
Mid-market	500	3,490	3,560	1,635	910	10,095
Economy		200	1,780	3,375	1,000	6,355
Budget	-		5	165	2,145	2,315
Total	2,075	9,550	6,780	5,355	4,275	28,035

Source: Otus & Co Advisory Ltd

Applying these valuations per room for each hotel category, the replacement value of chain hotels in France at €28 billion compared with €46 billion in Britain because of the preponderance of economy and budget room stock in France as well as the lower volume of chain rooms. The three categories that accounted for the highest investment value in France, up-market/full-feature, mid-market/full-feature and mid-market/basic feature accounted for 42% of the total replacement value of all chain rooms in France, but these three categories accounted for only 24% of the chain room stock. The differences in the supply profile of hotel chains in France and Britain were in the main a reflection of the historic differences in economic structure and economic policies. The replacement value of chain hotels in Paris and London was even more explicit. The supply profile of Paris produced a chain hotel replacement value of €10 billion compared with €15 billion for London.

Supply and Demand Performance: France

Table 12.7: French Hotel Supply and Demand Performance 1980–2008

	Total Hotels			Chain Hotels			Chain Share	
	1980	2008	CAGR	1980	2008	CAGR	1980	2008
Total rooms	400,000	540,000	1.0%	75,000	270,000	4.7%	19%	53%
Room nights available (m)	146	198	1.0%	27	99	4.7%	19%	53%
Room occupancy %	45%	48%		63%	63%			
Room nights sold (m)	66	95	1.7%	17	62	4.7%	26%	59%
Domestic business	17	26	2.4%	6	22	4.9%	26%	51%
Domestic leisure	16	19	1.1%	2	10	5.2%	18%	55%
Foreign business	4	8	1.7%	2	6	4.7%	20%	44%
Foreign leisure	29	43	1.3%	7	24	4.3%	33%	76%
Supply ratio	7.4	8.9		1.4	4.5			
Secular growth in hotel room supply	145,000	90,000		69,000	185,000		48%	206%

Source: Otus & Co Advisory Ltd

The supply and demand performance in France between 1980 and 2008 illustrated the enduring principle that the greater the penetration of hotel chains in any economy, the more that they dominate hotel performance and are the vanguard of the economic ascent of the hotel business. In the 28 years to 2008, unaffiliated hotels declined on all supply and demand performance measures and there are no economic conditions that are realistically possible that would reverse that trend.

Germany 1980–2008

Developments in economic structure and hotel demand

The dominant development in Germany over the period from 1980 was the reunification of West and East Germany in 1990. Both countries had experienced radically different development during the 41 years of separation. Whereas the economic growth of West Germany was electric, the East German economy ossified under communist rule. By 1985, state collectives in East Germany earned 97% of national income *(source:* East Germany: A Country Study, The Federal Division of the Library of Congress, 1987) Much of the economic activity was, like the other communist states, in primary and secondary activities in which productivity and capital investment were low. In 1985, 38% of the workforce was employed in the secondary segment and 10% was employed in agriculture. Of course, citizen services were state controlled as were most service businesses, which were narrow in range and focused mainly on serving the state and its collective primary and secondary activities. The state control of prices and wages eliminated access to personal credit, thus, except for the political elite, the population owned no appreciating assets and their ownership of consumer goods was limited compared with western standards of the time. Typically, housing was in large Soviet blocks of small apartments, built and owned by the state and it was not until after 1970 that new houses were built with indoor bathrooms, hot water and central heating. Hotel demand in East Germany was minor and controlled by the state and the Communist Party.

Politically, the reunification of the two Germanys was fast and effective, but the economic integration was slow and expensive. Changing the culture of reliance on the state was at the heart of the difficulties. The industrial infrastructure was outdated, while there were few venues for service businesses compared with western economies. The level and range of skills available in East Germany in 1990 was narrow and the standard of living and lifestyle of the East Germans were primitive in comparison with West German equivalents. The mammoth economic task was to convert communist East Germany to the social market economy of West Germany, which required investment. In the 17 years of re-unification till 2008 this involved the investment by West Germany of around 4% of its annual GDP, between €70 billion and €100 billion per year (Berg et al. 2005). Despite the investment of around €1.5 trillion, by 2008, East Germany had still not reached sufficient parity with West Germany and unemployment in East Germany remained higher than in West Germany as Table 12.8 illustrates.

Table 12.8: West Germany and East Germany % Unemployment 1991–2006

	1991	1995	1997	2000	2002	2004	2006
West Germany	8.0	9.0	10.0	9.8	10.0	9.0	10.5
East Germany	6.3	14.0	15.9	16.1	16.0	18.6	19.5

Source: Statistisches Bundesamt Deutschland

The integration of the structurally backward East German economy with the more structurally developed West German economy limited the structural progress of the reunified Germany. Otus estimates that over the 18-year period of reunification to 2008, the volume of total hotel room nights sold rose to 78 million, an increase of 19 million representing an average annual growth of 1.6%. By 2008, hotel chains in Germany accounted for only 55% of hotel demand compared with 66% in France and 68% in Britain. During the period, the four factors that are indicative of the shifting structural balance of an economy to service business progressed less than in France. Human and civil rights legislation expanded, as it did in most western economies, but in the case of Germany the major changes were made in the East where the restructuring and rebasing of the judiciary and the closing of the Stasi, the secret police, were landmark events. The social sciences accounted for a smaller part of undergraduate and postgraduate courses in Germany, particularly in applied social sciences. The expansion of ownership of appreciating assets such as homes, insurance policies and private pension schemes was slower than in Britain and France and this limited the provision of personal credit. The proportion of German citizens travelling internationally on package holidays grew strongly over the period.

The period of reunification for which employment data are available, 1991 to 2007, saw only marginal growth in the total number of German employees. The main focus of economic policies was on improving productivity in the agricultural and industrial segments, which accounted for almost half of East German employment and based on data from Statistisches Bundesamt Deutschland, Otus estimates that over the period, employment in these segments, the lower yielding segments for domestic business demand into hotels, declined, whereas the growth in employment was in citizen services and service businesses, the higher yielding segments for domestic business demand into hotels.

Table 12.9: Employment by Segment in Germany: 1991–2007 (millions)

	Agriculture	Industry	Citizen Services	Service Businesses	Total
1991	1.5	16.9	12.4	7.8	38.6
2000	0.9	14.8	14.0	9.4	39.1
2007	0.8	14.0	14.9	10.1	39.8

Source: Statistisches Bundesamt Deutschland and Otus & Co Advisory Ltd

Table 12.10: Employment by Segment in Germany: 1991–2007 %

	Agriculture	Industry	Citizen Services	Service Businesses	Total
1991	4%	44%	32%	20%	100%
2000	2%	38%	36%	24%	100%
2007	2%	35%	37%	25%	100%

Source: Statistisches Bundesamt Deutschland and Otus & Co Advisory Ltd

Agricultural demand into hotels

In 1991, agriculture and fisheries employed 1.5 million, mostly in East Germany, accounting for 4% of the total German workforce, compared with only 2% in Britain. The collective farm structure of the former East Germany involved little agricultural business travel, but in the early years of reunification there was a spike in the volume of travellers as the result of conferences and meetings about the political, economic and operational shift from communism to a social market economy. Otus estimates that in 1991, 2% of German agricultural employees, 30,000 were business travellers mostly in originating demand, but also at reunification meetings. German agricultural business travellers spent an average of seven nights in German hotels generating transient rooms demand and some packaged conference demand of 212,000 room nights for than 1% share of total domestic business demand. Over the 17-year period to 2007, employment in agriculture declined with the loss of almost half of its manpower as Western operating practices were applied in the East. Productivity rocketed and at the end of the period, agriculture accounted for only 2% of the total workforce. There was growth in concentration among agricultural firms, but the benefits it brought to the generation of hotel demand were limited by the overall reduction in the workforce. Consequently, by 2007, the proportion of agricultural employees who were business travellers increased to 2.5%, 21,000, down on 1991.

Mostly, they originated demand, but they were also involved in some industry-wide conferences and fairs. They spent an average of eight nights in German hotels generating demand mainly transient rooms demand, but with some packaged conference demand of 169,000 room nights down since reunification and accounting for only a trace of total domestic business demand.

Industrial demand into hotels

In 1991, industrial employment was 16.9 million, 2.5 times the number in France, to account for 44% of the German workforce due not only to the greater significance of the industrial segment to the German economy, but also because of the inclusion of the inefficient East German work practices. There was a low volume of industrial business travel in the former East Germany, but Otus estimates that in 1991, 6% of German industrial employees, a million, were business travellers mainly originating demand, but also with attendance at fairs and at conferences about the transition from communism to a social market economy. Although Germany exports a high proportion of its manufactured output and business travellers travel abroad, there is also a high domestic business travel from this source to the fairs and exhibitions throughout the country. They spent an average of 15 nights in German hotels generating both transient rooms demand and packaged conference demand of 15 million room nights for 53% of total business demand making it the largest segment for the hotel business.

Over the 16-year period to 2007, the industrial sectors – manufacturing, utilities, construction and mining – lost 2.9 million jobs as West German operating practices replaced the low productivity, low quality East German norm. West German and foreign companies became established in the East and significant investment was made in more effective technology. Although the total segment workforce declined, the bulk of manpower reduction was among blue-collar workers. The size of segment companies increased as did the number of white-collar employees, both corporate executives and professional employees such as engineers and designers, which increased the number of and attendance at industry-wide hotel based conferences, fairs and exhibitions.

A feature of Germany is the large number of industrial fairs held in the larger German cities to showcase technological, design and product innovations. For the period between 2006 and 2016 the Association of the German Trade Fair Industry (AUMA) listed a planned programme of 155 trade fairs and exhibitions from the entire citizen services and service business segments compared with 145 trade fairs for cars and consumer electronics, only two of the 91 industrial sectors with fairs planned. The fairs act as a magnet for both domestic and foreign business demand into hotels in the larger German cities. They concentrate a significant proportion of business travel and are a key factor in increasing the segment use of packaged demand into German hotels. By 2007, the proportion of industrial employees who were business travellers increased during reunification to 7.7%, still more than a million travellers originating demand, attending industry-wide fairs and conferences as well as travelling in the course of managing their companies. They spent an average of 16 nights in German hotels generating transient and packaged conference demand of 16 million room nights amounting to 47% of all domestic business demand and reinforcing its position as the largest segment for the hotel business.

Citizen services demand into hotels

In 1991, citizen services in Germany had a workforce of 12.4 million, a 32% share of the total employees. In the former East Germany, the volume and frequency of business travel from citizen services were very low. Thus, at the start of reunification, the volume of business travel that involved hotel stays from citizen service employees was heavily skewed towards West Germany. Otus estimates that 10%, 1.2 million of citizen service employees, were business travellers involved in segment management and attendance at conferences particularly from the former West German medics and academics. Collectively, they spent an average of seven nights in German hotels generating both transient rooms demand and packaged conference demand of 8.7 million room nights for a 30% share of domestic business demand. In West Germany, the organisation of citizen services was based on the Lander or states and this limited the volume and frequency of business travel that involved hotel stays and this approach was extended to the East. Over the 16-year period to 2007, the citizen services workforce grew to 14.9 million, well ahead of the national average rate of employment growth with the addition of 2.5 million jobs. Over the period the range and comprehensiveness of health, education and welfare services increased throughout Germany and particularly in the East. By 2007, the proportion of citizen service employees who travelled on business declined to 9.5%, but the total business travellers from the segment increased to 1.4 million with travellers involved in segment management and professionals as well as civil servants attending conferences and fairs. They spent an average of eight nights in German hotels generating transient rooms demand and packaged conference demand of 11 million room nights for 31% of total domestic business demand.

Service businesses demand into hotels

In 1991, service businesses in Germany employed 7.8 million compared with 12.6 million in Britain. Reunification had brought into Germany the East German population who were without home ownership, without savings, without access to personal credit and with ownership only of depreciating goods. Service businesses in communist East Germany were a peripheral activity that supported the state controlled collectives while personal demand for service businesses was microscopic. The East German housing stock was in a poor condition, owned by the government and rented to the citizens. At the same time the level of home ownership in West Germany was very low compared with the US and Britain. Thus, Germany started reunification with low levels of home ownership and low access to personal credit relative to other major Western economies. The West Germans were characterised by a high savings ratio, but low use of savings to buy services and develop their lifestyle, which limited the multiplier effect in the economy compared with the US and Britain. Thus, the German segment was not only smaller; it was narrower in its range of service businesses; it was more highly fragmented and more focused on local rather than national markets. Otus estimates that at the time of reunification 5.7%, 440,000 of German service business employees, were business travellers engaged in originating demand, executing contracts and servicing clients. There was less travelling on management of companies and fewer conferences than in the service businesses of France, which had a population three-quarters the size of Germany's. According to Otus, the segment business travellers in Germany spend an average of 10 nights in German hotels generating transient rooms demand and packaged conference demand of 4.4 million room nights amounting to 16% of total domestic business demand.

Over the period to 2007, service business employment grew to 10.1 million, one third fewer than the number employed in Britain, a country with only three-quarters the population of Germany. The historic thrust of service businesses in West Germany and even more so in East Germany, was support for corporate and government activities. Thus, sectors such as: corporate banking; wholesaling; distribution; professional services such as advertising, market research and accountancy; and much real estate management compared in size with other major western economies. However, policymakers had not focused on growing personal demand for most market services businesses and experience businesses to equivalent levels.

The root of this was the low level of home ownership. In 2005, only 42% of Germans owned their own homes (Toussant and Tegeder, 2006). At the same time, home ownership in Britain was around 70%. Thus, the majority of Germans lived in rented accommodation with no capital appreciation and there were few initiatives to grow home ownership. The typical loan to value for new mortgages in Germany was 70%, which limited the numbers able to accumulate a deposit, it made the average age of first-time home buyers higher than in Britain and the US and it limited any capital appreciation enjoyed over a lifetime (source: Combined Report, OSIS, 2005) The German approach to home ownership limited the scope and activities of German banks and mortgage providers as well as the insurance markets and the stock market. The market capitalisation of listed companies in Germany in 2007 amounted to 64% of GDP (source: www.worldbank.com). In contrast, the US accounted for 144%, Britain, 142% and France 108%. Another implication of the low level of home ownership was the reluctance of the banks to issue credit cards in Germany. In 2003, there were only 20 million credit cards, an average of 0.33 per citizen against an average of 1.25 in Britain (source: www.pbs.org). A greater proportion of personal spending in Germany was on buying consumer goods, so service businesses such as retailing were significant in size. Private health insurance accounted for only 7% of the cost of healthcare in Germany compared with 12% in France and 33% in the US (source: OECD, Health Data 2002).

The pattern of consumer expenditure in Germany entailed a greater proportion of leisure activities that were home based. Thus, out-of-home leisure activities in Germany were less significant than in other major western economies.

In 2007, cinema attendance per citizen in Germany was 1.5 against 2.7 in Britain and 3.0 in France (source: www.obs.coe.int). There were around half the number of casinos in Germany than in Britain. There were many fewer restaurants and the hotel rooms supply ratio was lower than in Britain and France. Otus estimates that by 2007, 7% of service business employees were business travellers, a total of 710,000 compared with 1.9 million in Britain. The German service business travellers were engaged in originating demand, executing contracts and servicing clients. Travel in the course of managing companies increased as market service companies grew, but attendance at conferences continued to lag the US and Britain. During the years of reunification from 1991 to 2008, the service business gap between Britain and Germany widened as economic policies in Germany focussed more closely on other segments as did the lifestyle priorities of the population. In 2007, business travellers from service businesses spent an average of 11 nights in German hotels generating transient rooms demand and packaged conference demand of 7.8 million room nights for 21% of domestic business demand, but still left it lagging far behind Britain where the segment generated 26 million hotel room nights.

Domestic leisure demand into hotels

In 1980, West German holiday taking was dominated by domestic holidays, most of which were not hotel based. Hotel based short breaks were embryonic at most and even in the 1990s it was not uncommon for city hotels to close at the weekend because there was no demand. The volume of packaged summer holidays, mostly to Mediterranean resorts and winter ski holidays, mainly to Austria, was already rising and had established Tui and Neckermann as the prominent tour operators in West Germany. In East Germany only a small proportion of the population took summer holidays in hotels and most of those who did were approved and subsidised by the state and the Communist Party. Otus estimates that in 1990, domestic leisure demand accounted for 16 million room nights into hotels in Germany for 27% share of all room nights sold. Throughout the period, foreign summer sun and winter sport packaged holidays taken by West Germans grew strongly and before reunification it had become the largest outbound market in the world recording 62 million outbound trips. By 2000, the number for Germany as a whole had increased to 74 million and by 2005, the latest date for which data were available, 77 million (source: UNWTO). More than 50% outbound trips were to Austria, Spain, Italy, France and Turkey.

The slow development in the economic structure of Germany, the low level of ownership of appreciating assets and low access to credit were key factors in the snail-like growth in domestic short break demand into hotels. Another factor was the virtual absence of German baby boomers as a distinct generation with a lifestyle built around high ownership of consumer goods and a high involvement in experience businesses. It is no accident that the emergence and significance of baby boomers in the US and Britain was linked to the growth in the structural balance of their economies. The absence in Germany of national thrust in demand for experience businesses as a whole and the hotel business in particular by this generation was a factor in the slower development of the German economic structure. On the basis of these trends, Otus estimates that in 2008, the domestic leisure demand in German hotels lost three million room nights over the reunification period from 1990 to 2008. Hotel chains captured only 31% of the leisure demand in to all hotels in Germany, below their share of hotel supply, but the concentration of the chains on business demand in the industrial cities limited their attraction to leisure travellers.

Foreign demand into hotels

Foreign visitors from western countries needed visas to enter East Germany, but that was only the start of the restrictions. They could only buy tourist packages offered by the state to travel on state-owned transport and they were allowed to stay only in state-owned hotels. They were permitted to visit only designated locations and were watched by the Stasi who sought to minimise contact between Western visitors and East German citizens. There were fewer restrictions on visitors from other Warsaw Pact countries who had the advantage of preferential hotel rates agreed by Communist Parties throughout the Soviet empire. West Germany was not a magnet for foreign holidaymakers due to the climate and the concentration on manufacturing. However, the high level of exports enabled it to attract foreign business travellers. This pattern remained throughout the period although the volume of foreign demand rose. In 1999, only 17 million foreign visitors arrived in Germany and stayed for at least one night. In the same year, 73 million arrived in France and 25 million arrived in Britain. By 2007, 24 million foreign visitors arrived in Germany, while the French total increased to 82 million and the British to 31 million *(source*: UNWTO). In 2008, foreign visitors to Germany accounted for 27 million hotel room nights, up by two-thirds from the time of reunification.

Hotel supply in Germany

Otus estimates that in 1980 there were 330,000 hotel rooms in West Germany producing a hotel supply ratio of 5.4, compared with 7.4 in France. Reunification as well as natural growth produced 435,000 rooms in Germany at the end of 1990 with a supply ratio of 5.4 blended from 6.1 from West Germany and 2.9 from East Germany. At a constant 1991 supply ratio, Germany would have needed only 445,000 rooms. Otus estimates that in 2008, total room stock rose to 545,000, to produce secular growth of 100,000 rooms and a hotel supply ratio of 6.6 still lagging the 8.9 in France and 8.4 in Britain. At the start of the period, hotel chains in West Germany had one third fewer rooms than Britain. Hotel chains in Germany reached 195,500 rooms by 2008, significantly less than the 270,000 in France and the 291,200 in Britain and this was reflected in the 36% concentration in Germany compared with 50% in France and 57% in Britain. As was the case with France, there was little historic detail available about hotel portfolios in West Germany until the early 1990s. In 1993, the 13 publicly quoted hotel chains with a presence in Germany accounted for only 37,200 rooms compared with 115,000 in France and 125,000 in Britain.

Kempinski was the only quoted chain operating in Germany that was German and at the time it had only 1,200 rooms in the country. Private German chains such as Steigenberger and Maritim had also grown, but none had developed a dominant position. The three largest quoted chains were Accor, with 13,385 rooms, Queens Moat Houses with 6,020 and the Saison Group from Japan, the owner at the time of Intercontinental and Forum Hotels with 3,240. The other 10 quoted brands including: Hilton, Holiday Inn and Marriott accounted for 15,290 rooms (Slattery et al., 1993). Rooms in up-market and deluxe hotels accounted for 36% of the quoted chain room stock, but economy and budget hotels accounted for only 17% with the remaining 47% at the mid-market.

Hotel chain supply profile: Germany 2008

In 2008, the market level/hotel configuration matrix of hotel chains in Germany was as shown in Table 12.11.

Table 12.11: Chain Market Level/Hotel Configuration Matrix: Germany 2008

	Resort	Full Feature	Basic Feature	Limited Feature	Rooms Only	Total
Deluxe	0%	2%	0%			2%
Up-Market	2%	29%	3%	0%	0%	33%
Mid-Market	1%	28%	16%	3%	1%	48%
Economy	0%	2%	2%	7%	1%	13%
Budget					3%	3%
Total	3%	60%	21%	11%	5%	100%

Source: Otus & Co Advisory Ltd

Chains were represented in 19 of the 25 hotel categories, but seven of these accounted for less than 1% of the room stock. The three dominant categories: up-market/full feature, mid-market/full feature and mid-market/basic accounted for 73% of all chain rooms reflecting a narrower supply profile than Britain and France. The non-rooms heavy configurations: hotel resort, full feature and basic feature, accounted for 84% of the rooms, compared with 68% in Britain and 40% in France. Unlike Britain and France, Germany did not have a major hotel city. Berlin, its capital and largest hotel city accounted for only 24,000 chain rooms, less than one third of those in London. In 2008, the five largest provincial hotel cities in Germany: Cologne, Dusseldorf, Frankfurt, Hamburg and Munich accounted for 53,300 chain rooms, 27% of the total. This pattern was radically different from Britain where the five largest provincial hotel cities: Birmingham, Edinburgh, Glasgow, Leeds and Manchester accounted for 33,410 chain rooms, only 12% of the total and in France where the five largest provincial conurbations: Lyon, Marne-la-Vallee, Marseilles, Nice and Toulouse accounted for 23,890 chain rooms, only 9% of the total. In addition to the six largest hotel cities the remainder of the chain rooms in Germany were located in 380 other conurbations. At the same time, in France chains were located in 983 different conurbations and in Britain 1,178 conurbations illustrating the very narrow geographic spread of chain hotels in Germany. The conurbation pattern of chain hotels in Germany also reflects its economic structure in the sense that the bulk of chain hotels were in the former West Germany and only a small minority in the former East Germany.

In 2008, the five largest provincial hotel cities in Britain had 13,260 chain rooms in the non-rooms heavy categories and in France the equivalent cities contained only 4,830. However, in the five largest German provincial cities there were a whopping 36,790 rooms in these categories. In 2008, these rooms accounted for 19% of chain hotel room stock in Germany. The prime reason for the high volume of supply in these cities is that they are the main industrial fairs cities. When fairs were occurring, the hotels were busy between Monday and Thursday nights. When there were no fairs the hotels had lower room occupancy. At the weekends the hotels had lower room occupancy because of the low level of short break demand. Accordingly, it is a challenge for these hotels to achieve collective annual room occupancy above 60%. For them to achieve and sustain a more effective 70% occupancy there would need to be a 15% uplift in the volume of demand, which is unlikely given the structural balance of the German economy. Alternatively, there would need to have been 15% fewer rooms and €1 billion less investment in the hotels. However, the most depressing announcement for the hotel business in Germany was made by in August 2008:

> 410 new hotel construction and renovation projects are currently in progress... Approx. 66,000 hotel rooms will be constructed or renovated in Germany within the next five years... More than 270 projects are first class or luxury hotels... In the capital of Berlin alone 34 construction and renovation projects are in progress. In Frankfurt/Main 15 hotels are projected and in Munich 13 new hotels will be opened within the next years... Two-thirds of the new hotel projects will be operated by hotel chains.

> (*source*: www.tophotelprojects.com)

The addition of this volume of new hotel stock without radical change in economic policies or the removal of more hotels from the market will increase the over-supply of non-rooms heavy hotels and further depress hotel performance.

Hotel leases in Germany

The problem of over-supply has been made worse in Germany because of the preponderance of leased hotels. There are several forms of hotel leases, but they all share the same three characteristics. First, there are two parties involved: the real estate owner and the hotel operator. Second, the hotel operator consolidates the financial performance of the hotel and pays a rent to the real estate owner. The owner assumes the capital risk and the hotel operator assumes brand risk and management risk. Third, the real estate owners' return comprises the rental income and the asset appreciation of the hotel over the period of the lease. The hotel operator, through the brand value and the management value brought to the hotel, contributes to appreciation in the asset value of the hotel, but does not participate in this benefit.

Most up-market and deluxe hotels have the longest lifespan and higher level of capital appreciation due to the higher investment in their built fabric and their more enduring locations. The range of lease structures produces different risk allocations between the hotel owner and hotel operator. Two common structures illustrate the range. First, full repairing leases with upward-only rent reviews is the most advantageous lease structure for hotel owners since after the hotel is constructed or acquired, the role of the owner is to receive the rent and benefit from the appreciation in asset value. For the hotel operator such a lease is an obligation to pay rent and to fund capital expenditure over the duration of the lease, normally more than 15 years. Invariably, during cyclical up-turns the hotel achieves a post-rent profit. However, invariably during cyclical downturns hotel demand declines and the fixed to rising rental payment can drive the hotel into post-rent loss. In this case the hotel owner continues to receive the rental income, but the brand value and the management value of the hotel operator is impaired.

The second lease structure, the turnover based lease, is a little more advantageous to the hotel operator. The rental payment is calculated as a percentage of hotel turnover and frequently the operator is responsible for funding the furniture, fixtures and equipment, while the owner is responsible for the built fabric of the hotel. Thus, the capital commitment by the hotel operator is in depreciating assets, whereas the owner investment is in appreciating assets. Nonetheless, this structure seeks to achieve a greater balance of risk between the hotel owner and the hotel operator. During cyclical upturns when hotel turnover is higher, the rent is higher and during cyclical downturns when the hotel turnover is lower so also is the rent. Thus, during the life of the lease, the post-rent income of the hotel operator is less variable than in the first structure, but there is still no benefit from asset value appreciation.

Of course, the risk allocation between the hotel owner and hotel operator depends on the level of rent as well as its structure and there are different views among accounting bodies about the significance of that risk to hotel operators. The US GAAP considers that the risk to hotel operators in leases is sufficient that the asset value must be included in its balance sheet as well as depreciated each year. Thus, the reluctance of US companies to take on leased hotels. The experience of hotel leases in Germany is that hotel owners have too frequently minimised their risk and hotel operators have too frequently maximised their risk, which has produced significant post-rent losses. The over-supply of hotels, given the structural balance of the German economy and the economic policies pursued, has forced losses for many hotels in economic downturns. The indictment on hotel owners is that they have been too greedy and the indictment on hotel operators is that they have been too blind to the reality of the hotel supply and demand dynamics in Germany. The more supply that is added to the market without changes in the structural balance of the economy then the greater and more frequent post-rent losses will be recorded in Germany.

Applying the same replacement valuations per room for each hotel category in Germany as in Britain and France, Otus estimates that the replacement value of chain hotels in Germany in 2008 was €36 billion, 20% less than in Britain and 30% more than in France. Also in 2008, the replacement value of the three largest hotel categories in Germany was 76% of the total compared with 62% in Britain and 42% in France providing another measure of the narrow focus of hotel categories in Germany. In 2008, there were only 37 German hotel brands. They accounted for 60,740 rooms. German chain hotels accounted for only 31% of all chain rooms in the country. No other major economy in Europe has a higher penetration by foreign hotel brands and none of the German brands have developed any credible portfolio outside Germany.

Table 12.12: Replacement Value/Room €m: Germany 2008

	Resort	Full Feature	Basic Feature	Limited Feature	Rooms Only
Deluxe	0.750	0.700	0.650	0.600	0.550
Up-market	0.280	0.260	0.240	0.220	0.200
Mid-market	0.175	0.160	0.145	0.130	0.115
Economy	0.100	0.090	0.080	0.070	0.060
Budget	0.050	0.045	0.040	0.035	0.030

Source: Otus & Co Advisory Ltd

Table 12.13: Chain Hotel Replacement Value €m: Germany 2008

	Resort	Full Feature	Basic Feature	Limited Feature	Rooms Only	Total
Deluxe	70	2,890	140			3,100
Up-market	1,120	14,495	1,240	25	40	16,920
Mid-market	205	8,685	4,610	790	115	14,405
Economy	55	300	360	1,010	135	1,860
Budget					195	195
Total	1,450	26,370	6,350	1,825	485	36,480

Source: Otus & Co Advisory Ltd

Hotel supply and demand performance

Over the reunification period from 1990 to 2008 the excess of hotel supply in Germany not only produced sub-optimal room occupancy percentages for the hotel business, but as expected hotel chains performed better than unaffiliated hotels, which mainly were small hotels in towns and villages where seasonality was high. Whereas hotel chains had 36% of room supply, they achieved 58% of total demand. As equally expected, hotel chains achieved the lion's share of business demand, both domestic and foreign because predominantly their hotel locations were urban. However, the chains share of domestic leisure demand was below par because their exposure to leisure locations was low. Typical of small unaffiliated hotels in towns and villages, the owners lived in the hotels, some of which had been in the same family for generations, they owned the hotels and had little or no debt and thus, they are able to survive on low room occupancy.

Table 12.14: German Hotel Supply and Demand Performance 1980-2008

	Total Hotels			Chain Hotels			Chain Share	
	1980	2008	CAGR	1980	2008	CAGR	1980	2008
Total rooms	330,000	545,000	1.8%	65,000	195,580	6.3%	20%	53%
Room nights available (m)	121	199	1.8%	24	72	6.3%	20%	53%
Room occupancy %	39%	39%		60%	60%			
Room nights sold (m)	47	78	1.8%	14	43	6.3%	30%	59%
Domestic business	21	37	2.0%	8	24	6.5%	36%	51%
Domestic leisure	15	13	-0.5%	5	4	-1.6%	34%	55%
Foreign business	7	16	3.3%	1	11	14.1%	15%	44%
Foreign leisure	4	11	3.4%	1	5	12.5%	13%	76%
Supply ratio	5.4	6.6		1.1	2.4			
Secular growth in hotel room supply		90,000			95,000			206%

Source: Otus & Co Advisory Ltd

Other European countries

In addition to Britain, France and Germany there are another 49 countries in Europe stretching from Iceland to Kyrgyzstan. In 2008, these countries accounted for a population of 665 million, 77% of the total population of Europe. Not only were these countries geographically diverse, but also economically and culturally diverse and also diverse in the size and structure of their hotel businesses. The major economic development since 1990 was the break-up of the Soviet empire and the establishment of 22 independent countries most of which developed democracy as their political structure and 10 of them: Bulgaria, Czech Republic, Estonia, Hungary, Latvia, Lithuania, Poland, Romania, Slovakia and Slovenia joined the European Union, while others such as Azerbaijan, Belarus, Georgia, Kyrgyzstan and Ukraine were primitively structured and poorer. Only very small, focused economies such as Andorra, Gibraltar, Luxemburg and Monaco had developed into full-blown service business economies, but their small size precluded domestic hotel demand. Consequently, throughout Europe there was a wide range of structures of the economies. Table 12.15 illustrates the extent to which employment in a selection of economies is based on agriculture and industry, the two segments that generate the lower proportions of domestic business and leisure demand into hotels. Thus, the higher the proportion of employment in these two low yielding segments, the lower the volume of domestic hotel demand.

Table 12.15: Agriculture and Industrial Employment: 2008 % Share

	Population m	Agriculture %	Industrial %	Total %
Britain	61,000,000	1	18	19
Sweden	9,000,000	2	22	24
Netherlands	17,000,000	3	21	24
Spain	41,000,000	5	30	35
Italy	58,000,000	4	31	35
Portugal	11,000,000	10	30	40
Russia	141,000,000	10	30	40
Poland	39,000,000	17	29	46
Romania	22,000,000	30	23	53
Kyrgyzstan	5,000,000	48	13	61

Sources: CIA Fact Book, EIU, Otus & Co Advisory Ltd

It is noticeable that after 18 years of independence the countries in the former Soviet empire were still challenged to reduce their exposure to agriculture and industrial segments to the levels of western European countries. It is also notable that none of the former Warsaw Pact countries had benefited from the sustained investment that East Germany received from West Germany. The transition to independent status, democracy and even membership of the European Union improved the performance of the economies and lifestyle of the populations, but they started from primitive levels.

The wide range of economic structure throughout the continent as well as the pattern of hotel demand was also reflected in hotel supply as Table 12.16 indicates.

Table 12.16: Hotel Metrics: 2008

	Low hotel demand segment employment %	Chain rooms	Hotel concentration %	Hotel room supply ratio
Britain	19	291,740	57%	8.4
Sweden	24	40,130	41%	10.8
Netherlands	24	38,710	48%	4.7
Spain	35	355,290	56%	15.4
Italy	35	80,555	12%	12.1
Portugal	40	25,130	26%	8.7
Russia	40	17,360	18%	0.7
Poland	46	24,950	38%	1.7
Romania	53	5,270	8%	3.2
Kyrgyzstan	61	180	9%	0.4

Sources: CIA Fact Book, EIU, Otus & Co Advisory Ltd

The relationship between economic structure, hotel demand and hotel supply is complex and as has been shown throughout this book reflects specific economic and social policies as well as the availability of capital. Broadly, in 2008 it was possible to identify three blocks of European countries in terms of the structural balance of their economies and in the extent of the economic ascent of their hotel businesses. First, there were the countries of north-west Europe: Britain, Benelux and the Nordic region, which in the case of Britain had already moved to be a full-blown service business economy, while the others were progressing towards that status. Generally, these economies had a lower proportion of employees in the agricultural and industrial segments, their domestic hotel demand was more significant and hotel chains had become more prominent. The second block of economies was in the Mediterranean region: France, Spain, Italy, the Balkans, Greece and Turkey, which had higher proportions of their employment in the agricultural and industrial segments and thus had a relatively low volume of domestic hotel demand, but they benefited from high proportions of demand from foreign leisure travellers, mostly from north-west Europe. With the exception of France and Spain, hotel chain presence in these countries was lower than in the more structurally developed economies and the chain presence was predominantly by domestic chains that had little exposure outside the country. The third block of economies was in central and eastern Europe. In 2008, they were characterised by high levels of employment in the agricultural and industrial segments, very low levels of domestic hotel demand, low levels of foreign demand, low hotel supply ratios and low penetration by hotel chains.

As the economies of continental Europe introduce new technology and work practices so the proportion of employment in the agricultural and industrial segments will decline. The two central issues are the speed at which this change occurs and the economic policies that are enacted in response. Without positive policies to create the conditions for new economic activities in citizen services and service businesses then structural unemployment will increase and the economies will spiral downwards as will domestic hotel demand. Only by the creation of new service activities will unemployment decline causing the economies to expand and become more complex. In turn, domestic hotel demand will increase and the economic ascent of the hotel businesses will progress. Historically, it has proved difficult for politicians to manage these processes effectively and indeed few of the significant economies in the world had become full-blown service business economies by 2008 and achieved significant economic ascent of their hotel businesses.

In this chapter, all data on employment in France from 1980 to 2003 was drawn from the University of Gronningen and from 2003 onwards from INSEE. All data on employment in Germany was drawn from Stastisches Bundesanmt Deutschland and Otus & Co Advisorfy Ltd.

13 The Economic Ascent of the Hotel Business: Future Options

Overview

The conventional approach

The conventional wisdom about the development of the hotel business is based on three metrics: historic trends in hotel revenue per available room (RevPAR), the current stage in the economic cycle, and the volume of planned hotel construction. Each metric on its own provides useful information. The problems arise when they are combined into the belief that changes in hotel RevPAR mirror changes in GDP in any economy and that the rate of hotel construction accelerates when GDP and RevPAR are growing and it shrinks when they decline. It has been convenient for many in the hotel business to accept this belief as a simple way to make sense of extremely complicated matters. However, like all superficial schemes, the devil is in the detail. The conventional wisdom does not take into account the complexities of economies, the realities of business and the diversity of social behaviour, but they cannot be ignored. It ignores any conception of the place of the hotel business in an economy. It has nothing to say about the economic ascent of the hotel business and it reduces the comprehension of the future of the hotel business to guesses. Central to the analysis in this book is the assumption that the hotel business is too significant economically to have the analysis of its dynamics and its future prospects reduced to three metrics that are producing too many flawed investment decisions, too many flawed development strategies and too many flawed marketing strategies.

The Otus approach

Drawing on details from four major economies: the USA, Britain, France and Germany, I have illustrated that, at any time, each economy has a unique structural balance expressed here as the numbers employed in each of the five economic segments: agriculture, industry, citizen services, market services and experience businesses. Each segment is different in terms of the type of work undertaken and thus, is different in terms of its economic significance, the reasons for employees to travel on business and the frequency of their business travel. The numbers employed in each segment also change annually. I have tracked the development of segment employment over time and the economic policies that have been influential in making the changes in the patterns of employment. As the structural balance of an economy moves towards service businesses so each emerging segment, on maturity, generates more hotel demand than the previous. Moreover, the greater the concentration of companies within each segment the more that the balance of employment shifts from blue collar to white collar and professional work and the more business travel that is generated. In parallel, as the structural balance of an economy moves towards service businesses and the numbers of white collar and professional employees increase so also does the leisure demand for hotels. The structural balance not only influences specific patterns of hotel supply and demand, but also the conception of the hotel and its relationships with its customers. To understand the development of hotels through history from the coaching inn to the basic feature hotel to the full-feature hotel, to the hotel resort we need to come to grips with the structure of the economy, the specific pattern of hotel demand that it generates and the specific pattern hotel supply it requires. The range of reasons for using hotels and the frequency of both business and leisure demand grows as economic structure develops. The more that the structural balance of an economy moves towards service businesses, the greater the diversity of hotel demand and the more categories of hotel that become available.

Over time, the structural balance of the US and British economies progressed from a heavy reliance on agriculture to a reliance on service businesses. Over the same time the structural balance of the French and German economies developed more slowly and had greater reliance on the industrial and citizen services segments. I have discussed the patterns and volumes of hotel demand that emerged at each time period in each country and explained why they emerged. I have analysed the volume and pattern of hotel supply over the same time periods to explain how the economic structure, economic policies, hotel demand and hotel supply are related. In particular, I have traced the emergence and growth of hotel chains and explained that they are integral to the economic ascent of the hotel business. Figure 13.1 illustrates the pattern of hotel development in the US from the start of the 20th century. It shows the growth in hotel room supply and the pattern of growth in hotel chain portfolios. It shows clearly that in the second half of the century, when the structural balance of the US economy progressed to service businesses, the volume of room supply increased most as did the size and significance of hotel chain portfolios. The chart also plots the rate of secular growth in hotel chain supply which illustrates a similar pattern, but with the caveat that from 1990 the rate of secular growth in hotel chain supply is slowing as an increasing number of brands achieve optimum size in the country. The pattern in hotel room demand was even more emphatic than the pattern in hotel room supply as Figure 13.2 illustrates.

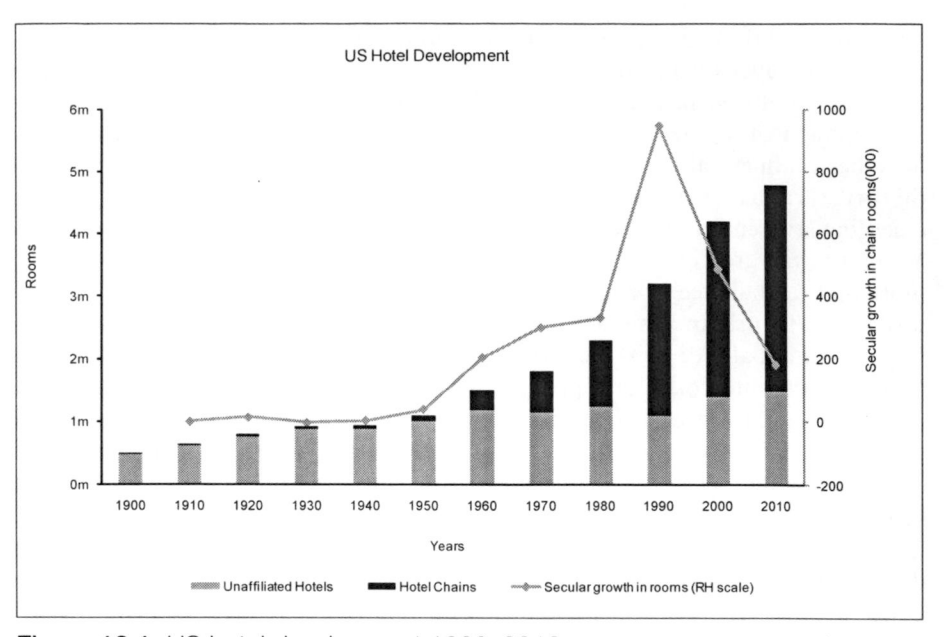

Figure 13.1: US hotel development 1900–2010

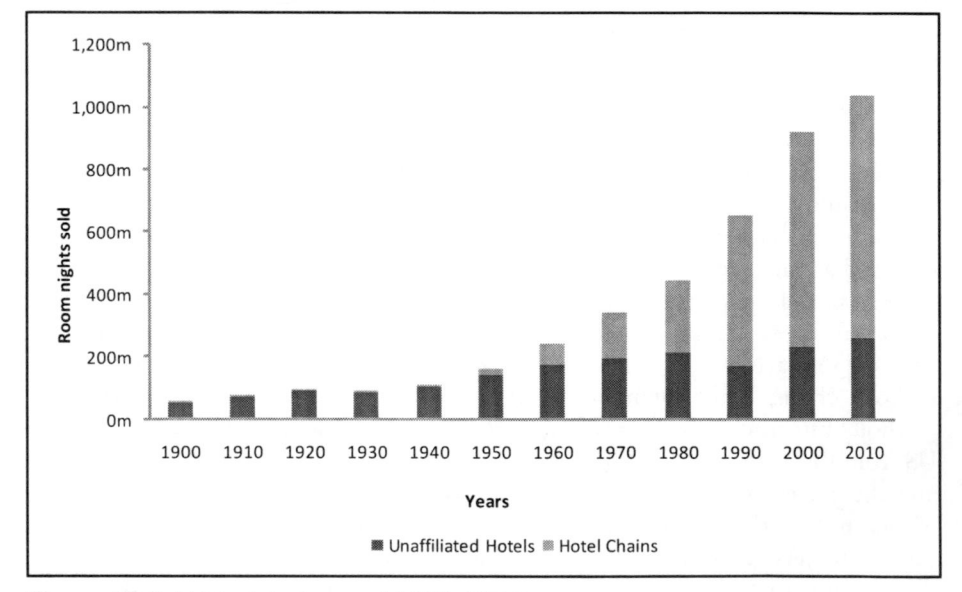

Figure 13.2: US hotel demand 1900–2010

The message of the Otus approach

The first message of this book is that to explain the pattern of hotel demand and supply in any economy more effectively we need to start with an understanding of its economic structure and economic policies. We need also to make sense of the sources and volumes of hotel demand and systematically to track the patterns of hotel supply to create a more effective understanding of the relationships between hotel economies, hotel demand and hotel supply. The conventional wisdom about hotel development has nothing to say about the issues addressed in this book. Yet these issues are crucial for understanding the place of the hotel business in any economy, of explaining why the patterns of hotel demand and supply exist at any time and providing the basis for understanding more systematically the future economic ascent of the hotel business.

Where next for economic structure?

Major economic, political, ideological and technological changes are followed by structural shifts in economies. The Industrial Revolution was the transition phase for the structural progression of the British economy from agricultural to industrial. The four critical events of the first half of the 20th century: World War I, ideological shifts, the Great Depression and World War II moved the structural balance of western European democracies towards citizen services, while the structural balance of the economy of communist Russia ossified, but a different governance of the critical events by the US propelled its economy towards service businesses from the 1950s. It took until the 1980s for Britain to make this transition to service businesses following economic trauma throughout the 1970s and radical change in economic policies from 1979. A feature of the historic shifts in the structural balance of economies is that the more developed the economy, the shorter time required to make a segment shift. The Industrial Revolution lasted for around 100 years. The shift to citizen services in Europe took around 50 years. During the same period, the US made two shifts from industrial through citizen services and on to service businesses, while it took Britain only the 1980s to make the shift from citizen services to service businesses.

The credit crunch and the recession of 2008 and 2009 were induced by malregulation and mismanagement in some financial service businesses in the US and Britain and spread fast to the other economies around the globe. It is clear, in spring 2009, that the major economies will not emerge from the credit crunch and recession in the same format as before. The G20 initiatives, as well as those of individual governments, have been designed to ensure that the context of 2007 will not be re-established. Thus, changes in the structural balance of economies can be expected. The high multiplier effect of the financial service businesses as well as the global spread of the collapse generated high levels of cyclical and structural unemployment, but before the credit crunch and recession started some of the major economies, notably France and Germany, were already suffering high structural unemployment, which exacerbated their problems when the recession took hold. As well as creating a new context for the financial service businesses, an urgent issue for governments, as the economies begin to emerge from the recession, will be to reduce unemployment and this will require the enactment of economic policies to create new jobs.

Governments have two options: first they can resist segment shift by subsidising employment in existing businesses, which before the recession were generating structural unemployment because of higher productivity, lower demand or both. An example of this is the initiative by the German government in 2008 to subsidise the scrapping of old cars to reduce the cost of buying new cars so that employment in car manufacturing could be sustained. Similarly, governments can create jobs in citizen services with the danger of higher taxes to support the over-manning. Such policies can only deliver short-term relief because economic development and economic realities are too powerful to be held back. The alternative option for governments is to enact policies to promote new demand into emerging segments and to encourage the creation of new businesses and new jobs for which there is emerging demand. This option involves segment shift as it did in Britain during the 1980s with the shift to service businesses. As the Great Depression heralded the peak of structural dominance of the manufacturing industry in the US so the credit crunch and recession of 2008 and 2009, with the regulatory changes being planned for the financial service businesses, could herald the peak of the structural dominance of the financial service business in the US and Britain. As the Great Depression acted as the catalyst that shifted the structural balance of the US economy to citizen services so the credit crunch and recession of 2008 and 2009 may act as the catalyst that shifts the structural balance of the US and British economies towards experience businesses. Simultaneously, the effect of the credit crunch and recession in other economies such as France, Germany, the Nordic countries and Benelux, could act as the catalyst to shift their economies to service businesses. Potentially, some of the economies that are grounded in the agricultural and industrial segments could also see a medium-term shift in the structural balance of their economies to the next segment, but for many of them the challenges are great and their structural development from primitive states will take many decades.

Experience business potential in the US and Britain

Governments are inexperienced in the economic policies to facilitate the shift towards experience businesses. Thus, there will be debate in the US and Britain as they decide on the new economic policies. Experience businesses include: airports, bars, bingo clubs, casinos, cinemas, coach terminals, cruise ships, events management, hairdressers, health clubs, hotels, nightclubs, passenger airlines, passenger coaches, passenger trains, private hospitals, private schools, private prisons, rail terminals, restaurants, sports businesses, theatres, and visitor attractions. Without supportive economic policies, the growth in experience businesses in the US and Britain will not transform economies over night. There are three supply movements that have started, but need to be accelerated. First, the movement of some citizen services to experience businesses, for example the growth of private schools, private hospitals, private prisons, transport terminals, airlines, train companies, bus companies and other citizen services with the capacity to become experience businesses such as parks and recreation. Second, the transfer of hobbies and non-business experience activities to businesses, for example the change of sports clubs to businesses. Third, there is concentration growth within experience businesses to create larger and more efficient companies.

The growth in demand for experience businesses does not rely only on positive government policies. In the US in the first decade of the current millennium, the move towards experience businesses was facilitated from the bottom-up, by natural growth in demand. The time had come for the experience businesses. The pattern in Britain was similar but the significance of the experience demand growth was less than in the US. In both countries the progress was supported by the increase in wealth, in the extent of ownership of appreciating assets and access to credit. There were no economic policies enacted specifically to propel demand for experience businesses. However, there were economic policies that constrained the growth of experience businesses such as the ineffective attempts by governments to promote tourism, the raising of the hurdles for foreign visitors to enter the US after 9/11, harsh planning hurdles for hospitality venues in Britain, policies to constrain casinos and other gaming businesses, and high travel taxes. Despite these and other negative policies, demand for experience businesses grew.

Travel is central to the development of experience businesses since demand for experience businesses requires travel from home to the experience venue. This is not new, the history of humankind can be expressed as greater proportions of the population travelling further and travelling more frequently. In the most structurally advanced economies the opportunities to participate in the diversity of experience businesses on a regular basis has only recently begun and with it the growth in travel within advanced economies and from the most advanced economies is invariably linked to other experience businesses. Few seismic events in advanced economies have been able to depress the motivation to travel for long. War, political ideologies such as communism and economic depression have imposed constraints, but they have not been permanent. Less seismic episodes are having shorter recovery times. Within two months of the London bombings in July 2005 hotel demand had recovered (source: TRI Hospitality Consulting, HotStats Briefing Data, August and September 2005). As economic structure progresses towards experience businesses lifestyle becomes more cosmopolitan and more out-of-home and private in-home leisure time declines.

Service business potential in continental Europe

Simultaneously, the effect of the credit crunch and recession in other economies such as France, Germany, the Nordic countries and Benelux, could act as the catalyst to shift their economies to service businesses. As the French and German economies as well as the Nordic region and the Benelux countries are moving towards market service business, they will require changes in policies to create the conditions for market service demand and supply to grow. We know what has to be done because it has already been achieved in the US and Britain when their economies were at that stage. Before the German, Nordic and Benelux economies can progress towards service businesses they have a challenge about the management of their economies. The social market economy was created after World War II to solve traumatic economic, political and social problems and has served the countries well. However, the structures and operating practices of the social market economies were designed for an era when manufacturing dominated the economies, lifestyle aspirations were home based and the economies were less diverse, less complex and their structure changed only slowly. The structures and operating practices of the social market economy are not well suited to the greater diversity, complexity and rate of change of a full-blown service business economy. Further growth in service businesses will require changes in economic policies, in the management of the economy and in the lifestyle that was common in these countries in the second half of the 20th century. Without the speedy development of service businesses, unemployment will remain stubbornly high and the aspirations of increasing numbers of the population to achieve a lifestyle based more on out-of-home leisure activities will be constrained. The challenge for the social market economies is how far and how quickly transition can be achieved without national disruption. The prospects for France will be easier. When President Sarkozy was elected in 2007 he received a clear mandate to change the economy and in the first instance to reduce prolonged high levels of unemployment. His administration began with policy changes aimed at shifting the structural balance of the economy towards service businesses, but the credit crunch and the recession stalled the process. Unlike Germany, France has a road map to follow for its post-recession development of its economic structure.

Industrial potential in the BRIC economies

If the structural balance of the emerging economic powers: Brazil, Russia, India and China (the BRIC countries) with a combined population of 2.8 billion are to benefit in the post-credit crunch and recession period then they will need economic policies that will reduce their heavy reliance on agriculture where they employ 45% of their combined workforce against only 2% collectively in the US, Britain, France and Germany.

Table 13.1: Employment by Segment: Brazil, Russia, India, China, 2008 (mill)

	Agriculture	Industry	Citizen Services	Service Businesses	Total
Brazil	20	20	51	5	97
Russia	7	20	39	2	68
India	272	54	109	18	454
China	332	193	224	23	773
Total	632	288	381	90	1,392

Table 13.2: Employment by Segment: Brazil, Russia, India, China, 2008 (%)

	Agriculture	Industry	Citizen Services	Service Businesses	Total
Brazil	21%	21%	53%	5%	100%
Russia	10%	30%	57%	3%	100%
India	60%	12%	24%	4%	100%
China	43%	25%	29%	3%	100%
Total	45%	21%	27%	6%	100%

Source: Economist Intelligence Unit and Otus & Co Advisory Ltd

Tables 13.1 and 13.2 illustrate the extent to which these economies are reliant on agriculture and the minor significance of service businesses in terms of employment. The BRIC economies employ 6% of their collective workforce in service businesses against 46% in the four advanced economies. The difference is also evident in the performance of the economies. In 2007, GDP per head in the US was $43,730; in Britain, $39,750; in France, $37,040 and in Germany $35,030. In contrast, the performance of the BRIC economies was poor and consistent with their economic structures: Brazil, $5650; Russia, $6930; India, $810 and China, $2000 (source: Economist Intelligence Unit, 2009) The crucial feature of these economies is the size of their population and the first initiative to progress the economies is to enact policies that will shift the structural balance of the economies to industry, which will also provide an impetus to citizen services and service businesses to provide support for the industrial growth. The shift will also need acceleration in international trade as well as growth in domestic demand for consumer goods. The BRIC economies have the capacity to become the factories to the world, a process that China has already begun. The more effective the BRIC economies are in achieving this structural shift the more pressure they will place on manufacturing in the advanced economies and the greater push this will provide for the shift in their economies to service businesses.

Potentially, other developing economies that are grounded in the agricultural and industrial segments could also see a medium-term shift in the structural balance of their economies to the next segment, but for many of them the challenges are great and their structural development from primitive states will probably take many decades.

The message about economic structure

The second message of this book is that after the credit crunch and recession there will be progress in the structural balance of more economies around the world than ever before. It will produce changes in employment and lifestyle at a greater rate and among a greater proportion of the world population than ever before. The issue is how long it will take for economies to change their economic policies and then how long it will take for the policies to have an effect. The slower the process, the longer it will take to recover from recession, the greater the rise in unemployment and the more severe the implications for humankind.

Where next for the hotel business?

Long-term secular global growth in hotel demand

According to the United Nations World Tourism Organisation (UNWTO) in the period between 1980 and 2008 international tourist arrivals grew to 924 million, up by 648 million, an average annual growth of 4.4%. Europe added 311 million; Asia Pacific, 164 million; Middle East, Africa and South America, 123 million and North America, 49 million. The anticipated structural development in economies around the world means that in the medium to long-term the increase in international tourist arrivals will exceed the historic growth.

The World Travel and Tourism Council (WTTC) estimates that in 2009, travel and tourism accounted for 9.4% of world GDP and projects that it will rise to 9.5% in 2019. In the process it will achieve average annual real GDP growth of 4% doubling its contribution by 2019 to $10,500 billion. Within this projection the performance of the four advanced economies and the BRIC economies travel and tourism GDP/head and contribution to GDP of each economy is projected as follows:

Table13.3: Travel and Tourism 2009 - 2019

	Travel & Tourism GDP/ head 2009 $m	Travel & Tourism GDP/ head 2019 $m	Real Growth in T&T GDP %
USA	4.5	6.8	3.3
Britain	3.3	6.2	2.9
France	4.6	6.0	2.4
Germany	3.2	4.6	2.5
Brazil	0.4	0.8	4.5
Russia	0.6	2.7	6.4
India	0.1	0.1	7.7
China	0.3	1.1	9.2

Source: World Travel and Tourism Council and the UN

Hotels will be a major beneficiary of the projected growth in the global tourism economy.

Patterns in short-term hotel demand recovery

When the US and British economies recover from recession and enter a new economic cycle not all previous markets will return to pre-credit crunch levels. There are three problem areas. First, financial services was a major market for both transient rooms demand and packaged conference demand, particularly in hotels at the up-market and deluxe levels. The introduction of heavier regulation and more prudent management of financial services will reduce the volume of hotel business and leisure demand previously generated and it is likely to take several years before the 2007 levels will be regained. Second, when the baby boomers began their careers in the late 1960s, they provided prime growth in domestic hotel demand in the US and Britain. Many of the boomers pursued careers in which hotel stays were a feature, while they and their families were responsible for significant growth in leisure demand. As the boomers are entering retirement they are being lost as a rich element of business demand, but that is being replaced and extended by younger generations of executives. A challenge for the US and British hotel business in the post-recession period is that the wealth and lifestyle that the boomers had accumulated was savaged by the credit crunch and recession. Their plans for regular travel and hotel stays during retirement were shelved and it is not clear when, if ever, the boomers will return to the hotel market in the same force as before. Third, we have already seen that, in the US and Britain, full-feature hotels are under threat from the reduction in demand for company-specific hotel-based conferences as well as the growth of restaurant chains and health club chains that have wiped out most local demand for restaurants, bars and health clubs in hotels. Because these changes in demand are structural and not cyclical, they cannot be expected to return after the recession. Thus, in the US and Britain there will need to be positive development in economic structure to create new business and leisure demand and this will have an impact on the pattern of new hotel supply.

New hotel demand from experience businesses in the US and Britain

The new hotel demand generated by experience businesses is expected to increase the volume of business demand. The pattern of business demand from experience businesses is expected to be similar to market services where the three client-facing activities of originating demand, executing contracts and servicing clients as well as growth in the number of business travellers involved in managing their experience companies will be at the core of transient rooms demand from the segment. Moreover, new packaged conference demand is also expected from growth in attending industry-wide conferences by experience business travellers, growth in company-specific conferences focused on training, strategic reviews and motivational initiatives from experience businesses and there will also be growth in individual experience companies hosting hotel-based conferences for their clients. It is clear that the shift to experience businesses will generate new business demand into hotels. However, without the impetus of supportive economic policies the growth in demand will be a medium to long-term change rather than a short-term transformation. The growth in white collar and professional careers in experiences businesses can also be expected to generate more leisure demand into hotels and the structural development of more economies will produce secular growth in foreign leisure demand as well as domestic leisure demand.

New hotel demand from service businesses in continental Europe

The shift in the structural balance of the French economy to service businesses will, as it did in the US and Britain, generate packaged conference demand from service businesses and packaged short break leisure demand as prosperity and access to credit increases and lifestyle becomes more cosmopolitan. The challenge for the French hotel business will be its under-supply of full-feature hotels. Otus estimates that in the medium to long-term, the growth in domestic business and leisure demand into hotels in key cities throughout France will require the most significant building programme of full-feature hotels of any European country and will drive the next phase of secular growth in hotel supply in France. The challenge in Germany is the reverse of France. The over-supply of full-feature hotel rooms in Germany will not be eliminated without significant growth in demand and that will not be achieved without the necessary changes in the economy and in economic policies. In the meantime, the continuing growth in full-feature hotel supply is a very big bet on the German government changing its economic policies and changing the social market framework to accommodate an economy whose structural balance is tipping towards service businesses. Early in 2009, as the short-term outlook for the German economy was for a decline of at least 5% in GDP and the coalition government was coming towards the end of its term, the odds looked long.

Too many hotel chains

The positive post-recession tourism demand prospects for the medium to long-term will have positive implications for hotel supply as a whole and for hotel chains in particular. However, there are three supply wrinkles that need to be ironed out for the benefits of demand growth to be achieved most effectively. First, a characteristic feature of experience businesses is that productivity hardly changes. There is no equivalent in experience businesses to the impact on labour productivity that the introduction of the assembly line had on manufacturing. Hamlet still takes the same time to enact and involves the same cast of characters as it did when first performed. Ball games still take the same time and involve the same number of team members as they always have. Flight times and train journey times have reduced little over the past half century. Similarly, a one-night stay in a hotel always lasts for one night. Attempts to reduce the time involved in hotel check-in and check-out, room servicing, meal production and meal service have produced marginal benefits in the time taken to deliver the experience, but the critical element in hotel productivity is the amount of time that the customer takes to experience the facilities, services and products.

In spite of this, major improvements in productivity can be generated from the corporate structure of hotel chains. Broadly, the larger the hotel chain the greater the synergies in demand generation, the greater the increase in operating margins and the greater the capital market synergies. There is significant scope for growth in concentration among hotel chains to capture corporate synergies and to propel the economic ascent of the business. At the end of 2008, there were too many hotel brands. The overall growth of hotel chains masked the fact that 126 of the 188 hotel brands with more than four hotels in Britain had less than 10 hotels in their portfolios. Together they accounted for only 18% of all chain rooms and most had little or no hope of becoming more effective on their own. Most countries are still at the entrepreneurial stage of hotel chain development. At the end of 2008 there were 148 hotel brands operating in France, 128 in Germany and 217 in Spain. The bulk of these brands were too small and generated too little cash flow to be able to deliver premium demand. They were also too small to buy in sufficient bulk to achieve premium operating margins and they had insufficient access to capital to grow their portfolios effectively and meaningfully. Of course, size is not everything. The dominant size of THF was not enough of a defence to prevent its acquisition by Granada in 1996. Its idiosyncratic portfolio structure meant that it was unable to produce enough returns for its investors. Thus, for the momentum of economic ascent of the hotel business to continue, hotel chains will need to develop more rational as well as bigger portfolios. The capital markets will play a critical role in this process since the more that they support short chains and unaffiliated hotels, the greater the risk to their investments and the more that they will inhibit the improvement in the effectiveness of the hotel business as a whole.

Too many obsolete hotels

The second supply issue about the future economic ascent of the hotel business is the problem of unaffiliated hotels. As hotel chains have grown in the US, Britain and France it has become increasingly difficult for independent hoteliers to access professional equity and debt to construct new unaffiliated hotels. Rather, they have been reduced to acquiring small, old hotels that are not attractive to the chains because of their physical state, their location or both. The front-of-house and back-of-house physical state of many unaffiliated hotels is problematic because their inferior performance over many decades has limited the capital available to create safe and modern facilities. It is for this reason that a much higher proportion of unaffiliated rooms are still without en suite bedrooms. Most unaffiliated hotels are basic feature hotels that rely on local demand for their restaurant and bar, which are declining markets as restaurant chains and pub chains expand. In less developed economies with lower hotel concentration, the access to capital has been easier for independent hoteliers and the hotel capital markets have been less efficient. Italy is an example in which its supply ratio is high at 12 and its hotel concentration is very low at 12%. In countries with a high level of hotel concentration, hotel chains build new hotels so there are progressively fewer unaffiliated hotels that are attractive to the brands. The issue is how quickly the worst of the unaffiliated hotels will be removed from the market. Sadly, there are no systematic data on hotels that are removed from the market, but the persistence of major banks in lending to independent and aspirant hoteliers to acquire unaffiliated hotels is limiting the rate of their removal. The biggest contribution that these banks can make to the further economic ascent of the hotel business is to stop lending to individuals to acquire unaffiliated hotels. Otus estimates that there are almost 50,000 hotel rooms in Britain alone whose physical state, redundant facilities and weak performance make their removal from the market overdue. The longer that lenders continue to lend on redundant hotels, the greater the impediment to the continuing ascent of the hotel business.

Hotel real estate ownership is too fragmented

The third supply issue is about hotel real estate ownership. Despite the growth in hotel brands in the US to account for 69% of total room stock at the end of 2008, the ownership of hotel real estate remained extremely fragmented. In

1985, Marriott owned 8,493 rooms, 13% of its total room stock. By 2008, the number of owned rooms was down to 1,044, but these accounted for only a trace of its total room stock *(source:* http://investor.shareholder.com). Like the other major chains, the endeavour for Marriott was to identify investors in hotel real estate and persuade them to give Marriott a contract to manage the hotel or to take a franchise. The net organic portfolio growth of the Marriott hotel brands throughout the 13 year period involved the negotiation and completion of an average of 125 management contracts and franchises per year. Consequently, the bulk of hotel development over the period was from real estate owners who affiliated their hotels to the major chains to maximise their performance. Many of the franchisees of the thousands of economy hotels owned only one hotel. Many of the mid-market hotels affiliated to chains by franchises and management contracts were owned by individuals and companies with less than five hotels.

The greater complexity of up-market and deluxe, full feature and resort hotels meant that a smaller proportion of these properties in the US were owned by individuals. Many were owned by real estate companies, institutional investors such as insurance companies and pension funds and Real Estate Investment Trusts (REITs). REITs were a separate class of company designed to facilitate investment in real estate companies. The REIT structure required, broadly, that 75% of annual gross income must have originated from real estate related sources; 75% of assets must have been derived from real estate, cash or government securities and at least 90% of REIT taxable income must have been distributed annually as dividends. In return, REITS were exempted from corporate income tax. REITs became a feature of the hotel business over the period and by the end of 2008 there were nine publicly quoted hotel REITs in the US. The largest in terms of enterprise value was Host Hotels & Resorts, which originally was spun off from the Marriott Corporation in 1993. At the end of 2008, Host owned 120 hotels of which 106 were in the US and of those all but three were at the up-market and deluxe levels. Hospitality Properties Trust, the second largest hotel REIT owned 290 hotels, mainly in the mid-market and all but three of its hotels were located in the US. Jointly, the two largest REITS accounted for less than 2.5% of the total US hotel room stock.

By the end of 2008, for major institutional investors, hotels were still seen as a minor asset class. They considered that the risk in hotel ownership was too great relative to other asset classes such as offices, residential or industrial in which the institutions had most of their investments. For this position to change, the prices of hotel assets need to fall relative to other asset classes or hotel chains need to become more effective in their performance to improve the returns on investment in hotels. There is no expectation that institutions will acquire substantial ownership in the hotel business without such changes. For the economic ascent of the hotel business to move on to a new stage it will require greater involvement by major institutions in the ownership of significantly more hotel assets. Without this, the hotel business will be restricted to small capital and the effectiveness of hotel chains in the capital markets will be restricted. The changes required by hotel chains in other countries will be even greater.

The message for the hotel business

The message for the hotel business from this book is that there are indications that we are about to enter a golden age in the economic ascent of the global hotel business. The Otus approach has shown that the hotel business in the advanced economies has come a long way since the agricultural period before the Industrial Revolution. The anticipated post-recession changes in economic policies will produce a larger scale progress in the structural balance of global economies than has ever been experienced. This in turn will propel strong secular growth in both business and leisure hotel demand. If governments do not enact economic policies to enable the shift in the balance of their economies, then not only will the hotel business suffer, but so also will the wider economy.

The growth in hotel demand will inevitably require growth in hotel supply, which will benefit the hotel chains. The impediments to the effective growth in hotel supply are that there are too many hotel chains, too many obsolete hotels and too many hotel owners. At the end of 2008, the four largest hotel chains: Intercontinental Hotels Group, Wyndham Worldwide, Marriott International and Hilton Hotels Corporation had portfolios of half a million rooms each. The growth in demand expected over the next decade as well as the international focus of these chains means that if they maintain their recent rate of portfolio growth then by 2020 each will have portfolios of more than a million rooms. The hotel business is about to become very much more significant.

Appendix: Hotel Supply and Demand Modelling

Introduction

There are insufficient historic data on hotel supply and demand in any country. Actual figures for the number of hotels, number of rooms, room occupancy, room nights sold, the volume of demand from domestic and foreign travellers or the volume of business and leisure demand are rare and not held on a consistent or continuous basis for the whole hotel market in any country. However, to elevate the understanding of the economic ascent of the hotel business beyond the qualitative requires an assessment of these details. Thus, a methodology to estimate the data is required. Otus has sought to be as systematic as the available data and the qualitative analysis will allow. Within the context of this book it has not been possible to develop such a methodology for each country. We have limited much of the historic quantitative analysis from the start of the 20th century to the US and Britain, the two countries for which most data and most historical detail are available and whose hotel businesses have achieved the greatest economic ascent. In the case of France and Germany, lesser detail is available on hotel supply and demand until later in the century and this has limited the extent of the earlier quantitative analysis of these countries. For most other economies, their economic structure is less developed and the details available on historic hotel demand and supply are even more patchy until recently and this has acted not only as a limit on the detailed analysis that can be undertaken, but also as an impetus to produce a theory that can help to make sense of the development of their hotel businesses.

Hotel supply modelling

The absence of a source of record on historic hotel supply data in the US requires the volume of hotel and room stock to be estimated. Data on hotel supply in the US at the start of each decade from 1900 are provided by the American Hotel and Lodging Association, but there is inconsistency in the numbers. It estimates one million hotel rooms in 1910, rising to 2.4 million in 1960 only to fall back to 1.6 million in 1970 and to grow to 2.1 million by 1980 and to add another 1.0 million by 1990 (*source*: www.ahla.org). The US government records the number of the hotels in the US in its census, available from *(source*: www.census. gov), but it does not record the number of rooms. Since the latter part of the 20th century, Smith Travel Research has estimated total room stock and hotel chain room stock in the US. I have also drawn on data about hotel chains from the American Hotel and Lodging Association's Directory, which was first published in 1931 and Hotels Magazine and its precursor publication, Service World International, which has published an annual list of hotel chains each year since 1966 *(source*: www.hotelsmagazine.com).The governments of some countries in Europe record total hotel and room supply. Examples include www.statisticssweden.com, www.statisticspoland.com and www.insee.fr for France. Whenever these have been available they have been used, but their total data are only available from the later years of the 20th century. Since 2000, Otus has tracked the detailed supply profile of all hotel chains in the 52 countries of Europe and since 1985, its precursor database tracked the detailed supply profiles of all hotel chains in Britain. However, there is no source of record on total hotel and room stock in Britain and these have had to be estimated from historic documents as well as economic and hotel business analysis.

Because the prime focus of this book is on long-term historic trends, the supply of and demand for hotels in the US and Britain at the start of each decade throughout the 20th century has been used for modelling purposes. Total hotel stock is rounded to the nearest 100. Total room stock is rounded to the nearest 1,000. The estimate of chain hotel stock, chain room stock and as a residue, the unaffiliated hotel stock and room stock, are treated similarly except from the later decades of the 20th century when better data were available for all hotel chains and actual numbers have been used. Estimates of global hotel room stock are drawn from the Otus records.

The hotel room supply ratio for a country is the number of hotel rooms per 1,000 citizens and it enables the density of hotel room supply in a country to be measured. All current and projected population statistics have been drawn from the United Nations (www.un.org). Two other measures are tied closely to the hotel room supply ratio. First, and broadly, the higher the supply ratio, the higher the proportion of the workforce employed in service businesses. Similarly, the lower the supply ratio, the less developed the economic structure of the country. This pattern occurs because as the structural balance of an economy progresses from agriculture through secondary industries to citizen services and on to service businesses so the proportion of the workforce in white-collar and professional careers increases. Because the activities in each segment are different they require different reasons for employees to travel on business and to spend different numbers of nights per year staying in hotels. The volume and frequency of hotel stays generated by each segment is different and increases as the structural balance of an economy progresses. Accordingly, for each segment at the start and end of each economic period, Otus estimates the proportion of employees who are business travellers and the average number of nights they stay in hotels in each year. It also estimates the reasons why employees from each segment travel on business. This also provides insights into the volumes of domestic leisure demand since, with the exception of retirees and the independently wealthy, leisure demand into hotels is derived from employed people and the greater the proportion of the workforce that are employed in white collar and professional careers then the higher the volume of hotel leisure demand generated.

The next closely related measure is that the more structurally developed an economy is and the higher the hotel supply ratio, then the higher the level of hotel room stock affiliated to hotel chains. In Table A.1, the US, with 53% of its employment in service businesses has a high hotel supply ratio of 15 and a high hotel concentration of 71%. Britain with a lower proportion of employment in service businesses, 49%, has a lower supply ratio, 8.4 and a lower level of hotel concentration, 57%. France, with a lower proportion of employment than Britain in service businesses, 31%, has a higher hotel room supply ratio of 8.9 due to the higher proportion of demand from foreign visitors and has a lower level of hotel concentration, 50%. Germany with an even lower level of employment in service businesses, 25%, has a lower hotel supply ratio 6.6, and a lower level of hotel concentration, 36%.

Table A.1: Hotel room supply ratio and hotel concentration 2008

	Total rooms	Chain rooms	Unaffiliated rooms	Service businesses employment %	Supply ratio	Concen- tration
USA	4,550,000	3,220,000	1,330,000	53%	15.0	71%
Britain	510,000	291,240	218,760	49%	8.4	57%
France	540,000	270,000	270,000	31%	8.9	50%
Germany	545,000	195,580	349,420	25%	6.6	36%

Source: Otus & Co Advisory Ltd and National Statistics

The number of hotel room nights available for a year is calculated by multiplying the average room stock in a country or in a chain by the number of nights in the year. In this calculation no deductions are made from total room stock for those hotels that close for parts of the year or for rooms that are undergoing refurbishment or are used to house hotel employees. For the purposes of this book in which the analysis is undertaken for the first year of each decade for each country, the total estimated room stock for those years is taken as the average since insufficiently exact data are available for the precise timing of new hotel rooms coming on stream and redundant rooms being removed from the market..

Hotel demand modelling

The measure of hotel demand efficiency in a country, a hotel chain or a hotel is room occupancy percentage , which is the number of hotel room nights sold expressed as a percentage of the total room nights available during any given time period. However, there are no credible and consistent country-wide data on total room occupancy. Firms such as Smith Travel Research have since the latter part of the 20th century provided an excellent service by collecting data on hotel room occupancy, average daily room rate and revenue per available room (RevPAR), predominantly from chain hotels, but not from all hotel chains. Because the collectors of hotel demand performance statistics focus mainly on chain hotels and exclude most unaffiliated hotels from their analysis, the room occupancy percentage that they record for any country is higher than the actual total achieved in any country because hotel chains invariably achieve higher occupancy than unaffiliated hotels. The higher the level of hotel concentration in a country the smaller the gap between the room occupancy percentage and the total achieved in a country and vice versa.

The volume of domestic business leisure demand for hotels in any country is a function of its economic structure. The more structurally developed the economy, the higher the volume of domestic hotel demand generated, to which there is one exception and one caveat. The one exception is nation-states such as Monaco and Singapore which have well developed economic structures, but which are too small geographically to generate any measurable volume of domestic hotel demand. The caveat is that although the more structurally developed economies generate higher volumes of domestic leisure demand, this is not necessarily spent in hotels in the home country. This is the case with north western European countries where since the 1970s there has been a progressively greater proportion of domestic leisure demand which has holidayed outside of Britain. The corollary is also the case. Mediterranean countries such as Spain, Italy, Greece and Portugal have less structurally developed economies and generate a lower volume of domestic leisure demand for hotels, but do attract high volumes of foreign leisure demand to their hotels because of climate and culture, which are factors unrelated to economic structure. The volume of foreign business demand into hotels in a country is also a function of its economic structure. The more structurally developed an economy the more trading relationships with other countries and as service businesses generate more business demand than any other segments of an economy so the more foreign business demand is generated. Data on foreign demand has been drawn from the tourism statistics of each country and from organisations such as the UNWTO and WTTC.

Total room occupancy has been low historically due to the high emphasis on the summer resort market where many hotels, attract only leisure demand, are unaffiliated to chains and close for several months per year when there is no demand. Chain room occupancy is higher than total occupancy due to the high exposure to urban markets that are open all year round, exposed to all sources of demand and investing more in generating demand. Room occupancy percentages used in the book are Otus estimates and are indicative rather than actual. No assumptions are made about yield management since there are no effective data on which average daily room rates can be estimated for countries as a whole or historically.

Bibliography

Accor (2007) *Reaching for the Impossible*, Accor.

Addison, P. and Jones, H. (2005) *A Companion to Contemporary Britain, 1939–2000*, Blackwell.

Ardagh, J. (1973) *The New France: A Society in Transition 1945–1973*, Penguin.

Automobile Association (1965) *Guide to Hotels and Restaurants*, Automobile Association.

Bachin, Robin S. (2005) 'From the city to the seaside: luxury hotels in New York, Atlantic City and Miami Beach', in M. Lamonaca and J. Mogul (eds), *Grand Hotels of the Jazz Age*, Princeton Architectural Press.

Banton, N. (1968) *The Structure of Commerce*, English University Press.

Beeching Report (1963) *The Reshaping of British Railways*, HMSO.

Berg, Stefan, Winter, Steffen and Wassermann, Andreas (2005) *Germany's Eastern Burden: The Price of a Failed Reunification*, Speigel Online International, accessed 09/05/2005.

Berstein, W.J. (2004) *The Birth of Plenty*, McGraw Hill.

Brendon, P. (1991) *Thomas Cook*, Secker and Warburg.

Briggs, Asa (1995) *The History of Broadcasting in the United Kingdom: Volume V: Competition*, Oxford University Press.

British Tourist Authority (1996) *The British National Travel Survey*, British Tourist Authority.

Broadberry, S. (1997) *The Productivity Race: British Manufacturing in International Perspective, 1850–1990*, Cambridge University Press.

Bull, F.J. and Richardson, C. (1962) *Hotel and Catering Law*, Barrie and Rockliff.

Bunch, Bryan and Hellemans, Alexander (eds) (2004) *History of Science and Technology*, Houghton Mifflin.

Burke, T. (1930) *The English Inn*, Longman Green.

Caterer & Hotelkeeper (1978), IPC Consumer Press, Centenary Edition, April

Chaucer, Geoffrey ([000] 1934) *The Canterbury Tales*, Gin and Company.

Courte, W.H.B. (1964) *A Concise Economic History of Britain*, Cambridge University Press.

Davidson, Lisa Pfueller (2005) 'Early 20th century hotel architects and the origins of standardization', in Molly W. Berger (ed.) *The American Hotel*, Wolfsonian-Florida International University.

Docherty, David, Morrison, David and Tracey, Michael (1987) *The Last Picture Show?*, BFI Publishing

Donzel, C. Gregory, A. and Walter, M. (1989) *Grand American Hotels*, Vendome Press.

Evans, H. (1998) *The American Century*, Jonathan Cape.

Eyster, J. (1988) *The Negotiation and Administration of Hotel and Restaurant Management Contracts*, Cornell University Press.

Foote, N. and Hyatt, P. (1993) 'Social mobility and economic advancement', *American Economic Review*, **43** pp. 364-378

Forte, Charles (1986) *Forte*, Sidgwick & Jackson.

Galbraith, J.K. (1929) *The Great Crash*, Allen Lane.

Glatzer, Wolfgang (1992) *Recent Social Trends in West Germany, 1960–1990*, McGill–Queens University Press.

Gregg, Pauline (1965) *A Social and Economic History of Britain*, Harrap.

Haldane, A.R.B. (1995) *The Drove Roads of Scotland*, Haldane.

Harris, J. Hyde, S. and Smith, G. (1986) *1966 and All That*, London: Trefoil Publications Ltd.

Health Insurance Institute (1965) *Source Book*, US Health Insurance Institute.

Hibbert, C. (1987) *The English, A Social History*, Norton.

Hilton, Conrad (1957) *Be My Guest*, Prentice Hall.

Jay, P. (2004) *Road to Riches or the Wealth of Man*, Wiedenfeld and Nicolson.

Johnson, H. (1987) *The Cunard Story*, Whittet Books.

Kaplan, Justin (2007) *When the Astors Owned New York*, Plume.

Kay, J. (2003) *The Truth about Markets*, Penguin.

Keynes, John Maynard (2007) *The General Theory of Employment, Interest and Money*, Macmillan.

Krug. J.A. (1945) *Production: Wartime Achievements and Recommission Outlook*, Washington, DC: US War Production Board.

Lacey, Robert (1986) *Ford*, Heinemann.

Loehlin, Jennifer (1999) *From Rugs to Riches: Consumption and Modernity in Germany* Oxford: Berg

Malthus, T.R. (1798) *An Essay on the Principles of Population*, Johnson.

Marriott, J.W. Jr. and Brown, Kathi Ann (1997) *The Spirit to Serve*, HarperBusiness.

Marwick, Arthur (1982) *British Society since 1945*, Penguin.

Mitchell, B.R. (1988) *British Historical Statistics*, Cambridge University Press.

Mitchell, B.R. (1998) *International Historical Statistics: Europe 1750 to 1993*, Palgrave Macmillan.

Monopolies and Mergers Commission (1989) *The Supply of Beer*, London: HMSO.

NEDO (1972) *Hotel Prospects to 1980*, HMSO.

NEDO (1976) *Hotel Prospects to 1985*, HMSO.

Olson, J.S. (2001) *Historical Dictionary of the Great Depression*, Greenwood.

Orwell, George ([0000] 1970) *Down and Out in Paris and London*, Harmondsworth: Penguin.

Oxford Economic Forecasting (2006) *The Economic Contribution of the Aviation Industry in the UK*, Oxford Economic Forecasting.

Pillsbury, R. (1990) *From Boarding House to Bistro*, Unwin Hyman.

Pine II, J. and Gilmore, J. H. (1998), 'Welcome to the Experience Economy' *Harvard Business Review*, July – August

Porter, Dilwyn (1997) ' "Never-Never Land": Britain under the Conservatives', in Nick Tiratsoo (ed.), *From Blitz to Blair: A New History of Britain since 1939*, Phoenix.

Price, R.S. (1993) *A Concise History of France*, Cambridge: Cambridge University Press.

Ricardo, David ([1817] 1821) *Principles of Political Economy*, John Murray.

Ritz, Marie-Louise (1981) *Caesar Ritz*, Bodley Head.

Roethlisberger, F.J. and Dickson, W.J. (1939) *Management and the Worker*, Harvard University Press.

Ruttenbaum, S. (1996) *Mansions in the Clouds, The Skyscraper Palazzi of Emery Roth*, Balsam Press.

Sampson, A. (1962) *The Anatomy of Britain*, Hodder & Stoughton.

Sandbrook, Dominic (2005) *Never Had it so Good: the History of Britain from Suez to the Beatles*, Little, Brown.

Sandbrook, Dominic (2006) *White Heat: A History of Britain in the Swinging Sixties*, Little, Brown.

Sante, Luc (1991) *Low Life*, Granta Books.

Slattery, Paul and Roper, Angela (1986) *The UK Hotels Groups Directory*, Cassell.

Slattery, P., Feehely, G., Savage, M. (1994) *Quoted Hotel Companies: The World Markets 1994*, Kleinwort Benson Securities.

Slattery, P., Feehely, G., Savage, M. (1993) *Quoted Hotel Companies: The European Market 1993*, Kleinwort Benson Securities.

Smith, Adam ([1776] 1904) *The Wealth of Nations*, Methuen.

Smith, E.M. (1927) 'America's domestic servant sortage', *Current History*, 27.

Steel, T. (1990) *The Langham, A History*, Hilton.

Taylor, D. (2003) *Ritzy, British Hotels 1837 to 1987*, Milman Press.

Taylor, F.W. (1947) *Scientific Management*, Harper & Row.

Toussant, J. and Tegeder, G. (2006) 'Security and insecurity of home ownership: Germany and the Netherlands', paper presented to the ENHR Conference, Housing in an Expanding Europe.

United Nations Statistics Division (2006) *International Industrial Standard Classification of All Economic Activities, Revision 4*, United Nations.

UNWTO (2008) *World Tourism Barometer*, Vol.6 No.3, October, UNTWO

Veblen, T. ([1899] 1971) *The Theory of the Leisure Class*, Unwin Books.

Williams, K., Williams, J. and Thomas, D. (1983) *Why are the British Bad at Manufacturing?*, Routledge.

Wilson, Kemmons and Kerr, Robert (1996) *Half Luck and Half Brains*, Hambleton Hill.

Woloson, W. (2005) *St. James Encyclopedia of Popular Culture*, Thomson Gale.

Wooler, N. (1987) *Dinner in the Diner*, David & Charles.

Index